The Lyndoniad

The Lyndoniad

William Guy

Rev. date: 04/28/2020

To order additional copies of this book, contact:
Xlibris
1-888-795-4274
www.Xlibris.com
Orders@Xlibris.com
811261

In Memoriam Robert D. Abercrombie

who taught me to see visions and to dream dreams

PREFACE

The poem or the poem in pieces, the fractured poem, which this volume comprises reflects a lifetime —almost 57 years—of reading and ruminating on the person and the career and the times of Lyndon Johnson. I was a senior in high school when John F. Kennedy was assassinated. I had been enraptured to be studying American history all during the fall of 1963 but I would say that some connection between that subject and my own life and time had been missing. The Founding Fathers seemed far more alive to me than my own President and his retinue and the world of Washington did. This feeling of disjuncture changed with the elevation of Lyndon Johnson to the Presidency, which I found electrifying. The present moment suddenly seemed to matter to me as it had not under President Kennedy, whom I found something of a cypher, and in Lyndon Johnson—I'm not sure exactly why—I saw American history embodied as a living force, a reality. I began to study him, his actions and his pronouncements as passionately, as obsessively as I had been studying the actions and the pronouncements of the Founding Fathers or the great triumvirate of Clay, Calhoun, and Webster under the tutelage of Robert D. Abercrombie at my alma mater Shady Side Academy. Like all of my contemporaries I'm sure I had my ups and downs with Lyndon Johnson during the next five years but I never doubted that he was the main man, the central figure of our historical moment. I am not sure when I became seized with the idea of writing about him in a literary way, I think it may have been as I was reading an installment of the PENTAGON PAPERS in THE NEW YORK TIMES while riding a bus into New York City from Princeton, New Jersey in the summer of 1971. It was many years before I saw my way clear to the form which my ambition to encompass Lyndon Johnson and his era would have to take, but the germ of that ambition had already been at work in me. I read everything about Lyndon Johnson that crossed my path—at the expense sometimes of the subjects that I was supposed to be studying. Thus I was fairly well steeped in the burgeoning Johnson literature before I even began my poem about him.

I must admit that I was stymied for a long time. Way back at the beginning, daftly, I had tried to imagine how one might do the LBJ years in a *War and Peace*-like novel. But even after I had realized that poetry was the only medium by which I might proceed with the work about Lyndon Johnson that I was sure I had inside me, I was still at a loss. Like Thom Gunn I had the feeling that there was something in Pound's *Cantos* that I could turn to account in this poetic project of my own which I envisioned, but the clue to that application of Pound's great epic to my proposed work was not immediately (and may never have become) apparent. In the meantime I had written GRAVITY'S REVOLT, a long novel, and DEFUNCTIVE MUSIC, a volume of poems. In the latter, without quite knowing it, I had hit upon the tactic that would serve me in my poem about Lyndon Johnson: wholesale stealing after the fashion of Shakespeare rifling Plutarch. To invoke this case, i.e. to compare myself to Shakespeare, is no doubt to put on airs ludicrously, but thinking about his audacity in plundering Plutarch gave me the big breakthrough that allowed me to write a poem about Balanchine by stealing word for word (always moving the words around to make them scan in English) Kleist's ÜBER DAS MARIONETTENTHEATER (in a translation because at that time my German was a bit sub-par). I had tried and tried to write about Balanchine, always puppeting Kleist's ideas about genius—the result was never very good. With Shakespeare's example in mind I finally saw that I had to just make Kleist my own, appropriate him since he had unknowingly prophesied Balanchine. So I had to do also, I later realized, if I was going to write a LYNDONIAD. Above all I needed to appropriate raw historical materials. Revelation came to me in a plane stuck on the runway waiting to take off once in Pittsburgh. I was reading Doris Kearns Goodwin's book on LBJ, a long speech of LBJ's in fact which she had gotten down in her kind of shorthand during one of her amazing pre-dawn "psychoanalytic" sessions with the great man. In regard to my particular problem of how to begin the poem I wanted to write about Lyndon Johnson, some still small voice above the tarmac that night said "Copy out only that [meaning the speech that Kearns Goodwin had gotten down] and save expense." Or "Sin boldly, boy." Not that the copying out is ever easy—it is not inexpensive in that sense, the usual great pains must still be taken, the words that one is taking over must be sculpted and shaped so as to scan. But why try to render Johnson in false coinage of my own fashioning, I wondered, when he had so incomparably rendered himself or, as I came to realize as I now was able to make some progress, when he had been reflected and illuminated and revealed in the words of so many of the people who surrounded him, the players of the Johnson era? Copy out only those words and save yourself the expense of seeking another way. And so I did, from oral histories and minutes of the meetings of potentates and phone conversations. I relished the prosodic challenge of making the prose of these kinds of sources sing. If Richard Strauss had claimed that he could turn the telephone book into music if commissioned to do so, I reasoned that I ought to be able to turn the flat prose of politicians and statesmen into poetry.

It would have been one thing if I had only stolen the *ipsissima verba* of historical figures from the public record but I went farther in what I suppose was my greed to know and to figure forth Johnson. I would say that I borrowed passages from historians and writers about Johnson except how would I ever have been able to return them, repay the debt? The operative word must be that I *stole* passages from them. There was an element of prosodic curiosity in play here similar to the one I mentioned above in connection with the utterances of public figures, i.e. could I turn prose scenes and paragraphs into poetry or how could I turn them into poetry? It wasn't as if I was thinking that I would never try to publish a LYNDONIAD, but in the early years of composition there was a sense in which I wasn't "serious" yet, I was just amusing myself, seeing what I could make of many different kinds of material, playing somewhat giddily around. The poems or rather the tesserae of the long poem of mine that resulted in part from these thefts from historians are always "different"—they have to be in order for there to arise what I think of or rather feel on my pulses as "Guy scansion," my characteristic rhythm. I had to change words, I added phrases to sharpen meanings, I had to make these passages mine. But still the basic element of theft is undeniable. I lifted passages from books about Lyndon Johnson. "Bad poets imitate, good poets steal" or some such words are the gist of a famous dictum of T.S. Eliot's. He was probably talking more about what Virgil did with Homer (sometimes one can wonder whether Virgil ever invented a single "original" phrase of his own, i.e. one that he had not stolen from Homer). Such echolalia was not accounted a crime among the ancients. And the history of Elizabethan drama is one of purloined letters. To read the old King Lear play over which Shakespeare wrote his own is a startling experience. I mean the Bard had no qualms. HAMLET is said to be made over from an old play too although the original has never surfaced. And to return to an example that I have used before: Shakespeare seems to have had his copy of Plutarch open on his desk for copying (i.e. theft) when he was composing Enobarbus's famous speech about "The barge she sat in" for ANTONY AND CLEOPATRA. What greater precedent than mighty Jove then if one aspired to compose an historical epic? It's called poetic license or the immorality of poets whose sole motto might be "All's meet with me that I can fashion fit."

I would hope that any historians who recognize pieces of their work embedded in my poem the way the ancient relief sculpture of Hercules and the Nemean lion is embedded in the tomb of Giorgio Arberini in Santa Maria sopra Minerva in Rome would take my re-cycling of their work as the highest compliment I can pay them, a mark of my utmost admiration. Witness the good-humored reaction of Erich Heller in the preface of his book of essays THE DISINHERITED MIND to a piece of thievery that had been visited on him:

It is only to avoid the suspicion of plagiarism that I should like briefly to relate—apropos, perhaps, the Nietzschean theme of metamorphoses—the following curiosity. Part of my essay on Karl Kraus was originally written for *The Times Literary Supplement*. It appeared anonymously (as used to be the custom of the journal) on the front page of No. 2,675, dated May 8, 1953. I was surprised as well as flattered to discover much later that with this article I had contributed not only to the T.L.S. but also to the poetry of Hugh MacDiarmid (Dr. C.M. Grieve), the renowned Scots poet. His poem 'And above all, Karl Kraus', from his cycle *In Memoriam James Joyce*, consists of 157 lines of which 149 are taken from my essay—with their essential identity preserved—even though they suffered a little breakage in the process of being lifted up into the poetic mode. My slight anxiety that this transference may be detected by some readers and ascribed to me as plagiarism is caused by the (may I say deserved?) notoriety of Hugh MacDiarmid's poem. It was selected, without acknowledgement of my T.L.S. essay, for the Penguin Book *The Mid-Century English Poetry 1940-1960*, which enjoys wide circulation. I have sometimes wondered whether this episode should not serve as footnote to my essay 'Rilke and Nietzsche' with its discourse on the relationship between poetry and other forms of linguistic expression.

Could I perhaps hope for a like equanimity on the part of those whose work I have appropriated wholesale and I hope "lifted up into the poetic mode"?

If I had written a prose book, a book of history about Lyndon Johnson, I would have cited all my sources, but I have instead written a poem where footnotes would be extraneous and intrusive. For the record I will cite those historians and writers and memoirists and biographers whose work I can remember pillaging. They are: Doris Kearns Goodwin; Richard Goodwin; Harry McPherson; Rick Pearlstein; Joseph Califano; Clark Clifford; Randall Woods; Robert Dalleck; Tom Wolfe; Charles DeBenedetti; Paul Keith Conkin; Theodore H. White; Godfrey Hodgson alone and as a member of that estimable trio of Hodgson, Lewis Chester and Bruce Page; William Appleman Williams; Ronnie Dugger; Marshall Frady; Bobby Baker; Townsend Hoopes; Horace Busby; Booth Mooney; Kai Bird; Loren Baritz; Taylor Branch; James C. Thomson; Harrison Salisbury; Larry Berman; Eric Goldman; Michael Honey; Jonathan Darman; Robert Pisor; Lloyd C. Gardner; Bill Moyers; William Leuchtenburg. The problem is that I know I am omitting others. The composition of THE LYNDONIAD has gone on over many years and as I have gathered all the pieces together and re-arranged them now for publication, I have sometimes wondered where some of the pieces came from. I truly have no idea concerning some of them. They simply sound like me or like poems I might have written. I offer my apologies to anyone whom I have omitted from my list of notables above.

I owe thanks to my wife Vicki for having humored me all these years in what must have seemed to her my obsession with a President whom she can remember despising during our undergraduate years at Duke University. She now gives me credit for having kept my eye on LBJ even during the years when he had gone into eclipse and disgrace, ignominy. She was my companion of course when I finally visited the LBJ Ranch, the Johnson family home in Johnson City, and the LBJ Library at the (I must say awe-inspiring) University of Texas. This trip was revelational in many ways. And it was profoundly moving in our tour of the ranch to find ourselves among people who retained affection for and continued to admire Lyndon Johnson just as I did, and to find in the docent who was leading us around the fabled property a woman whose knowledge of Lyndon Johnson probably far surpassed my own.

I must thank the staff of the LBJ Library for the help they have extended to me on a number of occasions. My original contact person was an impressively knowledgeable and extremely helpful intern. When her term was up and as I continued writing e-mails asking for help, I had the extreme good fortune to land on the desk and in the hands of Ian Frederick-Rothwell who has been my go-to man at the LBJ Library ever since. With his deep knowledge of the archives and of the ways to tap them, he has with great good humor handled all my sometimes crazy requests and questions and always given me astute answers that have sent me on my way for a while, until my own obtuseness has led me to ask him further questions.

Finally I take pleasure (and probably demonstrate infantile vanity) in noting what I consider strange little ticks of destiny that to my mind linked me to Lyndon Johnson from the beginning. My father and Lyndon Johnson were born on the same day though nine years apart, both of them in Texas. They were twins by extension. During the years of my early adolescence there lay on a little shelf under a table in the front room of my grandparents' house a copy of LIFE MAGAZINE with Lyndon Johnson on the cover of it. Stray copies of LIFE got marooned and left around in many households I'm sure during this period. People just forgot about them. With time the colors of the covers faded. I loved the front room of my grandparents' house for its rank of windows looking out on the neighborhood. I never failed to visit it whenever I visited their house, sometimes twice a week, Monday and Saturday, for lunch. Invariably I glanced at and even, I suppose, contemplated the picture of Lyndon Johnson which this room contained. I could not miss it on the way to the front windows or on my way back out. This cover was my introduction to the man. To say that I was looking at Lyndon Johnson twice a week for years is a simple statement of fact. But I like to think that he was also in some sense looking at me, sizing me up in the inimitable Johnson manner, marking me for what has turned out to be the biggest work of my life. I hope I have been worthy of it.

1.

With LBJ triumphant in Atlantic City 1964 I had to muse
Amid the ghosts of pin-up beauties (what a strange place),
I thought long thoughts back to 1948, back to
That infamous campaign when many loathed both him
And everything they thought they knew for sure
That Lyndon stood for. Not a few of those who loathed him
Then converted, some sincerely, some because
He'd gained such power that they had to "come on over."
Now he stood astride the pinnacle where every US politician
Deep down inside hoped to be some day as he himself
Once told me. I had been with him throughout those sixteen years
And it remained the strangest tossup in my mind,
I couldn't say yet whether blind ambition only
Was the motivating factor of this man's life or
An equal part of some abiding wish to make life better
For the poor folks striving upward. There was something
That impelled him, he ran harder than the average man
(than any man!) toward goals which even his incisive mind
May not have clearly understood—I mean, did anyone
For certain know what prompted Lyndon Johnson?
On election eve in Austin he would say he'd spent
His whole life getting ready for that moment.
Such a statement seemed a fair enough summation,
Simple fact, but what infinitudes of tumult, shifting
Inner plate tectonics of emotion and of striving it omitted.

2.

And this the man that in his study sits:

...For if I'd chosen any other way,
It would have started World War III.
It was the thought of World War III that kept me
Going every day--or of avoiding it--
I saw what this was doing to my programs
And I hated that the most--and I have seen
Who knows how many thousand boys I loved
Get killed and felt responsible for them--
But all that horror I've accepted
To have kept at bay the horror of that war
Which would have ended all we've known.
It started up among the intellectuals you know,
Just two or three of them at first stirred up the doubt,
But then the columnists came in,
The New York Times--then *Newsweek* followed,
Life and *Time*. And then *The Post*.
And then the doubt spread till it seemed
That all the people were opposed.
Then Little Bobby started in, he made this his cause.
He got Martin Luther King in on his payroll,
And so the Nigrahs got stirred up--
If they came out into the streets he'd get them more,
And then the Communists joined in,
And they control the national networks as we know
And all communication outlets,
There are the FBI reports that prove just that.
The Communists' desire to be the rulers of the world
Is like the lawyer's wish to someday be Chief Justice.
And if we don't stand up to them they will do it,
We'll be slaves. Now I'm not one of those
Who looks beneath the bed at night for Commies.

But I think I know how power in this world works,
And I have seen when someone's weak
How someone strong for sure will step into that vacuum,
And that's exactly what the Communists have done,
They saw the soft spots in our liberal professions,
The reporters and the teachers and the preachers.
The opponents of the war went on these jags
Which first arose among the Communists in fact,
Then found their way across the world in time to us.
The first jag was that we had killed civilians.
The next jag was we had to stop
The bombing, try a pause out.
The first pause in the bombing came
When someone from the Communists, some diplomat
Got talking to some influential person on our side.
Bobby Kennedy sat right here at this table
And assured me that he knew
That if we held the bombing up good things would happen,
Something positive would come of it.
And so I called a pause.
We wrote North Vietnam but got the letter
Thrown back next day in our faces.
In came Wayne Morse and he told me
That the Soviet ambassador had told him
Such and such a thing would happen
If we halted all the bombing.
They told Fulbright too and Clark,
They told Mike Mansfield, Church and others,
Then Mac Bundy and Dobrynin went to lunch
And damned if Mac did not start advocating peace.
Fortas was against the pause and so were Rusk and Clifford.
So was I, I didn't want us starting off the way
I knew we'd tend to look, like some weak sister, with concessions.
But I also didn't want to have the books say
I'd ignored a chance for peace

And so I pulled the bombers back,
But nothing happened. Is it just
Some strange coincidence whenever my advisors
Have some contact with a communist,
They're always quick right after that to offer me advice?
And then believe me, you will always see
Dobrynin's car in front of Reston's house
The night before some blast against us
Runs next day in Reston's column.

How can it be, and after all that we've accomplished...
Yet I know the people out there really love me,
All this talk of how I'm lacking in charisma--
It's invention, an invention of reporters--
They all tell you that I lack it, that my talks are uninspired,
Too "presidential," missing sparks, the face
Looks all but paralyzed they say, the muscles of it,
And those frozen smiles that simper, dull,
Dishonest preacher's manner, I can quote you
Their descriptions, yet deep down I know
The people out there love me after all
I've done for them, how could they help it?
It was some minute percentage
That had given up, lost faith,
And yet this small group--exhibitionists--
Were getting all the headlines,
Men in uniform were serving,
I got letters from them, hundreds every day,
That they supported...they weren't marching round
With placards in the streets with cameras on 'em.
They were just there dawn to dusk defending freedom.
The problem is they sabotage me
Every time I go to make a speech about the war.
The *St. Louis Post-Dispatch* will start to write
The week before about how terrible my public speeches

Are if that's my destination--they don't seem
To have an inkling that I once taught elocution,
Was debate coach, just about the best in Texas--
They will say the war is wrong and that the bombing
Is atrocious, make the people start to wonder,
Build this prejudice against me in the run-up
To my speech and soon the people say why bother
If it's all so uninspired, why even bother
Going down to hear the speech so pretty soon
There'll be no crowd, the press will gleefully report
How small the crowd, how dull the speech was,
All their prophecies come true, they work these wonders.
Now I'll admit the magic cycle might be broken,
It's the cycle which has fed me all my life
And I'd be willing to admit there's something
Wrong with it right now. It goes like this:
If you work harder than the rest, then you get power.
Having power you can do good works for people,
That's its purpose, and if you can do good works,
The people love you, you spend power
But it all comes back redoubled
In the form of people's love, and their support,
You shouldn't lose. You start with no chips,
Then you've got you this big pile if you've been smart.
What I can't understand at this point though...
In 1964 I bested even FDR, who was my daddy
In the deepest sense, I got the people's love,
We got the turbine really humming,
Power, energy, and good works
As the outflow and the inflow people's love.
But if you interrupt the current...
That's what's missing now, the love part,
And without it I get worn down.
I'd have thought...
Who's ever given them such laws,

So many jobs? You take the Nigras.
I've been fighting for them every day
Since I came into office, I have spilled my guts out
Getting them the Civil Rights Act first,
I gave them everything I had,
I gave that speech before both houses.
I had my dream too you know. I dreamt
That every child no matter what the color of his skin
Would have a nice house he'd grow up in,
Each day eat a solid breakfast, have a safe
And decent school he could attend and at
The end of it a good and lasting job.
I tried to make conditions such
That this would not just be some idle sort of
Politician's snow job. I asked little in return.
A bit of thanks. Appreciation. Recognition.
What I got instead was riots--rage erupting.
Everything I'd dreamt of was in ruins from these riots.
Take the students. I fought hard
To get them scholarships and loans,
For better schools and better teachers.
What I've gotten in return is student cohorts
In the streets deserting classrooms, singing songs
About the kids I've killed each day--
What do they think, that I take pleasure in
These deaths? I just don't understand
These young folks, can't they recognize
That deep down I'm just like them?
I despised cops just like they do in my youth,
And I dropped out and made my way to California
Just like them--I'm no conformist--all the people
I hung out with in the days of FDR
Were what you might have called the radical elite,
Not hidebound bureaucrats--we really meant
To overturn the world and had no patience for delay.

And then the poor have turned against me,
They have made me out as villain when the Congress
Cuts my programs. I remember once
A house in Appalachia, worse than Texas in my youth,
The seven kids all sickly looking, swollen bellies,
And I promised both the parents
That I'd make things better for them,
They seemed happy hearing someone say
He cared about their prospects, which were dismal,
I felt happy we might start to make some progress,
Then I turned around to leave, I saw
Two pictures on the wall. The one was Jesus
On the cross, the other picture was
The face of JFK, that suntanned face,
That placid smile. Now you can say
What things you like about old Jack
But he did nothing, almost nothing
For the poor man, so that picture felt to me
Like someone slapping me in public,
It insulted me, betrayed me.
Then there's critics in the Congress.
Take Bill Fulbright. Fulbright's problem,
Fulbright's gripe is that he's never going to get
To run the State Department, that's the job for him,
He's feeling bored up on the Hill
And so he makes a lot of noise to staunch the boredom.
He wants the nation to take note of William Fulbright,
And the fastest way to get that kind of notice
Is to assume the role of critic.
Whichever way I moved on Viet Nam
He would have had to be against me--for attention.
And then besides Fulbright,
There are all those squawking liberals on the Hill.
They squawk because I never went to Harvard,
Since I can't be JFK, and since I can't be friends

With their friends, I don't move in fancy circles.
And I'm keeping Little Bobby from the throne.
The Great Society's accomplished ten times more
Than what the New Frontier just on its best day
Ever dreamed of, that fact rankles most of all.
They simply had to find some issue
They could use to turn against me.
Vietnam became that issue, this despite the fact
That they're the ones who got us in
That whole great stinking mess to start with—
Limited war was their idea, little wars of liberation.
And then you have the columnists,
They've turned on Viet Nam from sheer self-interest
Since Pulitzer Prizes don't get given out
To those who praise administrations,
They get given out to those who dig up dirt
And make sensations--truth be damned.
The story's always pitched to win the favor of
The writer's higher-ups, they're like a wolf pack
In attacking me when I make tough decisions,
Herds of sheep among themselves, to one another.
They always will follow the bellwether sheep,
And that means Lippman and Reston.
As long as those two stayed with me,
I seemed to be OK, but once they left me
In pursuit of fancy prizes, that was it,
The others left me in succession,
In a pack, a Gadarene swine pack.
But the more they screamed and squawked,
The more determined I became to stick it out,
To be like Lincoln who's revered now
Since he persevered through troubles
In his conduct of a war.
These people say South Vietnam
Is not a country with a boundary you can point to

Though that boundary was created in Geneva
And was recognized by nations--fifty nations.
And the North was fully recognized as sovereign
In its own zone by the communists--that's settled,
There are two zones. People say it's not aggression
When it's North against the South, it's all one country
Just because some people think so, that eliminates
The boundaries. But let's talk about aggression:
When a man walks in your house and that man's
Brandishing a gun and that gun's cocked,
I think the name for that's aggression.
And that's exactly what the North did
When it walked into another person's house--
South Vietnam. It's just bad history
Perverted by the Harvards and the Galbraiths
When you say that's not aggression,
It's pure ignorance of all that went before
For thirty years. Before the Communists took part,
You didn't have an insurrection.
Ho's been communist throughout his adult life,
Got trained in Moscow, he's the founder of
The communist regime in Indochina,
He's their Jefferson and Adams.
Thousands of guerrillas moved
From North to South awaiting word from Ho.
The myth that these professors have
Of some nice family feud is just pure crap.
The decision to renew the fight
Came from Hanoi in 1959.
The NLF was organized by communists in Hanoi.
There may be some free movement of the forces
But there's no doubt where the main direction
Comes from--it's Hanoi. As for the argument
That it's been our aggression, not the North's,
Against the people of the South's will,

That's sheer nonsense and naïveté, the elections
They've just had have clearly demonstrated that.
And there's the fact that they've been struggling
In this war, a large proportion of the South has,
They've displayed a steadfast will
To keep themselves from going commie,
And when certain critics say the peasant's
Suffered under governments we've propped up,
Just compare that to the way the Vietcong
Has made the peasant village suffer,
Killing teachers, doctors, lawyers.
Some now speak of a consensus
Of the well-informed best writers
That the Vietcong-supporting side
Is larger in the South.
They should recognize the stake that LaCouture has
In interpreting the evidence that way,
The academics and the journalists make money,
Sell their papers pushing that line
While ignoring any other, disagreeing
With their government.
Then they read each other's pieces
While the rest of us, the uninformed in their minds,
Read benighted CIA reports, intelligence,
Security reports compiled by men
Whose only goal is finding out what's going on,
The State Department, DOD.
I believe that we are quarantining dangers
To the world's peace over there just like the smallpox.
Just like FDR and Hitler, just like Wilson and the Kaiser.
What I learned about the First World War
In college was that lack of any demonstrated strength,
Reserves of stamina on our part
Got us in there in the first place,
That the Kaiser only made some crucial moves

Because he knew that he could count the US out.
And then I learned in Congress, on preparedness
Committees, and from FDR himself,
That we were telegraphing messages
Susceptible of misinterpretation
By the Japanese and Hitler, that the Wheelers
And the LaFollettes, the Lindberghs
And that whole America First crowd
Were as much as telling Hitler he could move
And never factor us as part of his equation.
I learned history at first hand in the Congress
Back in those days. Even I was almost swayed
By all that liberal debate, I signed
The Ludlow Resolution which demanded
That the people get to vote
Before this country went to war--
Hitler could have taken over Europe in the time
That it was taking us to vote.
I ran down and took my name off those
Who'd signed it when I came back to my senses.
I felt silly. I believe our vacillation
Was what caused us to get caught up in that war.
And so I knew that if aggression
Got a toehold in the south of Vietnam,
There'd be no stopping the aggressors,
They'd take over Southeast Asia
Down to Singapore at least, perhaps Djakarta.
Now I know these academics think
That all they have to do is write a treatise
On the absence of the threat
And it will vanish overnight,
The row of dominoes won't fall.
The impotent academics keep on talking,
In the meantime you have Moscow and Peking
In steady motion, an expansion of control

Is taking place, before you know it
We'll be fighting in Berlin, and so we're back
To my first specter, World War III.
Which is for real. It's not some joke.
Although I recognize the argument
The enemy's diverse, the communist threat's
Not monolithic, I know nationalism's strong
And might move mountains in the end,
But I'm sure communism's stronger,
They have leadership, materials, and training.
I wish it wasn't so, the world would be a safer place.
But look at Hungary in 1956, in came the tanks
And they prevailed, the crunch of tanks
Defeated faith, superior force
Will vanquish spirit in the end.
Some have this little fantasy of Vietnam united
As a bulwark stemming communist aggression,
Of democracy that's founded on a social revolution.
I would like to know the last time
That a social revolution came to pass
Within a country that was carved up by a war.
The Bolshevik in this case can't be cited,
It was altogether different.
And Vietnam is somehow going to stand up
To the Communists in China? That's pure nonsense
Of the kind you hear from Fulbright,
Bull from Fulbright. Slightly less bull
Than the claim that Dulles made when he said
Laos was a democratic bulwark.
None the less a disavowal of the facts,
Of how the Communists control things.
You've got to get the Communists out completely,
Then there's time perhaps to talk
Of making Vietnam a bulwark.
Still the accusation I find most unfair is that...

You would think to hear them talk
That my intention was to bomb groups of civilians.
There is nothing I try harder to prevent.
I pick the targets one by one myself each day.
I know the generals would have bombed
Without discriminating targets,
I made sure I reined them in, there was no
Saturation bombing, I enforced the strictest limits,
I had more control of generals
Than any other president in history and yet...
War means destruction. We've rebuilt
As we've proceeded though,
And we meant the Mekong River
Delta project as another TVA for them--
We're modernizing Vietnam society.
Some talk of land enclosure is a good thing
But I see it as enclosure of the spirit
Since the promise of America has always been
Our freedom from enclosure--new frontiers--
I liked that phrase--but it's dependent on
Technology. The Vietnamese will never
Be the same again I know, but they've had
New worlds opened up to them, more choices.
They'll get freedom from their ancient superstitions.
You can't talk about the quality of life
Till they have food and basic minimums provided.
We will get those things to them
Once we can get this conflict settled.
Our tradition is benevolence. I'm sure of that.
But still it seems I'm being chased on all sides,
Some stampede from all directions closing in,
The people come at me,
They say we have to give up Vietnam.
Inflation's booming, I see trouble up ahead,
We'll have more riots in the spring.

There's this whole mob who's hot
To run me off the edge, the angry blacks,
You have the demonstrating students,
Welfare mothers, these professors up in arms
And those hysterical reporters. Bobby Kennedy
Is plotting to regain his brother's throne.
The magic of his name makes people
Come out in the street and start to dance.
After thirty seven years of public service
I deserve more than this plain
That I'm left standing in alone
With these stampedes on every side.
And there's this dream I have, it's somewhat
Like a dream I've had since childhood.
I'll be lying in the Red Room of the White House
And I know the head I have is still my own head
But the body from the neck down's all
Emaciated, withered, Woodrow Wison's
Body partly, it's the way my grandma was
In her last years too, she was propped up
In our house with lots of pillows
After having had a stroke, and I can hear
All my advisors in the next room
As they divvy up what once had been
My power, hear them fighting, Califano
Says my legislative program should be his,
The foreign policy is always claimed by Rostow,
Arthur Okun says he'll formulate the budget,
Christian says he'll handle dealings with the public.
I can hear them but I cannot give an order,
I can neither talk nor walk within this dream,
I'm just this lump, I feel exposed.
But no aide seems inclined to offer
Any least protection, so I wake from having had
This dream all sweaty and I start to walk the halls,

I have this little pocket flashlight,
I go downstairs and I look
At Woodrow Wilson's portrait hanging on the wall,
And I sometimes even touch it just to make sure
He's the one who had the stroke, the one who's dead,
That Lyndon Johnson's still alive.
I get some peace from this but not for long,
When I wake up it all resumes,
What caused this bad dream in the first place...

3.

--We're like the damn cow over the fence in Vietnam.

--Yes, I'm confronted. I don't think
This country's people ever wanted me to run,
Turn tail and hide, but if we lose,
They'll say that I'm the one who lost it,
I've pulled back. What kind of shape is that to be in?
I do not want to commit us to a war,
That's number one fact. There's a study
Being done now by the biggest experts out there,
They are trying to determine if Malaysia, also India
Might fall if we pull out,
If our prestige will suffer sorely
If we just get out and let some conference fail,
Some thing like that. And did I tell you
What old Moursund said last night?
He said Goddamn it, there's not anything'll
Tear you up as quick as pulling out of Vietnam,
There's only one thing all Americans
Want for sure: prestige and power.
I said yeah, but I don't want to kill those folks.

He said he didn't give a damn about those folks,
He said he didn't want to kill them in Korea
But to stand up for America, we had to.
There's only one thing that a man in
Johnson City or in Georgia can't forgive,
That's being weak. Now I think
Goldwater is the leader, you got all of them
Are raising hell about it, hot pursuit
And let's go right in there and bomb 'em.
You can't clean it up, this situation's hell
I'll tell you that.

--It'd take a half a million men, they'd all
Be bogged down there for maybe ten more years.

--We never did clear up Korea yet.

--We're still right where we started there,
Except for 70,000 of them buried.

--Except for this damn thing in Viet Nam
We're doin' fine, we're doing wonderful,
The indices, the businessmen, the tax bill's
Working out just right and only 2.6 percent
Of married people jobless.
You've got 16 of the youngsters unemployed,
The kids are dropping out of school
And then they go off on a roll, but then
My poverty addresses that whole problem,
It gets organized, there's money in departments,
One administrator sitting over all and then
We'll really get results, go in and clean up
These damn rolls, 300 million dollars more
Than what was budgeted is all that it requires,
Down in Kentucky we got fifty kids there

Teaching beauty culture, how to do up
Linda's hair and then they'll get themselves
Real jobs in three more months
Instead of paying out four billion on relief
For doin' nothin'. No more
Unemployment compensation payouts.
People working. But I've got to find a man
For Viet Nam. And tell me this:
How did the Congress take it when we bombed them?

--They don't know about it yet.
But I think all of them would sign off if they did.

--We're going to continue with reconnaissance
As needed, and we're sending in armed people
And will shoot back if we're shot at.

--That would be what Moursund said you have to do.

--Mike Mansfield's got him this fine
Four page memorandum says
We're getting in too deep,
I'm going to start another war.

--I think I share some of his fears.

--I share them too but I would say
The fear the other way is greater.

--I do not know what the hell we're going to do.
I didn't ever want to get messed up out there
To start with. All the brain trust types keep saying
We'll lose everything in Asia
If we lose South Viet Nam
But I don't buy that.

At the same time we're now in there
And I can't quite figure out how you'd explain
We're coming out, they'll think you're whipped,
That you've been ruined,
It's disastrous every which way.

--I believe I have to say that I did not make this commitment.
It was Eisenhower, Dulles got us in--
I can't quite say that.
And we oughtn't to have stayed in.
But we're in there now by treaty
And the question's one of honor for the nation.
We are there and being there
We must conduct ourselves like men,
That's number one. And number two
We must remember our own principles
And sympathize with people wanting freedom.
If the communists will leave the South alone
And give them freedom, we'll get out.

--The American people would not want
To stay in there forever, they would understand
Agreements all around, they have the sense
To see we're only saving face.
We can't just walk away and leave those people stranded.
On the other hand if we were going to get out,
I would call the crowd that got rid of Diem
And have them get rid of these people we have now
And put some fellow in there saying
That he wished to hell we'd go
And then we'd have us our excuse.
Just put some old freebooter in there,
I can't think now of the man's name,
I've been thinking of some sort of hellraiser.

And I think if he took over,
He'd be asking us to go.

--How important is it to us?

--Not a damn bit since we got these missile systems.
From the standpoint of psychology...well, maybe.

--Yes. And from the standpoint that we're party to
A treaty.

--Yeah, but we're the only ones who are abiding by
The treaty, you have other countries just as bound
As we are. They do nothing.
There are several others in there
Who were party to it too.
This whole damn thing's one great big headache.

--I spend all my days with McNamara, Rusk,
Mac Bundy, Harriman, and Vance and they all think
We've got to show some force and power.
They do not believe that China will come in,
They're like MacArthur in Korea.
They don't know of course for sure,
They feel we haven't got much choice,
That we are treaty-bound, we're in there,
It's this domino will kick off all the others
If it falls, we've got to get set for the worst.
I don't agree with Morse,
He wants us simply to get out.

--But what he says reflects the sentiment of many.

--Yeah, that's right. The people don't know Viet Nam
From diddley-do and they could care less.

--But then you go and send our boys out there...

--We got enough hell over losing thirty-five
Of them this year. But you've got Hickenlooper saying
We've just got to stand and show our force
And put in men regardless, come what may,
And no one disagreed with that.
I can't do anything on just the information
I've got now. Who can I talk to?

--I think everyone around you
Has his mind made up already.
They're too fixed in their opinions.

--To be fair I'd say that Rusk has tried to pull back.
He thinks Laos now is crumbling though
And Viet Nam is wobbly.

--Laos hell. That place aint worth a damn.
It's ten times worse than any Viet Nam
You've ever heard of.
There are some Vietnamese
And you can beat them on the head
And maybe then they'll go and fight,
But it's impossible in Laos, just a rathole.
To return though to the subject of that man
You need to send there: why not get
Old Omar Bradley and some senior people like him
With some sense. Perhaps not military.
Let them go out there and fool around
And smell and get the atmosphere

And come back here and tell you what they think
Before you take some drastic action.

--Don't repeat this but our biggest problem out there
Still is Lodge. He just aint worth a damn,
Can't work with any-bodd-y.
First we get the U.S.I.A. man
To put on all the radios
And get 'em to be loyal to the government
And fight and stop deserting,
Then he calls the U.S.I.A. man and says,
"I'll handle radio myself, to hell with you."
So that knocks that guy out. So I send in CIA,
The best guy out there, but he says of course
"I'll handle all intelligence,"
And so we lose another man,
And then he wants a new Assistant Chief of Mission.
Give us names we say. He gives them
And we pick the very best one, send him out there,
Soon enough Lodge picks some kind of fight
With this guy whom we've sent to run the war for him.
Even McNamara goes there and they work out
These agreements, issue orders, McNamara
Sends in stuff, but Lodge takes charge of it himself,
But he is not a take charge guy
And all that stuff just gets stacked up.

--He's never followed through on any one thing
In the twenty years I've known him,
He's a bright, intelligent fellow,
But he thinks that he's the emperor out there
And that he's dealing with barbarians
He can order what to do.
I have no doubt that he's the one
That ordered old Diem be killed.

—Now that was tragic. We've lost everything since then.

--Why don't you get some man out there who's pliant,
Who would do exactly what you said right quick?
Lodge is living somewhere up there on cloud nine.
The best thing you could do would be to ask him
Don't he think that it's about time he
Came back home to the States.

--He'd come right back home against us
And he'd be out there campaigning
On this issue every day.

--God A'mighty he'll be back here to campaign
Against us anyway. I know that.
When the time comes.
Why not give him some good reason?
It would be just like MacArthur who
With all the power he had
Still couldn't damage Harry Truman.
Everybody said he's mad because the President
Removed him though a lot of people
Thought that he was right.
Just let old Lodge be like MacArthur.
Then his blows won't do you damage.

--There's not a damn thing we can do.

--I've wept and fasted over this
Because we're getting in there deeper,
It's my country getting pulled in,
Pretty soon you'll have the Chinese coming in,
A danged conventional war with them,
You'll have Korea on a bigger and a worse scale,
It's the damnedest mess on earth you can imagine.

The French spent all that money, theirs and ours,
Lost all those men, and in the end
They got the living hell whupped out of them.

--I would agree with what you've said,
I think the Chinese will come in
Although our people say they doubt it.
There's this memo here from Mansfield
That I've mentioned. He accuses me
Of pique and saving face at every essay of
De Gaulle's. Well, we're not piqued,
We asked de Gaulle to give us blueprints.
He don't have one. Aint no party to this war
Who's going to sign on now to neutralize.
He says we must continue to maintain our strength
And get into position. What does that mean?
We have gotten in position.
We lack military allies we can count on.
Hell, I know that. We should think about
Appealing to the UN.
They don't do a goddamned thing.
And we should entertain proposals for a conference.
We've been ready to confer with anybody anytime,
But Ho Chi Minh and all his boys will not behave,
And we send word out every week through
Proper channels, we tell Khrushchev
That we're ready to get out and to remain out
If they North will stop these sorties
On their neighbors. They say "Screw you."

--You can't let this situation simply go on drifting.
It gets worse. You've got a real good case
For having us get out, a somewhat
Weaker one for having us move in
Although I know that moving in

Is more consistent with American reactions,
People understand that better.
But getting out will be a mess
And it will be a good bit worse to some extent
Than where we are now.
I'm not clear how much the Russians--
They must surely want to cause us
All the trouble they can think of--
Is it true that they're at odds somehow with China?

--Yes they are, but they'd go with them in a fight,
They've got that Communist philosophy that binds them.
We've done all that we can do to have them help us.
They contribute very little.

--They'd be foolish to contribute very much
Because they see us pouring money down that hole
And we don't even get good will back.

--You've got all these politicians, you've got Nixon,
You've got Rockefeller saying move up north. And even Ike.

--You know there's no way we can move there.
Hell, we've tried that from the infiltration standpoint.
Our results have been disastrous.

--Nixon, Rockefeller, Lodge, they all say move.
Goldwater. Ike.

--And bomb the North and kill old women, children,
Innocent civilians.

--No, they say pick out an oil plant or refinery.
We would take selected targets.

Watch some trail when they come down it.
Intercept them. Bomb them out when they come in.

—You know that kind of talk aint worth a hoot in hell.
That's just impossible. We tried it in Korea.
We had got a load of old B-29s, increased the bomb load,
Sent them over there and dropped bombs
Day and night, and they would say
They'd knocked a road out in the night
And in the morning they'd be people,
Crowds of people moving over it again,
Same full scale traffic. You can't stop them.
We controlled the seas and air then absolutely
And their people still got through.
You can't control it.

--They'd impeach a President though if he ran out
On this I think. Don't you agree?
Outside of Morse each one I've talked to
Says go in including Hickenlooper.
Everyone. Republicans. I don't see any way
Of getting out unless they tell me to.

--We got to get a man in there to ask us
To withdraw--a man in charge.

--I know you're right but we can't do that.
That'd fix us in the world's eyes pretty bad.

--But we don't look too good right now.
You might look good if you go in with all
Those troops or for a while, but I'll say this:
It's going to be the most expensive thing
We've ever gone for.

--I've got me a little old sergeant at the house,
He's got six kids, and I hold him up
As my picture of the Army and the Air Force
And the Navy when I think of this decision,
Sending him there with those kids of his at home
Gives me the chills. And what the hell gain
Is there for us if I send him?
I just haven't got the nerve
And yet I can't see any out.

--God knows I'd like to help you if I could.
We're in the quicksand to our neck.

--Well, I'll be callin' you again.
You know I love ya.

4.

I had heard the old men talking on the front porch
In the evening, they would gather round my Daddy
Who was sitting in his rocker, holding court
And holding forth, you'd have these old men
In their faded denim overalls, their elbows
Always resting on their knees, they seemed
To contemplate the floorboards, they might
Shift their quids and spit from time to time
But not move otherwise, like wooden decoy ducks,
The fields a-glow behind them passing into dusk.
There would be this same scene every summer night
And I would hover in the doorway
As the wave of talk would oscillate,
The wind might seem to fan it into fervor
When discussion turned to Wall Street,

To the grip in which the potentates and powers
Held this country by the balls.
Those men were living off our sweat, they didn't know
What real work was, they just clipped coupons,
Wrote debentures down which our men couldn't spell,
They ripped the shirts right off our backs
So that the guy who grew the maize
Did not get his share, they were cancerous,
Were leeches, we could make them cease
To matter if our management of money really worked.
But they controlled the banking system.
Just remember: if the revolution comes,
Then they'll be shown to be its prime cause
And its victims, I believed that when I heard
My Daddy say it and I still believe it now.

5.

-- No single speech will be enough to reassure the country,
We will have to face up to the fact
That we are changing our past policy,
Not just continuing.
We are asking all Americans to bet more
To achieve less, we're engaging in
A much more massive effort,
Both political and economic.
We may have to change our mission in Saigon,
Change how it's organized.
And governmental structures here at home
May have to change too.
Early victories are out and early casualties
Are likely to be heavy.

--We need to get the government in Saigon to assure us...
There will be time later to decide that this won't work
When we have given it a good try.

--We won't get out, we will double down our bet
And end up lost among the paddies.

--I would rather keep our policy the same
And waffle through than just pull out.
I think the country is prepared to take grim news.

--The nature and integrity...the firmness of
Commitments is the main thing.
They will make our stance toward Russians
Something real, they back it up,
And if the leaders of the Communists believed
That we would not see this thing through,
It would be dangerous, de-stabilizing.
It is crucial to convince them of our firmness,
More important than what other nations
Think of us, non-Communists that is.
And I remain more optimistic toward
Our prospects in the war, I think
Our increments of force will make guerrillas
Of the VC, they cannot use major forces
For attacks upon the GVN...confronting them
With difficult decisions. An increased
US commitment doesn't mean the war is changing,
We've already gone a long way in the air
And on the ground without an escalation statement.
I'm not sure we need to make it too dramatic
When we send in greater forces.

--Still, to call up our reserves involves some drama.

--If we had sent in 50,000 men in 1961,
Hanoi might not be moving now against the South.

--We cannot count on stability prevailing in the South.
Saigon has no roots in the countryside.
Do not rely too much upon the government.
If we think that the area's important,
We may have to act alone, do what is needed
Irrespective of the government, what it wants.

6.

This was just a desperate bind that he was in
To tell the truth, he needed first of all to rally
Some support but only rally it so far
Because he knew that if he really stomped them up
And said "We have to go and kill those little slanty-eyes,
Let's go out there and smash 'em," he'd be riding
On a groundswell, they'd be clamoring
To win the war decisively, to end it, get it over with,
The only way to do that was invade North Viet Nam,
Which risked a bigger war with Russia and with China.
We thought at first that we might win the war
By all this bombing--he gave up on that quite early
Though I think he never said so.
So the only way to do it was invade,
But if you did invade, you risked the bigger war,
And so you couldn't, so you had to try
To rally your supporters for this half war,
Which was tantamount to getting half a hard-on
With a girl you had the hots for.
It was difficult and worse than that was crazy
And I think the situation drove him nuts,

Made him impatient, and impatience was behind
His calling doubters nervous Nellies.
That phrase hurt him worse than anything he said
Because at that time questions nagged
At all these families with their draft-aged sons in college,
What the hell was this damned Asian war about,
Why were we fighting it, and if we had to fight it,
Why not win it, why not get the damned thing
Over with at once, don't mess around with someone's
Fifth rate jungle army, playing paddycake.
The war's no longer being fought by pros
The way Jack Kennedy had led us to believe
It could be, fought exclusively by people
Wearing green berets and so on, some elite corps,
We were smarter and could hit and get away
With such precision, we could come out clean
From all these wars of local liberation.
Now it's taking many thousands of draftees,
The whole thing changes. It's at this time
When he's failed to give a thorough explanation
And no proper preparations have been made
Because he doesn't want to stir the country up
And he's afraid that those in Congress will curtail
Domestic programs if a full scale Asian land war's
Getting started that he calls these fair dissenters,
These dissenters who were asking valid questions,
Nervous Nellies. This was terribly disturbing,
Yet I understand the bind that he was in then,
How to half-lead his supporters, those who
Would have liked to be such, into war--
I guess this falseness of position should have warned him.

7.

We Southern liberals may have misconceived it,
I'd be willing to concede that, we believed
In integration, men of good will making
Common cause and putting down the racists
Whereas Moynihan contended that the problem
Was a class of untermenschen, urban
Working people boiling with the pressures
That beset the urban poor except that
This group had it worse because their skin
Was also wrong, and they kept getting
More delinquent, anti-social, more resentful,
And the old approach, the rhetoric
From circa 1950, all that stirring sort of stuff
Of get the shackles off the Negro, let him run
The race of life no longer fit the situation.
That's exactly what we thought though,
We would set a sort of super YMCA up
To help them, saying you can go to school now,
We will educate you, train you, we will
Build you better housing, but we hadn't
Really fixed it at the base, we hadn't
Thought about security and money
Or cohesiveness of families
Or the power money gives you.
Either money or the bomb were means
To power in this country, they'd resorted
To the bomb with some success-
I mean by riots--but the riots meant
The Polacks on the line at River Rouge
Weren't going to stick with Walter Reuther
And the governmental people who supported
Spending money on the Negroes.
There's a certain coalition that we've barely

Held together, it's the slenderest majority
That's gotten us such progress as we've made
Comprising labor, intellectuals, and Negroes,
And the bosses of big cities, their machines,
The urban poor. The riots scared
A lot of people in this group or they
Offended them, they saw it as the government's
Response...let's put it this way:
There were speeches which expressed our deep concern
About the very groups that carried out the riots,
Taking their side, saying we knew how it was
And that the riots would continue--understandably--
Until conditions changed, and so
We funneled money their way,
We "rewarded all those rioters."
That's what some stalwart former coalition members
Heard as what their government was saying.
Tear the cities up and you'll get more attention.
It was fatal for the Negroes losing this group
As their allies. Who'd support them then?
Just believe me, ot the people in those office buildings there,
L Street NW, because they're scared
And always have been of the blacks,
They're simply middle class white workers
Who don't want to live near blacks
Or go to school with them.
The coalition was the Negroes' only hope.
But you've got coalition members now convinced
That their own government is unconcerned
With their plight, that the Negro's now the focus,
Only focus of attention. Then a President's
Commission sits in session and produces
Its report. What does it say?
That it's the fault of all those racists
Who had heretofore been coalition members,

They're the ones who caused the riots.
You can understand why they'd say
We'll go vote for Richard Nixon
Or some guy who understands us even better
Like George Wallace. So the President
Was being pulled apart by contradictions,
There were Southerners who said
"By God you've got to tell them, Lyndon,
We can't have these kinds of riots in the streets,
And there were others, anguished liberals
Who were telling him again that this whole thing
Derived from Negroes being poor, what good's the call
For law and order till you alter those conditions.
He was hearing these positions but accepted
Neither one of them completely,
So his message came out garbled.

8.

He's simply more alive than all the others,
Those professors, you take Galbraith, you take
Schlesinger, politicos, the bureaucrats
In Washington, I've been around them all
And they don't really have a clue what's going on.
You saw those people he was speaking to,
You saw it in their eyes, he made them feel
That something real was being shown them
For the first time in their lives,
They just can't not respond to something
He calls up, my heart was pounding,
I was mesmerized with all those people screaming,
You can almost say you love him
Though in fact you know he's just a little shitass.

It's the vigilante ethic with apocalyptic overtones:
Whenever your community's in crisis
You must intervene directly and with violence
If needs be--that's the dark side
Of the moon of our tradition.

Let 'em go ahead and say that I'm a racist,
Makes no difference, they's whole heaps of folks
That feel the same way I do. Race
Is what is gonna win this thing for me.
Let's say a nigger down here comes up sidlin' to
Some white gal, tries that stuff they do up North,
We gonna shoot him or we bust his head in half,
We do not tolerate that business, niggers
Know for sure what happens, let 'em
Try and start a riot here, the first one
Picks a brick up gets a bullet in his head right quick,
And then you ease yourself on over to
The next one and you say to him, all right,
Pick up a brick. See what he does. You shoot
A few down and you got the whole thing stopped
Dead in its tracks. Now Bob McNair, South Carolina,
Don't go in for all that roughneck kind of talk,
He's one 'o your nice boys. Old Carl Sanders there
In Georgia. Now I like Carl though I'm not sure
He likes me and I got nuthin'
Gainst the way he runs his state except that
He's another nice one, wants to moderate proceedins.
But he found out you can't do that.
Ivan Allen over there, they knocked him
Off that car you know when he was tryin'
With those rioters to talk nice.
Ought to have done a damned sight more,
There's too much dignity in government right now
When what we need's a little meanness.

You elect some kind of steel mill hand as guvner,
Then you'd see--you want to talk about
Ignitin' revolution. Damn! You'd see a lot of shootin',
Tearin' down and burnin' up and lettin' blood,
He'd simply go ahead and do it, wouldn't
Think about it first, he wouldn't have to sho enuff.
What I've been telling folks for years
Is there'll be fightin' in the street some day,
The rightists and the leftists, blacks and whites.
Hell, all we'd have to do right now
Is march us up there to Montgomery,
To the courthouse, take control of it
And lock up several judges and by sunset
You'd be seein' revolution East to West,
We'd turn this country right around.
We got part of it already, got the workin' man
And now we're gonna get the other part of it
You watch, we'll get the high hoi polloi,
They gonna come around, you'll see, they'll say
I'd vote for him if I felt I could trust him,
If I felt sure he would not be getting tamed up there
By Washington like our boy done--Lester Maddox.
These here liberals and intellectual morons,
They got nuthin' to believe in but their theories,
They lack faith in common people--hell,
A lot of them don't even like real people
When you scratch 'em down to basics.
When the liberals and the pointy head professors
Say that we lack common sense, they mean
Us people. They don't realize just what
Solid information you can get from some man
Drivin' him a truck to make his livin',
You don't need to go and ask some kind of egg head.
The fella on the street has got a better mind
And instincts than your sissy britch professor

Up at Harvard who will say our folks are votin'
Out of ignorance for me. Just who they wantin'
You to vote for stead of me? This here's a secret.
Nixon, Johnson, all them big boys, they don't hang
They high priced breeches on the wall so's they can
Do a flyin' leap to put them on 'em every morning,
They's the same as you and me, they get dressed
One leg at a time, they like the folks in
Chilton County, all them good folks I got
Standin' there behind me, you don't think
I got this power on my own, it's cause a' them,
They see me standin' up to all them slick-hair
City boys up north, it's really them,
They know I'm standin' up for them,
The whole world's heard of Alabama now,
The big politicos is worried, even Paris France
Has heard of Alabama, they afraid we gonna hurt 'em.
Lemme tell you somethin': they deserve to hurt
Cuz they hurt us so long, I'm kinda sick and tiyud.
The Republicans are meetin' now in banks,
They got to figger what to do 'bout us down here,
The Chase Manhattan and the Wall Street crowd,
They holdin' secret meetins in the biggest banks of all,
Not little biddy banks, discussin' what to do
With Guvnuh Wallace and his state of Alabama.

9.

Increasingly it gravitates to two centers--Power--
Other empires have dissolved--unlike the previous
Aspirants to hegemony the Soviets are animated--
Bald fanatic faith that's antithetic to our own,
Seeks to impose an absoluteness of authority

Enveloping the world--the conflict therefore
Is endemic, will be waged by methods violent
Or non- as its expedience will dictate,
There's this specter of increasingly terrific
Mass destruction, every person faces swift
Annihilation should the conflict enter
Phase of total war--STOP--on the one hand
All the people of the world yearn for relief
From this anxiety of looming mass destruction,
On the other hand extension of dominion
By the Kremlin makes it possible the coalition
Adequate to stand up to the Kremlin
Can't be mustered--this Republic and its
Citizens ascendent though its strength may be
Now stand in gravest danger--all the issues
That are facing us--momentous--this destruction
Or fulfillment of the civilized ideal--
It is apparent--greatest jeopardy Republic
Ever faced--of free society--of reconciling order
I now sing--and of the need--participation.
Order absent mid the nations and the Soviets
Are seeking to impose one, their possession of
Atomic weapons backs up their design and it
Increasingly is jeopardizing us, it adds great strains
To this uneasy equilibrium devoid of any order
Which exists and raises new doubts--how long
Nations go on tolerating tension--order may be
Sought on anybody's terms--the risks
We're faced with--total struggle--total victory
Can never be attained since our democracy's
In process--risks still crowding in upon us.
Still the Kremlin seeks to bring the free world
Under its dominion, it subverts by infiltration
Or intimidates, it seeks to swallow up
Our institutions turning all of them against us.

Our material and moral strengths are obviously
Targets, labor unions, civic enterprises,
Town halls, schools and churches, our opinion-
Makers, mining all within...make them be sources
Of confusion, take advantage of our doubts
And our diversities, the merits of our system,
Rights and privileges that all free men enjoy
Are opportunities the Kremlin takes advantage of
To do its evil work--we can't retaliate, prevent,
Since it's our democratic scruples
Which define us while morality for them
Is "that which serves the revolution."
Never miss an opportunity to insult or
Revile us in the world, they cast dishonor on
Our country or our motives or our methods
At the same time they seek overwhelming
Military force the will to use which they claim
They possess alone--in saying we lack such
A will they call us decadent and doomed...
In local incidents encroaching for the sake
Of short term gains and to induce
Defeatist attitudes in us. Since both sides
Have atomic weapons but mistrust each other,
Premium is placed upon surprise attack
Against us...they know we would never
Carry out preventive war against them,
Our unwillingness to use atomic weapons
Any time unless attacked makes them prefer
Piecemeal aggression...take for granted
Our unwillingness to ramp up our attacks
Unless attack is made on us...we are immobilized,
Confused, our inability to weigh things
And to choose, pursue a firm course
Based on rational assessment...there's the risk
That we may therefore be prevented

Or delayed in needful measures...risk
That allies also lose determination,
A descending spiral sets in far too little
Far too late, our options narrowed,
This the greatest risk of all...at several
Vital points of pressure we must give
The Kremlin evidence of willingness to make
Of any pressure point which we can't hold
Occasion of a global war, full-scale
Annihilation...it is bad enough to have
No better choice than to give in or to
Precipitate this total global war
At all these pressure points, but risk
Is multiplied by weakness it imparts
To our position in the cold war
Which we must win, not appear in it
Irresolute and desperate as
An alternating pattern...

10.

All our bombings, our deployments must be
Linked up in the long term with, support
This settled outlook: to contain Communist China,
Which is threatening to undercut United States
Importance, our effectiveness...all Asia
Could be organized against us...an instinctive
Understanding in our country of the threat
Some coalition Chinese-led...to our security...
Defensive...we're thrown back on mere defensives...
Understanding of this threat is interwoven with
Perception that the U.S. has a view
Of how the whole world should be moving,

Of a need for a majority of all the other
Peoples to be moving in the same direction
We are if we mean to meet
Our national objectives...this the role
That we've inherited and chosen for ourselves...
To move the world as best we can
In this direction we prefer but cannot do so
If some powerful and virulent and contravening
Nation is allowed to set its section
Of the world up in accordance with
An outlook that is hostile to the openness
And freedom we believe in and promote.

11.

Before we turn and let this country go we should consider
Using our own troops to counter all the communist insurgents
In the South I don't anticipate a re-run of Korea.
I believe that it is possible at least that one or two brigade-
Sized units sent to do specific jobs perhaps in six weeks
Might be just the kind of medicine that's called for.

12.

To wait he said might be to risk more turmoil,
And a "popular front" might develop
And the US might be forced then to withdraw.
If the USA was forced to leave the region
With its tail between its legs, then this defeat
Would be disastrous through the world,
Not just in Asia.

13.

Almost all the actors made miscalculations whether high
Or low or in the middle echelons and whether dove
Or hawk or something in between them, there were
Errors to be made by all concerned. I cite one simple
But conspicuous example late in 1964 or early 1965:
Peace-seeking planners in the State Department who
Opposed the bombings of the North that we'd projected urged
That we send ground troops in instead of bombing,
Troops would give us better leverage when we bargained,
Troops increased our "chips" they said, would give us
Something to negotiate about (withdrawing them)
Whenever conferences toward peace would get convened,
If we pulled troops out we were making some concession.
At the same time air strike option boys, the military types
Remained dead set against American participation in
"another land war in Asia" like Korea. They were joined
In this position by civilians who proclaimed themselves
"for peace" but who believed that it would
Soonest be achieved if we bombed Hanoi
Into swift negotiations, made them hurt, made them
"cry uncle." By the end of '65 what did we have?
The worst of both worlds. Ineffective costly bombing
Of the North, ground forces growing in the South
And no negotiations even vaguely being mooted.

14.

At some point late in '65 already we were stuck
In Vietnam and in an article, an analytic piece,
I up and said so, spoke of dangers in the offing,
This was when the White House constantly

Assured us we'd be out of there in two years—
Not the President himself perhaps but others.
But my article appeared about a day or two before
The press pool flew down to the Ranch
To have a weekend with the Man Himself.
We had a routine sort of briefing in the morning—
That was Saturday—then they said "the lid was on,"
Which meant that nothing more officially was scheduled
For that day so we were free and we were lounging
In the driveway when the President drove up
Toward us at truly breakneck speed in that white
Lincoln Continental with the top down which he
Ripped around the ranch in—you could wonder
For a moment what his strategy for stopping was,
He did slam on the brakes though and he leaned across
And opened up the right front door—we stood there
Dumbly watching what he'd do next—he yelled
My name (last name only) out abruptly,
So I got in and we sped off down some dirt road,
Not a single word exchanged, I guess two minutes
Had elapsed before he slammed the brakes again—
A screeching halt, a stand of trees, then he got out—
He didn't turn the engine off, he left his own door open
And he walked about a dozen feet I guess
And then he stopped and pulled his pants down
And proceeded then to defecate in full view,
Then he wiped himself with bits of leaves and grass,
Then pulled his pants up, took his seat behind the wheel,
Drove off again at breakneck speed up to the cohort
Of reporters who were standing there, they hadn't
Really moved, and I was motioned out, the Presidential
Lincoln then roared off and still no words had passed
Between us, I was stupefied, embarrassed, feeling numb.
Perhaps I wanly smiled. I can't remember any questions
Which my colleagues might have asked, they must have

Wondered what had happened. So did I though too.
A message was delivered. I could say that much.
"I know he's never going to end this war," was one
Clear thought though I was reeling for the most part.
How could I ever find a way to write about what happened,
What I'd learned, who would believe me? Who was crazier,
The President or me? I knew he'd never end the war,
I had the proof, Ahab's insistence on the rightness of
His mission, yet there was absolutely no way I could tell it,
I was baffled by the knowledge. And tormented.
Maybe that was his intention all along, to make me mute.
He had succeeded in a sense and he could laugh at that,
He'd made of me a party (guilty party) to this outrage.

15.

His senior advisors were sure we were headed
Correctly in Vietnam and all the members
Of the legislative branch were in agreement.
It was rare to find a voice that counseled caution
Or advised that we not do it.
The support for our involvement there
Was really overwhelming. Lately
Some have started thinking or believing
It was Lyndon Johnson's war
Or at the very least, with evil
His intention, he expanded it
Or had been plotting all along to make it wider.
There was no such plot from Machiavelli's book.
Few experts thought in 1965
That we should not send in our troops,
There seemed to be no other way.
To put it very bluntly he was told

The Viet Cong were outright winning
And no matter what he'd said in his campaign
He had to take some drastic action.
If the people then complained
That they'd been hoodwinked by his statements,
Well, would they have rather had us lose the war?
And he himself was feeling guilty.
"We've kept our guns above the mantle
For a long time," he would say,
"With what results?
They are killing our men while they sleep in the night.
Can I ask our men to fight with one arm
Tied behind their backs? How can I
Not give them the maximum support?
The Viet Cong blew up Pleiku.
Mac Bundy's out there. He calls in
And tells me how much now they're all of them
Agreed—Max Taylor, Westy—
It was time for us to bomb them.
We retaliate against North Vietnam
Because Hanoi directs the Viet Cong in action,
It supplies arms and it infiltrates more men.
They are the same…"

It was just before the first big escalation
And a bunch of us were down there in the morning,
He had called us for a meeting.
He asked each of us, he went around the room,
"Would you advise me?"
If I ever saw a man more torn apart
Than he was torn with us that morning,
I can't think who he might be.
And almost every man would say
"I'd put more troops in, I'd do
Everything I could to hold them back."

It was unanimous opinion.
He announced that he was sending
50,000 more men in: "combat support troops."
More would probably be needed later on—
An understatement—this was only the beginning.
He did not disclose the full extent
To Congress at this time. Was that dishonest?
Well, perhaps no more dishonest
Than his hero FDR in '41.
Except that his dishonest actions turned out well
And LBJ's have turned out badly.

16.

The first I ever heard of Lyndon Johnson was a story
From the governor himself, "It was in 1936
And Lyndon Johnson came down here
To pass his NYA funds out, and I had called him
To my office, I said Lyndon, you've been
Passin' out this money and I know you plan
To give grants next to Prairie View.
Now I have just done me some research,
There's no other Southern state
In which the NYA director's
Given money out to nigras
At a nigra kind of school.
Your future's lookin' mighty fine,
I think you might go very far,
That's why I thought I ought to tell ya
Texas simply isn't ready
For this kind of grant
I hear you plan to make.
I want to help you.

Lyndon stood up,
I stayed seated at my desk.
That booger said I do appreciate
Your having called me in,
There were important things
I could have done this morning
But I thought I ought to take the time
To see you since you're governor of Texas.
I felt honored to receive the invitation
And it's been an inspiration
Learning how a man like you
Whom we all know to be a Christian
Would apply his Christian faith
Toward human beings in his state,
It's very touching." Allred told me
He was not sure how at this point
This whole thing was comin' down,
He said he stood up from his desk,
He meant to pin old Lyndon down,
He wasn't going to let him leave
Until he got some kind of statement
Of intention. Lyndon headed toward the door
But then he turned back toward the governor
And said, "And in the light of this example
You've presented of the way
I ought to act toward whites and nigras
I'm returning to my office,
I will send my grant to Prairie View
This very afternoon,
It will be doubled."

17.

This civil rights thing: I came in, the bill was up there,
I could not say I'm against it, tear it down.
I haven't called a human being, haven't done
A thing that's vicious that I know of,
But when things get so damned bad
That I cannot do somethin'else,
I have to send the FBI in. They investigate.
I haven't ordered paratroopers in
Or sent divisions. I allowed some Navy boys
In little white jackets, I gave them the run
To look around with FBI and local law officials.
My relations with the governor of Mississippi
Aren't too bad, we talk a few times every week,
I try to help out. I had Hoover down there.
I am doin' what I can to carry out my oath of office,
At the same time not be ugly, mean or vicious,
Be considerate of fellow human beings
While I try to lead the nation. I can understand
How this is playing out in Mississippi
And in Alabama, Georgia, I've spent
56 years in it, I've been living it,
I'm trying now my damnedest,
But I've got to walk this tightrope.

18.

"Don't be thinkin' '68 George, 1988's
The year we both should think of,
You and I will both be dead and gone by then.
You now got ignorance in Alabama, George,
But you could change that, you could help

Your people clarify their minds,
And your own President will help you.
After all what do you want to represent
Your life's achievement when you're dead?
Some big old monument of marble
Saying here lies George C. Wallace,
He built up, he had a vision and he edified
His people. You could have that
If you chose it, now's your chance.
Or would you rather have some scrawny
Pine board box sunk down real deep in caliche soil
That says here lies a man who kept on hating?"

19.

The first time I met Johnson when I came up here
To Washington he said "You ought to know my thoughts
On everything," and so we toured the world in talking,
We discussed the looming prospects of another war for instance,
That was everyone's concern then, we went on
For Ninety minutes, at the end he said
"And then there are the Nigras."
This was 1948. He said "The Nigras fought the war,
They filled the war plants, built the bombers,
They did this and they did that and now they're back
And they won't take this shit we're giving them
Much longer. I'm still hoping that we can
But I'm not sure that we will make the system
Answer their demands but if we don't,
The streets I'm sure will run with blood."
I'd never heard a person talk that way
Because in Texas it was not like Mississippi
Where the presence of the black folks

Could be thought of as a threat.
I arrived here after driving through the Deep South,
Alabama, northern Georgia, you could just feel
That relations there were different than
The way they were in Texas, something shuddered there,
There seemed a kind of thickness, it was something
That I knew we'd have to deal with, I had had
A sort of instinct, but it took these words of Johnson's
As the spark I'd say, the fundamental lessons
That you learn in life occur in milliseconds,
There's a sharp flash or a rending of the veil,
You see the whole world in a different light,
Your paradigms have changed,
That tiny millisecond's really like
A great gulf in your life, once you're across it
You look back—except you can't look back—
To how you used to think and I had understood
Instinctively what Johnson was evoking,
That's the only way I *could* know
When he talked about how streets would run with blood.
But I was soon back out in Texas on campaign stops,
All those little towns, and race was not arising
As a topic, not at once, these were the helicopter stops
When we'd come swooping out of nowhere,
We were working on East Texas which was one place
Where you might see three or four blacks in the crowd.
There was a noontime stop in Cleveland,
Lathan Abram was involved somehow,
That pleased me, I would not have thought
That he'd turn out for Johnson since his family
Were among the better off, he'd been a friend of mine
In college, quite a track star and in football
He excelled at wide receiver. He was married
To a girl who was a friend of mine as well,
I knew them both. Poor Lathan

Died a little later in Korea. That was sad.
But in these tank town stops the helicopter circled
For a while to build excitement, draw the crowds out,
Then it put down on an empty space—
In terms of structures it was empty—by the railroad depot,
You would have a flatbed truck or he might give
Some kind of speech from off the depot building's porch,
There was the sunlight glare and dust,
And there would be one pair of tracks
Ran by the station in a straight line
East and west or south and north
And they would shimmer in the distance.
Desolation. If you're standing there where Johnson is,
The track is to your right, right by your feet,
And there's the right of way, a space of twenty feet
Beyond the track and then there's woods,
Deep piney woods since this is East Texas,
Not my home turf let me tell you.
There was a broad slope of grass and it gave access
To the station, I can see it to this day,
And there may well have been a parking lot
Of clay or maybe not, the need
For making lots was not perceived back then,
And so the crowd was comin' in and Lathan
Started introducing all the big wigs from the county,
They had come there, then when Johnson
Finally stood up at the microphone,
He didn't start to speak and that meant trouble,
It was take off for the woods time,
You did not know what offended him
Or got him out of sorts, you only knew
Not to be seen by him, avoid the big man's
Sight lines, I could hear him this time saying "No, no, no"
So all the panic buttons sounded, he was in place,
Nothing seemed to be the matter. True,

The crowd would not come close this time,
Sometimes he'd try to draw a crowd in closer,
But that didn't seem to be the problem this time.
He came out with it at last. "I won't start speakin',
I don't care if people have to miss their lunch
But I won't speak till those Americans"—
He gestures to his right across the track—
"Come over here, till they are standing over here
With these Americans"—he gestured to his left—
"This is America, that's not the way we do things."
To say the least he'd really gotten my attention,
I looked over to his right, there was a dribble,
Very small, of local black folks, lots of kids,
Some older kids, some adult black folks,
It was hard to tell exactly, four or five deep,
They were spilling from the woods on to
The right of way, but that was not the total,
There were more, there were a lot more sort of
Skulking in the woods behind a fence,
You couldn't pick them out exactly since
The undergrowth was just as tall as they were,
So the number of the black folks who'd turned out
To hear this speech was somewhat larger
Than the numbers who were out there
In the right of way, and the numbers in
The right of way weren't bad, this was a fair-sized
Crowd of blacks, but they were here
And then you had the crowd of white folks
Over there, it was a color line division
Pure and simple and he said this
And I don't think either side, since what he'd said
Was so enormous, neither side was really sure
What they had heard, they all just froze there,
Nothing happened.
So he spoke again, he ran at it again

And he was sounding rather put out,
Even angry. "All right, move now, you Americans"
While pointing at the blacks, "come on,
Cross over to this track." And he was being that specific
With his orders. What you saw
Was maybe 25 or 30 of those blacks head for the woods,
Crawl through that fence or crawl across it.
But there were maybe three or four who stayed
And one who stayed was very old,
A white-haired black man. And the three of them
Kept holding to their ground with what
For strategy in mind I couldn't tell,
And I felt fascinated by them, by the courage
They were showing, were they simply buying time
Or were they really ready to be sacrificed for others?
I myself did not know what would happen next
Though I was very well-positioned to observe
And all the white folks to my left were standing rigid,
They appeared to be in coffins, they were looking
Straight ahead, not looking over
Where they knew the blacks to be.
And so he made another run, he made it
After all that happened, after all that didn't happen,
He could see as well as we did, he came at
The thing again and that old white-haired man
He kind of sidled sideways, you could not say
He was slouchin', he was walkin' and he left
Where he was standin' by that fence
And he came over to the edge of where the tracks were,
He was standin' on a tie's end and he stopped,
He kind of ducked or bowed his head
Which as I took it meant "That's all you gwine to get
But you got me." And I assumed
He must have been quite well-respected, ß
He was well known, he was old and not afraid

Or if he was afraid he figured
Nothing bad would happen this time, so he came.
We had the woods, though, full of blacks still,
They began to creep back slowly, they never
Showed themselves, these black folks,
You could see them standing back
Behind a tree though, you could see their eyes look out
Behind a leaf and there were boys up in the branches
And the one old white-haired man
Beside the railroad tie and now because
The one old white-haired man continued standing,
Two or three more black men edged
In his direction, they felt safer.
And you had that crowd of white folks
To his left, they hadn't moved.
And there were Democratic loyalists,
Supporters of the Fergusons,
And Johnson finally started with his speech.
When it was over, you had Lathan and the big wigs,
They went up and told him "Good job," shook his hand,
But no one else came up to speak, the big wigs had,
But no one came up from the crowd.
I was not detecting animus against him,
I was not sure what it was. So we
Spun back to our hotel in several cars,
I drove in my car. It was one of those old
Southern places, big wide breezy porches, with the fans
Hung from the ceiling, kept things cool,
And I came in and I could hear him down the hall
And he was bellowin' for me before I entered.
I went down there to his room which had a parlor
And a bedroom, and he took me to the bedroom,
All his clothes were comin' off,
He was about to take a nap,
But he was wired up, all excited,

All his energy was boilin'up and over.
He was takin' off his socks,
And when I came into the room,
He asked how many votes I thought we'd get
From Cleveland, Texas, I just held up all ten fingers,
I did not show much conviction, I did not think
We'd be getting very many. He said no
And shook his head, he held up one hand,
All five fingers in the air but then
He took one finger down. And he was smilin'.
He had really stuck it to them.
He had looked out there and seen that separation
Of the races, I did not think what he'd done
Would help our chances very much
But he did not care. If his gesture toward the blacks
Lost the election, he would live with that.
He didn't do a thing like this again
In this campaign, but then the stars
Were not aligned a second time the way
They were this day in Cleveland,
With that crowd of all those black folks holdin' back.

20.

God damn it old Jim Crow has laid a collar on
More smart men sure enough than if you sentenced them
To chain gang work in Georgia--take Dick Russell:
If he hadn't had to wear that Jim Crow collar,
He'd be sitting at this desk instead of me now.
And I'd like to ask Ben Tillman, Pitchfork Ben,
How it had felt to throw the office of
The President away to keep on hating.

21.

His program was the New Deal and the Fair Deal
In excelsis, to the limit, underlying all his efforts
Was our favorite mantra: growth, the non-
Disruptive way to solve all social problems,
Since we thought the pie was big enough for all
And growing faster than the population grew.
This did not work for FDR or Harry Truman,
And it also did not work for Lyndon Johnson.
It's the capitalist's classical assumption
(and his prayer) that growth will slubber o'er
A multitude of sins, like the inequities,
Insane use and insaner distribution of
Resources, growth will meet the cry
Of everyone for goodies, more of same.

22.

There's this talk that I'm conservative,
I've heard it, that we're going back to Ike's ways
Now that I'm in charge, economy and slashing
Of the budget for the sake of slashing budgets
Pure and simple. Don't believe it. First, I understand
Expenditures must rise to match
The growing population, but there's more to it
Than that and you can find it in my record,
I'm a Roosevelt New Dealer. JFK
Was too conservative for my taste I would say.

23.

Chickens are as dumb as you can get because
They eat and never stop, then they start shittin'
While they're eatin', then before they know
What's hit them, they're there knee-dip
In their own shit. They don't stop though.
They keep eatin'. That's the way the AMA is.
They've been eatin' all these years
And now they're knee deep in their own shit.
That's no secret. We all know that.
We can see it. I'm not worried.
They can't stop this health care bill of mine I'm sure.

24.

--We're going to send Marines in
To protect the Hawk battalion at Danang
Because they're trying to attack
And knock them out there, local troops
Just can't protect them. All the military men
And all the Joints Chiefs, all the everybody else
Have asked around and gotten clearance.
I suppose they haven't cleared it yet with you
Since you've been sick.

--No, not a word.

--I guess we've got no choice in this
But it sure scares me. I think
Everyone will say "We're off to war
Because we're sendin' in Marines."
Of course if they try an attack,

Then they will have themselves a fight
As sure as hell, our boys won't run.
But we're tied down then.
But if they don't fight and they ruin
All those airplanes, I'll catch hell
For not securing them. The last time
Those guerrillas made a raid,
I caught hell then.
So it's a choice and it's a hard one.
Every day I got Westmoreland saying
"Send on those Marines puh-lease."
And I got Taylor and the Joint Chiefs.
Ditto McNamara, Rusk.
"Please send them on"
And so I told them,
"Go and clear it with the Congress"
But I've got to know what you think.

--It's the damnedest thing I heard of, Mr. President,
We've gotten in so far, its scares the daylights out of me.
I don't see how we start to back up now
Because we're in it. We keep getting pushed on
Forward, forward, forward.

--That's the truth. We're losing more men every day
It's getting worse.

--And those Marines,
They'll soon be killing friendly locals,
They'll begin to shoot at everything
That comes around those airplanes.

--Airplanes aint worth one good damn, Dick.
They scare ministers and leaders of the countries.
Bombing anything. They did it in the Ruhr.

And they can do it where there's industry I guess.
But they can't do it in the barracks.
I had hundreds of 'em over at a barracks,
There were twenty seven buildings,
They set only two on fire.
It's just the damnedest biggest fraud I ever saw,
Completely phoney. Don't go gettin' any hopes up
That the Air Force can defend us.
That's the trouble I'm in now, the men can fight
If they see daylight down the road.
But Viet Nam, there aint no daylight.
None at all.

--The road has no end. There's just nothin'.

--And the more bombs you go droppin'
You're just scarin' other nations,
You're just makin' people mad.

--We're going to wind up with the people mad as hell
With us, the people that we're savin' bein' in there.
It's the worst mess that I saw in my career.
It's the worst mess you could possible inherit.

--But they won't say I inherited the mess,
They'll say I made it.

25.

Before I left for Viet Nam, I heard from Senator Russell.
"Look into that free-fire-zone stuff, will you,
I don't like the way it sounds
Because the people there are animists,

They feel deeply for the land in which
Their relatives are buried.
I suspect it doesn't do us one damned bit of good
To move them from their homes although I know
It's for their safety. Georgia people feel the same way.
When a big dam's getting dedicated down there
And they've moved a lot of farmers out
To make way for the reservoir,
You won't see me puffed up among the big wigs
On the dais taking credit.
I don't want the farmers seeing me
As occupying platforms built on their land."
I presented these concerns to our commander in Pleiku,
I asked him whether he was worried.
"Not at all. These people lived in filthy huts,
Now they're in sanitary houses.
And we protect them from the VC."
That case evidently closed, at least in his mind.

26.

In Vietnam the mettle of the macho boys
In Washington was being sorely tested,
Their big pricks, since they'd been shown up
By the Bay of Pigs fiasco, then the President
Got treated like the bear whelp that he was
By big bad Khrushchev in Vienna, had to save
Or to regain the face he'd lost there—Vietnam
Became the place he'd take his stand,
Show he was manly—schoolyard posturing
That beggars comprehension as a basis
For conducting our affairs, but there it was.
The Indochina expertise we needed

To discern our way was lacking, Vietnam
Was first an adjunct of our embassy in Paris.
Our Saigon embassy, the Vietnam desk
In the State Department—both were staffed
By Foreign Service personnel whose whole
Career experience was Europe, they all spoke French,
And so in Vietnam by cast of mind and by their language
They were limited to dealing with the upper crust
In cities, they knew nothing of the peasants
In the country. And the shadow of the "loss of China"
Warped what was reported from Saigon,
The old career hands could remember how the ones
Who'd sent in frank reports from China
Got mauled later when the Senators held hearings,
Thus they played down Viet Cong strength
And the weakness of Diem to save their skins.
And even if they had been fully honest in reporting,
Nolting never would sign off on any pessimistic cables,
Any expertise in Vietnam got banished.
To be sure in time some talent was developed
But the more an issue rises in importance,
Then the more the folks who really understand it
Are excluded, shoved aside, as senior staff men take it over.
The frantic skimming of a briefing paper
In the back seat of a limousine's a poor excuse
For real deep-seated knowledge, and such papers
Can in time get marked "too sensitive" for experts
To review them, and in Vietnam the experts—
For the most part pessimistic—were replaced by cadres
Of the "can-do" types of guys, the "loyal"
Energetic fixers who had not been "soured by knowledge."
In early 1965 I told an older colleague of my doubts
And he assured me that the best step we could take
For self-protection and advancement of careers
Was just to "steer clear of the growing Vietnam mess."

But he was thought of as a "can-do" guy,
And now he's highly placed in Vietnam
To clean the mess up.
Internal doubters did in time appear
Despite the banishment of experts, they appeared
And they persisted, but a strange dynamic
Neutralized them: the domestication of dissenters.
There was a twofold clubbish need at play
That drove domestication: on the one hand
The dissenters wish to stay aboard the ship
And on the other hand the non-dissenter's conscience.
Dissent was somehow made to feel at home
Though on the low end of the ladder.
Someone higher up might even speak of
A dissenter as his "favorite dove"
And thereby flatter him, make him feel wanted.
At its worst, its most insidious, this syndrome
Even neutralized George Ball who had become
An institution, they encouraged him to speak up
As the in-house devil's advocate
At each stage of the escalation process,
He'd be asked to speak his piece, to make his
Argument, to fight the fight for righteousness let's say.
The advocates of further escalation soothed
Their consciences, considering the dovish option fully,
Thus the club was kept intact and all unpleasantness
Was muted, they were gentlemen discussing
These grave matters, and the fact is maybe Ball
Restrained them somewhat speaking up, who knows
How headlong our descent into the quagmire
Might have been without his input. Still,
Dissenters got reduced to mascot-status
Or to playthings, butts of humor and affection
(condescension?) for the group of inside do-ers.
"Here comes Mr Stop-the-Bombing" LBJ would say

When his last doubter Moyers entered rooms
For meetings. Thus he'd pat him on the head.

27.

One whole generation overlearned
The lesson Munich may have represented.
Interventionist emotions of the former
Isolationists now focused in on Asia
In relation to what Westerners construed
As the Establishment's, the Easterners'
Too great a stress on Europe.

28.

That's just him, you have to face the fact
That that's the way he is,
You have to take him warts and all.
He was a bully, sadist, lout, a truly
Wretched human being, a brutal person.
Every lapse of his from civilized behavior
Was intended to subject
Another person to his overweening will,
I'm sure you've heard of how
He'd take men to the privy to continue
Conversations while his bowels moved,
This was patently a test he staged to see if you
Could take it, an initiation rite
For would-be followers and aides,
He stuck your face in it to see if you had
Stomach for the job. Pure domination.
Did he ever take Mac Bundy in for this?

I couldn't tell you. But there's much more
To consider than this boorishness of his,
The way he treated other people
Like some dog he brought to heel.
He may very well well have been the biggest bastard
Pure and simple but colossal, he inspired
Such strong attachments in the people
He misused, the very people who could
Tell you, who had tasted what he was.
There was a certain kind of masochistic fun
That came from working for this man,
You just stood up to him, did not cringe,
Had to tolerate the barbs, did not talk back.
There was no future talking back to Lyndon Johnson.
Except Liz Carpenter perhaps, who'd sometimes
Snap back. But we had to learn to live with him
On terms that we could manage.
I cannot imagine sitting down to eat
Some kind of meal with JFK, but you
Could not avoid a lot of meals with Lyndon,
You were in his life in that way
And without doubt he was fully into yours
Since in a real sense he embraced you as his family.
He was Daddy. Daddy had at times to blow off,
Then he'd turn around and hug you. Was capricious.
But through all remained your Daddy. Was capacious.

29.

Up close he was a most attractive man.
You didn't get that from the TV.
John Wayne plus, all tanned and rugged.
Tough and charming and so well dressed,

Which was not what I'd expected.
He was what I'd say a President should look like.
He was not like some plain person idly walking
Round the block, he had this presence,
Had this purpose, and he really was enormous,
You weren't ready for the size of him,
It took away my breath when I first
Walked into the room and met this man.

30.

Kennedy looked fine, made fancy speeches
But did not get too much done
And when a senator would come to him
And say I'd like to help you, Mr. President,
On this one, but they'd kill me back at home,
He'd mildly smile and simply say "I understand"
And let the man go, off the hook.
But in the case of Lyndon Johnson...
Well, he knew first off the senator
Would make that lame excuse if Lyndon let him,
But he didn't, he'd forestall the song and dance
About the problems back at home,
He'd tell him all about the flag by God,
The story of our country, how the country
Needed his vote on this one issue right away
And he would grab the man's lapels,
He'd dust him off and send him back out
Through the door before the senator
Could figure out what hit him--
Not before he'd pledged his vote though.

31.

Oh God! Of course there's no way to describe it,
Just exactly what the Johnson treatment was,
It might be badgering, cajolery, and promises of favors,
Threats implied were in there somewhere,
It left everyone who got it feeling helpless,
It bewildered them. You knew
He hadn't answered any question
You might ask him. It was…
Suddenly this stream would start to flow,
More like this torrent, this Niagara
Falls of eloquence that drenched you,
It was that strong, like some potent force of nature.
It could be case of salesmanship
Or sometimes self-defense. But I suppose
He did it sometimes just for practice
Or to garner your good will.

32.

The CIA was no help
As we gathered up our data for the meeting,
They could churn you reams of texts,
On top of that they churned you summaries
Of texts, top secret stuff, but in the long run
They could not say how the Chinese
Or the Russians might react if we took
Measures that were needed—massive bombing
And the mining of their harbors
For an early and victorious end
To war in Vietnam.
Intelligence was no help

So the Joint Chiefs did what they were paid to do,
They reached conclusions of their own,
They thought the risk of intervention
By the Chinese or the Russians wasn't
Great enough to make us curtail action,
On condition that we act without delay.
McNamara and his coterie of whiz kids
Disagreed though, and of course they ran the show.
The Joint Chiefs thought that we were
Simply piling forces on in Vietnam
For no good reason while the whiz kids
Thought that we were acting rightly.
This dispute was what had caused the Chiefs
To ask to see the President in private
To present their point of view—
To which the Secretary finally acceded.
For the meeting we prepared a map,
We mounted it on plywood,
Then we coated it with acetate
On which the Chiefs could illustrate their comments,
Making marks on it with grease pencils.
It was going to be my job
To set this whole contraption up,
Then leave the room, and so I did,
I left the first room with the Chiefs inside conferring
While they waited for the President to see them.
When the call came for the Chiefs to move,
I fetched the map and waited in the hall with them
Prepared to set it up.
The President came out and he was all charm.
Also big at six foot three and on the order of
250 pounds, he dwarfed each chief whom he
Now greeted, he made many friendly comments
In a Texas accent more pronounced
Than any you could pick up

When you heard him on TV
As we got led into his office by the President himself,
I held the map board as they entered,
Looked between them for the easel
We'd been promised as a prop for it.
There was none, which the President picked up on.
He invited me to join them and to stay there
In the room while they were talking,
"You can stand right over here." And so I did.
A human easel so to speak, I held the map up.
He positioned me beside a bank of windows,
Then arranged the Chiefs around me
In a circle, he did not ask them to sit,
It was an awkward sort of set-up from the start,
It augured ill as General Wheeler started talking.
The President was peering at the map,
He had his arms crossed. General Wheeler
Thanked the President for letting us
Present our point of view
Which was avoidance of a land war,
Use of air and naval power. More decisive.
We would isolate Haiphong through naval mining,
Set blockades along the coastline
And we'd also bomb Hanoi.
General Wheeler then asked Admiral McDonald
To describe just how the Navy and the Air Force
Would combine. The Admiral did so.
General McConnell then explained that we would
Have to execute this plan with great speed,
That we'd have to make the North believe
That we could make their punishment
Much worse unless they sued to us for peace.
The President appeared to listen closely,
He would nod at times, he asked
The other generals of the Army and Marines

If they supported this scenario,
It was their troops who'd be fighting
On the ground. They said they did.
He turned his back a moment, deep in thought
Or so it seemed, but then he whirled around
To face us and exploded, almost made me
Drop the map. He screamed obscenities,
He cursed us out by name, he heaped
Such ridicule upon us for our military counsel,
Called us dumb shits, pompous assholes,
Used the F-word as an adjective more freely
Than a young marine in boot camp
Ever would have, he reminded us
The free world's weight was resting on his shoulders.
The buck for starting World War III
Was being passed by us to him he said.
The tantrum then was over, he resumed
His calm demeanor, crossed his arms,
He'd meant to punish us, to cow us
And control us. He continued with profanities,
But they were more soft-spoken,
He said something like we all knew
He did not care much for what we might
Advise him, he disparaged our abilities,
Then he said he was expecting just the same
To have our help and he suggested
That we put ourselves in his shoes:
Five incompetents had offered him
Their "military wisdom,"
He was going to let us go through
What he'd gone through when five idiots
Advised him. He reminded us
The whole damned world was what he had
To think about each day, that it was time to see
What kind of guts we all had. Then he paused

As if to let those points sink in.
You felt the tension like a drumhead.
He just eyeballed us for maybe half a minute,
Then he turned and asked Buzz Wheeler
What he'd do if he were President.
Now Buzz was not an easy man to shake,
He took a deep breath, then responded very calmly
He had known what he was facing when he came here:
A titanic force in Johnson who was venal and vindictive.
He had known the stakes were high
And he now realized he'd been set up,
That the President had been prepared by McNamara
Fully in advance and that this meeting was a fraud,
A mere charade. Buzz nonetheless said
"Mr. President, I cannot take your place,
There's only one man who can understand
The awesomeness of choices you've been faced with."
Diplomatic was the tack that Buzz was taking.
"I do not know all that you know,
I cannot say what I'd do if I were you.
With all respect, sir, it is you and you alone
Who must decide."
The President, apparently unmoved,
Put this same question to the others,
What they'd do if they were him,
And each man echoed Wheeler's comments
More or less, they followed his lead.
I was not sure that my arms were going to hold out
As I held on to the map, I guess its weight
Was thirty pounds, but it was feeling like a ton.
When the generals got finished,
Then the President looked sad first,
He was something of an actor,
Then he suddenly erupted yet again,
He yelled and cursed, he used that language

I've described, expressed disgust with our naïveté,
Said no military idiots could talk him
Into starting World War III, then
"Get the hell out of my office." Conference over.
The Chiefs of Staff had clearly done their duty.
They were well aware of what kind of
A military error we were making.
They had pressed on past rebuffs,
Civilian masters in the Pentagon rebuffed them,
They persisted, they'd presented their position to
The ultimate commander, he'd rebuffed them now,
Insulted and demeaned them.
"This has got to be the worst thing
I could ever have imagined."
Thus spoke Admiral McDonald
As we rode back to the Pentagon this day.
And thus the country was committed
To the loss of more than 50,000
Sons of this great nation.

33.

We came to Texas and this St. John Harwood fellow
Who was here last night got Cliff to make a speech
At Texas Law School and they gave a little dinner party first
And Bob Montgomery was there and Terrell Maverick,
Other friends of ours from old times, and I asked them
What they thought got into Lyndon with this war,
Why did he do it, I was really quite worked up.
I'm quoting as exactly as I can, as I remember.
Bob Montgomery replied, you should have had
Much better sense than not to know what Lyndon's doing.
From my knowledge of what's gone on

When he got into the White House
Plans were well advanced to knock hell
Out of China with the a-bomb.
He said Lyndon said the military men
Were riding so high at that time that Lyndon said
If they were so hell-bent on getting into war,
He'd let them have one, but they'd have to fight
The thing out on the ground so that they'd know
What making war was, he was not about to let them
Just go flying over China dropping bombs on them
And so forth, and he was scared of course
Since Russia also had the bomb, he had enough sense
To remember there were two who had the bomb
And both could drop it. And the strange thing was
When we were out in California later—
Cliff was speaking out there too—I asked
Rex Tugwell what he thought got into Lyndon,
That same question, and by God he answered
Pretty much the same way, said essentially
The same thing Bob had said.

34.

Internal doubters and dissenters got assigned
To putting fires out, small p.r. jobs
As the controversies worsened since
By virtue of their own doubts certain men
Were deemed best able to "massage,"
These men could draft benign responses
To the more important critics,
Write "conciliation-sections"
For some presidential speeches,
Meet at great length with complaining delegations,

Outraged Quakers, academics, rabbis,
Clergymen and housewives.
My senior colleague was assigned to meet the most
With A.J. Muste, Norman Thomas, I was point man
When the Women's Strike for Peace came.
We had orders: keep these delegations off the backs
Of those who were concerned with making policy
(and therefore had no time for any doubters).
My most discouraging assignment was to write
WHY VIETNAM, a White House pamphlet.
In a gesture toward my conscience, as a sop thrown,
I fought mightily to have the title
Followed by a question mark but lost

35.

The President asked the group if there was anyone who doubted
It would all be worth the effort. "We could not afford
To let Hanoi prevail," said General Taylor. General Wheeler
Said that he concurred most forcibly with Taylor.
He reported the unanimous opinion of the Chiefs of Staff
That losing Vietnam meant losing all of Southeast Asia,
Every country giving way, they all would gravitate
Toward China as the power on the upswing in the region.
John McCone expressed concurrence as did Rusk,
Conveying understated vehemence to boot.
Then the President observed that any need we felt
To wait was just a function of the weak and wobbly
Southern situation—an attack would be unwise
Until we stabilized our base.
The President as well as Rusk and McNamara
Emphasized the point that no one had to think about
How much this war was going to cost,

That money would not be a problem.
Rusk recalled that it had cost us fifty thousand
Just to kill a single communist insurgent
Back in 1947-48 when we were fighting them
In Greece and thought that no amount was too great
If it meant that we would win in Vietnam.
But Taylor then remarked that we weren't short at all
On funds. But then the President observed
By way of closing: what disheartened him the most
Was that we'd had our A-team out there sixty days
But that we still were losing ground.

36.

I don't think any reason has been given
That will satisfy the people of this country
As to why we haven't closed down Haiphong harbor.
And why we're leaving those petroleum dumps intact.
Now if the public finally says that they believe
We ought to give up Viet Nam, it will not be
For fear of China or of Russia, it will be
Because they think our boys are being left
To fight out there at grievous disadvantage,
We don't take these simple measures to protect them,
We don't bomb these sitting targets.
Nobody wants to kill all those civilians
In Hanoi or in Haiphong,
But we all think our boys deserve
A fighting chance when they fly sorties.

37.

If he openly discussed the escalation of this war
And built consensus, he'd wreak havoc with his programs.
Once he got the programs passed, though,
He still shied away from openly discussing
Escalation--if he faced up to it publicly,
He'd somehow be confirming his worst fear:
We were committed to a long term type of war
That would involve him in its ruin,
So he put off facing up to that reality,
Had recourse to denial. He pretended
We were fighting just a brief war
That required no explanation, that would end soon
And would not spell his destruction.
This was involuted torture of avoidance.

38.

Don't kid yourself, the Communists
Are working every day to split this country,
They're there mining all within the highest
Counsels of society, the government.
McCarthy's methods may have been all wrong
But he'd identified the threat because there's no way
These professors could be offering
Their independent judgment, they've been duped,
They've got these starry-eyed assumptions:
The advantages that Communism offers.
They're romantics. Worse than that,
They're downright crackpots.
And the Russians are in constant touch with
Senators who stand against the war.

They have them over to their embassy for parties.
And the daughters of the staffers of
Those Senators date Russians.

39.

Either we believe in other people's right to self-determination,
Or we believe in someone's right of imposition (meaning ours)
Of "an arrangement of the parts."

We got to pick us someone good before he takes over,
So he won't ask us to leave, so that we won't be asked
To get out when the wrong man takes control.
The way I see it Ky is gone, he's at his last gasp.
Hell will break loose when he goes.
But what we need there is a government
That we appoint ourselves and can support.

Just keep our troops and our equipment
Out of riots, don't go gettin' us involved.

Even if we haven't got a government in Saigon,
Let's keep going. We're committed
And we will not be deterred.
Stave off debacle. Pick up pieces. Even if
There's no democracy in Saigon,
Don't let Communists take over.

Many people in America have given up believing
That the effort and the sacrifice are worth it,
We have lost some basic cohort of support
Which I cannot see us regaining.

How could any country that's as powerful as we are
Not be able to impose its will on some state
That's as weak and undeveloped as the North
Of Viet Nam is? What is Johnson doing wrong
Is all they're asking, let's just get the whole thing
Over with or get out, no more "measured force"
And patience. It's ridiculous for this to take so long.

The maximum deterrence that we can
Against the Communist aggression
With the minimum of costs. This explanation
Won't change anybody's mind, but it will warn them
What to look for in the future.

But the people don't have any sense of
Sacrifice or deep participation.
No necessity impels us.

But it's not just Viet Nam, the fight's
For freedom from political oppression
And from economic want around the world.
How can they say that we're the villains?

40.

As Medicare and Medicaid
Began to pay for nursing homes,
He talked about some filthy ones
He'd seen, he was concerned
That public dollars not be paid
To put our seniors into "rat holes,"
He was meeting with a task force once
Of experts, he invoked the kind

Of place you wouldn't "want your mother
Close to," as his voice rose,
He began to talk of honoring
Your father and your mother,
What was written in the Bible,
Then his eyes lit up. "I called
You fellas in here, I want nursing homes
Where people in this country can serve out
Their older age and have a little bit of joy
In those last years and I want places
That will meet their special needs,
We need flat floors designed for wheel chairs,
Special handles on the bath tubs, in the showers,
For the safety and the dignity of old folks.
And when you think about the toilets…"
He leaned over on his left rump,
Leaned his elbow on the chair arm,
Took his right arm, strained to twist it
Far behind him, s tarted grunting now
And poking with that hand
Way back behind him… "don't go putting
Any toilet paper rack where they
Can't reach it, where they have
To wrench their back out,
Maybe dislocate their shoulder,
Get a stiff neck just to get
A piece of paper." He then
Brought his right arm forward.
"Stick it right here by their side,
Perhaps in front of them
Where they can reach it easy."
He stayed tilted on his left haunch
While he said this not to make too fine
A point, and he kept staring at those experts.

41.

He had a great capacity for penitence,
It always came right after he'd exploded,
There would be these great eruptions of emotion,
Then the great calm coming after.
If he happened not to like what you were doing,
You could easily get skinned by him alive,
But then he'd turn around and hug you
Moments later, there was no predicting.
I had witnessed his behavior many times
But only one time as recipient of wrath
Or as its target. My experience was peculiar.
We'd had a long meeting to discuss Israel.
At the end of it he said "I have invited Nassser
To the White House." I replied to him
I knew that he had done so, I'd seen stories
In the paper. My suggestion was "I wish
That you'd remind him that it's even more
Important that the Straits of Tiran
Should be kept open than the Straits
Of Sharm al Sheik because the Straits
Of Sharm al Sheik are right off Israel,
They can handle those themselves.
To keep the Straits of Tiran open though
They'd have to launch attacks
On southern Yemen, other countries."
Some sort of strange cloud came across
His eyes at this point. I now realized
That I'd probably reminded him
Or shown him how he'd missed a crucial
Geographic point, i.e. had slipped up.
I had seen him getting angry,
All the yelling, all the shouting.
This was altogether different, of another order,

I saw his eyes become opaque
As they would do sometimes
If he was very angry but did not express
His feeling. All he said to me so softly—
And it really was Elijah's still small voice
In which he said it— was
"Would you like being President one day?
I mean just try it."

42.

Harry Truman might come up
With something truly scatalogic.
I once asked for his philosophy of life
And he produced me quite an answer:
"Never kick a fresh turd round the back yard
On a hot day." HST was very prim
Discussing sex though, he could almost seem
Embarrassed. Not so Lyndon.
Someone asked him what he thought
Of Jerry Ford once and he answered:
"Jerry's economic program is the worst thing
That has happened to this country
Since some guy invented pantyhose
And ruined finger-fucking."

43.

When you listen to the talk of Richard Nixon
You can sense a kind of phoniness
When he attempts profanity, he tries it on
For size to seem a tough guy.

But with Johnson his profane talk's
Just a part of him, it's simply a component
Of the magic, of the poetry let's call it,
Or the black keys of the keyboard
He keeps playing all the time, it isn't
Out of joint at all, it just keeps flowing
With the rest of what he says,
He'll use that language
When he's talking to a preacher
And it doesn't seem discordant,
And the only time some phoniness creeps in
Is when he tries to sound too pure,
Too Presidential.

44.

The President was in bed in pajamas once receiving
A be-suited Richard Nixon, this was early in the morning.
Lady Bird came in then in her dressing gown.
She greeted Nixon warmly, then she crawled up into bed
Beside her husband for the visit to continue.

45.

I'll tell you one thing, Lyndon
Never says a word he didn't hear
His pappy say since old Sam Ealy
Was a country man, he talked just like
The country. There was one more way
That he resembled Lyndon:
When he had business to discuss with you,
He'd get right up before you nose to nose

And sometimes grab you. You've seen Lyndon
Do the same thing many times.

46.

He arrived here lugging his belongings in a cardboard suitcase.
That was 1931 or thereabouts…

47.

When I was young in Congress,
I was out to get some bridge built down in Texas,
I've forgotten where it was,
All I remember was I wanted it,
I needed it so badly, I was up against
Some congressman, debating him for money,
In the end I got that bridge,
But this debate had made a fool
Of my opponent, I had really laid it on him,
This guy never could forgive it
Or forget it. Speaker Rayburn called me in
And said "Young fella, look, you've got yourself
A bridge, you've got an enemy for life too.
You didn't need to cut this fellow down so bad,
You could have gotten you the bridge
Without the enemy." And that was how I ran
The Congress later, Mr. Sam had helped
This young man, this young red-hot
See the light. You didn't have to make
The other guy eat crow.

48.

I got Ex-lax in this pocket over here
And I got aspirin in the other.
I work seventeen hour days.
And all I'm asking you to to work is sixteen with me,
Then for sure we'll get that boy
Down on the corner there a job.

49.

There remains a fatal flaw here though,
We are *giving* them the troops while only *praying*
For their proper use and for diplomacy perhaps.
We're only hoping yet again that it will work.
We "only" give them 80,000 troops right now
And that's important, we're postponing
Any call-up of reserves with all the baggage
They entail, but then the generals will come back
At the worst time asking more—I mean in 1968.
Providing 80,000 troops means we've acceded
To the whole request in essence while pretending
We've resisted, drawn some line. They will "accept"
The 80,000, but in six months we'll get messages
That say the need remains 200,000.
There's an appetite that's infinite in play here
Which we've only been appeasing,
We have not applied real pressure,
So the military war continues growing
With no diplomatic progress getting made,
It's like the Blob, the war's "philosophy"
Needs hashing out right now because at present
Every different group's proceeding on assumptions

Of its own and we keep getting dragged in deeper.
At the very least the President should give
Westmoreland limits just as Truman
Gave such limits to MacArthur. If Westmoreland
Is to get 550,000 men, he should be told
He'll get no more and that we mean it.

50.

I can see why he would think that
The opponents of his tax increase
Were sacrificing national wellbeing
On the altar of political advantage.
And it's true that with the wealth it had
America should not have put off
Paying for a war or made the poor pay
In effect for it by cutting back
The programs meant for them.
This was a scandal. But the President
By playing it too cute had brought
This avalanche of troubles on himself,
He should have 'fessed up back in 1965
About the costs he knew were coming.
If the people who were critics two years
Later had been told about and signed off on
The costs set out back then, then they'd have
Had no ground to stand on in opposing
What he asked for. But he'd told them
We'd be through by '67, maybe sooner,
So that when he finally coughed up
All the facts at that point, leveled,
They cried foul, got understandably indignant.

51.

The Congress doesn't need to know
How many troops I'm sending
Into Viet Nam right now
If I can get them out by next year.

52.

Vietnam was less a fight against
Some enemy or enemies abroad…
It was a struggle which we waged
Among ourselves about our values
And our interests and the meaning of
Our country and its purpose.
First our leaders were proclaiming Vietnam
A vital interest—they informed us.
Then the nature and the cost
Of our commitment got debatable.
Debate about the subject hinged
On symbols not on literal survival.
Vietnam got argued out in terms of
Munich and Korea—what they meant—
The Cuban missile crisis, Nuremberg
And so forth. Likewise dominoes
And enclaves, what it meant to fight
To liberate your nation and from whom.
And most ferociously the fight
Was waged in moral terms, perceptions
Of Americans as persevering people
You could count on, would we really
Stay the course (would we be blindly
Persevering)? This whole congeries.

Could we define our policy correctly?
What relation did the means bear
To the ends and also individual conscience,
How far it could be extended,
Free debate within democracy
And how accountable the men
Who served in office were.
In addition to a war in Southeast Asia
Which was shattering people's lives
We fought a metaphoric war among ourselves,
A rabid conflict over meaning, Vietnam
Became a "proving ground," a "showcase,"
An "experiment," a "test"
Of what Americans could be
Or rather should be. We were fighting
For an answer to that question,
Just what kind of people we were
Quintessentially. Brute force?
How did the violence define us?

53.

We can question all the wisdom which has
Got us where we are but we are there
And we must face it. It's primarily a contest
For allegiance, we must show them we can
Lead them to a better way of life.
Although a lot of lives are lost, we are
Primarily engaged...we're leading people
Toward a modern world they almost
Haven't heard of. By comparison
The Viet Cong's a nuisance, a mosquito
We must fend off, we must demonstrate

Above all to the Communists that wars
Of liberation will not work.

54.

The effectiveness trap, the effectiveness bind.
It's a trap that keeps a man from speaking out
Or speaking often, it prevents a man from offering
A protest resignation or believing his dissent
Might have an impact from the outside.
Your effectiveness: a mystic sweet communion
Of your training and your style and your connections.
The most ominous complaint or observation one can make
About a person is "He's losing his effectiveness."
To preserve it, to maintain it, you must carefully decide
Where you are going to buck the mainstream.
The temptation not to speak or just to meekly acquiesce
Whenever great ones have appeared is overwhelming.
Thus you live to speak and fight another day
Or so you reason to yourself. And there is no one
Who's immune to this temptation, it's the need
To keep oneself plugged into power.
Even those whom one would think of as secure
In their positions have to think twice
Lest they rashly snip the cord. And resignation?
Well, it's really not an option
When you haven't go a back bench to retreat to,
There's no refuge for resigners.
So you justify maneuvers you'll be making
To remain, you justify that constant trimming.

55.

Of course in retrospect the whole thing's hard to fathom,
Why we went there in the first place, we were
Ridden by obsession that the Communists
Were somehow monolithic,
They were going to go and Bolshevize the world
And if we didn't hold the line in Southeast Asia,
This would spread. It was absurd.

He spoke scornfully of those who would
Attack him for the buildup of our forces over there,
He called them bellyachers, whiners.
At the same time one adviser on the Joint Chiefs
"Would have bombed Peking tomorrow."
He was getting it from both sides.
It perplexed him that the North Vietnamese
Could fail to understand our motives.
As he saw it he was pictured in Hanoi
As some big wheeler dealer emperor
Whose only goal was conquest.
What he really wanted most to do he said
Was to improve the way of life
In Southeast Asia, not spend all that money there
On bombs and bullets.

By 1967 they all felt themselves beleaguered
In the White House. It was LBJ who mainly
Set the tone for this, he overcompensated.
If he heard some charge that this was just
Our client in the South, our little servile puppet state,
Then he would make outlandish claims,
Like "there's democracy at work there,"
Or he'd ask when was the last time
An election held in Boston

Would have met the stringent standards
Which the South of Vietnam was being held to.
Bobby Kennedy was always on his mind in this
Or right behind his shoulder.
As to reports the war there wasn't going well,
He'd ask how people could believe that.
"We just took out all their power plants last night,
The North can't hold out six more months."
Much talk like this. I did not think
That he believed those things himself
That he felt forced to say, that he believed them fully,
But he thought he'd somehow counterbalance
Undermining noises he was hearing in our country,
He was making this big effort then
To bully and cajole North Vietnam, he thought
He'd bring them to their knees or to the table
To negotiate. But not if they heard
Opposition protests back at home.

He would say "It's not the hippies
And the students and the Commies
Who concern me, they'll raise hell
But they cannot do lasting damage.
It's the right wing that's the real beast.
If they ever get the notion in their head
I've started selling Vietnam out,
They'll wreak havoc and the escalation needed
Just to calm them will exceed
The wildest nightmares you could conjure."
His constant fear was always of the right.
He never really understood the left,
That is the New Left. He epitomized
The generation gap. He always asked
"What in the hell do these kids want?"
Or "Don't they know that they're American?"

He'd ask in something close to real despair.
"What a mistake, it's almost tragic,
To attack the only country that they've got.
When the ordinary John Q./Joe Blow dies,
There may be 25 or 30 of his neighbors
Who remember him in some way—insubstantial—
And he's got relatives of course
Who may recall him—also vaguely.
But the only thing that gives him immortality
Beside what he believes—
Although he may be atheistic—
Is his standing as a citizen of something
That was going on before him and
God willing will survive him by a long shot.
When he says I'm just Joe Blow, that name
Survives him for a brief while on a tombstone,
Although I must say if you go to see the tombstones
Down in central Texas, you may have to rub real hard
To get the dust off—even then you cannot
Really read the name it's so long gone,
They take that from ya, even that
Does not survive, you have no name.
But if you say I'm an American,
What that means is I'm immortal like this country,
This Republic. So these demonstrators shouting
In the park then, they're attacking,
They impugn the immortality
Of most of those poor bastards
Who have ever made the lists up of this country."

Their whole life style was so different
From his life style as a young man.
You would graduate from college,
You'd take care to comb your hair
And tie your tie right, get a pressed suit,

Make the rounds in search of work
Which you'd find quick. The long hair
Bothered him a lot, the sloppy clothing
On these kids when he could look around
The White House and the aides
Were pretty close to his ideal
Of what a young kid coming out of school
Should look like, all-American and clean.
I don't know where he thought
The kids outside, that is the demonstrators
Came from, maybe Mars for all I know,
Or maybe Neptune.

He said to me "I just don't understand,
Who are these young folks who are pitched
In opposition to the war, I never meet them.
Any young folks that my daughters
Bring around are never like that."

There was this split, this great dichotomy,
The people who supported him on civil rights
Opposed him on the war.
Not all but many. Mary Rather
Went to work for him the last year,
She had worked for him in past years
On the Hill, she said the bliss she got
From working on the Hill had disappeared,
The downright fun, that in the White House
What was left was only horror.
She just hated every minute,
She just couldn't wait to get out
Of the White House since she saw him
Being torn apart, ground up.

And one night, it was midnight,

He was finally eating dinner by himself,
I think the news had just gone off
And I went in to him and said
"I love you, Daddy." I went over
And I sat down in a chair
And he was reading,
And I saw the tears rise up
And then subside.
I sat there with him
Maybe 30 minutes longer,
And he never let me know
He knew that I was there beside him.
He was torn up, he was caught up,
So consumed by it. And it was deeply painful
To behold a man who so much loved
The company of people.
We'd just sit like that with him
So many nights, he seemed to like
To have us present if we never said a word.

He did, we must remember, come from flag country,
So when he got to Vietnam it was my country
Right or wrong, it was my loyalty
To these United States like World War I
Or World War II. It warped his vision.
When you look at all that talk about
The body count, how much it made him suffer,
Drew him over to the situation room
At three or four o'clock AM to see how many
Planes were lost, he was a man bound on
A wheel of fire and torment…
But I never got a sense that he had feelings for
The other side, how many people did
Vietnamese lose in the South and in the North,
How many Viet Cong had died.

It was always only our lives, it was our folk
And those other people didn't seem to figure.

The dissent, the disagreement over Vietnam,
The arguments got into everything.
His "family," that is his cabinet, his inmost
Circle of advisors felt the pressure.
A meeting one day of the cabinet was over
And he asked us "Any questions?"
Which he'd never done before.
So there was silence. So he asked us all again:
"Does anyone have anything
He'd like to bring up further?"
And so I said, "Yes, I have something,
Mr. President." The silence grew more deathly
As the junior member brashly opened up.
"My son, who's fourteen, and some friends of his
Were coming at me hard the other night,
They wanted reasons for the war in Vietnam,
I did my best to give them answers,
But I did not win them over.
I could see these young men thinking
They might have to serve as soldiers
But for what? I wonder what you might have said
If they'd been asking you these questions."
I could see Dean Rusk and McNamara thinking
"Oh Christ, why would he be asking that
At this point?" Still the President
Took half an hour to answer, but the answer
Made no sense, and I was shocked.
If he had given that defense of Vietnam
Before the public, they'd have laughed him
Out of court. Now several of us
Got to talk with him again when we had found
This set of answers unpersuasive,

He arranged for us to hash this out with Rusk
And other cabinet officials. But this cohort
Wasn't any more convincing. It was awful.
So whatever reason Rusk and LBJ
Had for the war, whatever way they had
To make themselves believe that it was right
They couldn't make known to the public,
They weren't even half-way competent explaining.
And I think that this incompetence
Affected how they viewed the outside world
When it began to lodge its protests,
Made a kind of siege mentality
Their *modus operandi*
As it should have been I think
If they could not explain their own war any better.

56.

When Johnson and Rayburn appeared
In the President's office that afternoon,
He informed them both benignly they's been
Good boys and were getting Papa's blessing.
He was treating them as equals
With an element of cunning, sneaky malice,
To disturb Sam Rayburn's settled state of mind.
I'd say he admirably succeeded.

57.

I took--what shall I call him?--a more
Delicate disciple of my predecessor with me
To the bathroom to discuss stuff

While I sat there on the toilet.
He could not look, you'd have thought
He'd never seen those human body parts before,
He turned his back, he kept his distance,
I could scarcely hear a word that he was saying,
I kept straining, then I finally asked
If he could just come closer for the sake
Of conversation. It was ludicrous. Instead
Of turning round and walking toward me,
He maintained polite discretion of a sort,
He kept his eyes, his face averted, he advanced
Backwards with these mincing little
Rickety kinds of steps, he almost fell
Into my lap by moving blindly in the end.
You know I had to ask the question
How that man had made it so far in the world.

58.

Kennedy would share with you
The details of his conquests, LBJ
Was much more close-mouthed,
Almost circumspect, respectful.
LBJ would use that scatologic language,
He would joke of sex in general,
Using language of the barnyard,
But his escapades were not for being shared
Whereas the President regaled you with specifics.
He was not without a certain charm and wit
When he would do so, he went into
Almost clinical complexities describing,
Still he struck me as a sort of boyish braggart
Next to Lyndon. Lyndon loved

To get the gossip on his boss though.
I was over at the White House once
Discussing legislation with the Boss
And as our sessions often did,
This one concluded with the candid recitation
Of a recent sex adventure by the leader
Of the free world.When I got back
To the Capitol they told me that the V-P,
Mr. Johnson, then presiding in the Senate,
Had been calling, three or four times,
It was urgent that I speak to him at once,
The very moment I arrived back from
The White House. I rushed over to the Senate.
When he spotted me, the V-P waved me forward
To the dais where he sat conducting business.
I became at once the cynosure of all eyes
In the building let me tell you, I could
Feel them beaming in on me,
The regular reporters, all the senators,
The visitors above us in the gallery
As I approached the dais, LBJ
Was leaning forward really focused
And he whispered in my ear his urgent question:
"Has ol' Jack been gettin' much pussy?"
His eyes continued sparkling as I whispered
Back to him the latest Presidential exploit,
All the details, though he kept his face
As carefully, I'd even say as piously composed
As if the two of us were speaking of
The arms race with the Russians.

59.

--I just don't believe we can't take 15,000 men
Who have been sent there as advisors,
Add on top of that 200,000 men from Vietnam
And keep the status quo in place the next six months.

--Well, the only thing that scares me is
Their government could up and simply quit on us,
Or there could be another coup,
At which point we're invited out.

--There very well may be another coup,
But there is nothing we can do that would prevent that.

--There is one thing we could think about
Or ask Bob to consider, some small stiffener,
A couple of thousand more men
Who could give the needed psych--
Not that they're needed now to win
But that they'd show we think
The damned thing could be done.
The problem's mostly state of mind.

60.

There was one force superseding all the rest
And that of course was wishful thinking.
I partook of it myself at many times
And most acutely in the fall of '63
When we were struggling with Diem
And thinking maybe now for once,
As we were dealing with a client,
We could use our economic and our military help

To gain some leverage, not be led around
On nose rings by the likes of Chang Kai Shek
Or Syngman Rhee. If we could prove that single point,
I thought the war in Vietnam might very well be worth it.
Later came the kind of wishful thinking
Which the air strike planners practiced
In the fall of '64: they were convinced
That after six tough weeks of strikes
We'd have the North come crawling to us,
They'd be begging us for peace talks.
And what, as someone asked once
In a meeting, if they didn't? Well,
The answer was we'd bomb another four weeks
And that add-on would be sure to do the trick.
Or consider what one of the very highest echelon
Of figures in the White House said to me
When I had drawn him into private conversation
At a party, I expressed to him concern
About the vaunted air-strike option, its effectiveness.
He assured me that I didn't need to worry,
He was sure a neutral government would rise up
In Saigon and then invite us out politely.
There was a strain of wishful thinking
That sustained us after air strikes had begun
In '65 and '66: we'd be in conference
After six months all the "architects" assured us
And this escalating spiral would be over.
The basis of their hope was that "It simply can't go on."

61.

Doubt, dissent and expertise were neutralized
When policy got made, I'd call

Executive fatigue a crucial factor.
The toll responsibility exacts
Is both emotional and physical and it's compounded
When one's service gets extended,
Four to seven years the tenure.
Few executives complain and health
May well continue unimpaired, that is
The physical variety of health—
Emotional's more difficult to gauge.
But what's eroded by this deadening fatigue
Is any freshness of capacity to think
Or to imagine, that rare asset of
A new administration in its first years.
The fatigued concocter of our policy becomes
A kind of prisoner of his narrowed
Point of view and clichéd rhetoric,
Increasing irritation and defensiveness
A product of his lack of sleep
And lack of family times—a lack of
Patience. Much bad policy gets made
And then compounded, there is neither
Any time nor any temperament
For airing new ideas, stale procedures
Just continue getting mashed, low grade
Toxicity of pulp. And just below
The basic level of executive fatigue
There lurked the notion of curatorship
That seemed to reign at State.
The way the average bureaucrat
Conceived of his own job led to inertia.
The "desk officer" received or he inherited
A policy toward Country X or Y
And he regarded it as his prevailing function
To preserve intact that policy,
Un-tampered with, undusted, under glass,

And pass it on to his successor.
Such chaste curatorial service
Is what earns you your promotion
In the system, you maintain the status quo,
Steer clear of trouble. The inertia
Such a system tends to generate of course
Can sometimes slow rash innovation.
All too often it maintains the deleterious
Momentum of unwisely entered into
Bad commitments.

62.

The storm of modern change could blight in decades
And diminish something cherished and protected by
All generations past. Our population
As it grows has swallowed areas of beauty.
There's a dark side to technology from which
We all of course have greatly benefitted.
Uncontrolled, the waste which it produces
Threatens soil and water, wildlife, the environment
Without which there can be no life at all.
We are responsible. Societies which benefit
From industry must exercise control,
And yet our conservation must be something
All-encompassing, not merely some reaction
Of protection after damage has been done,
And it must not derive from love of nature only
Though that love of nature matters.
We're concerned with man's relation to the world
In its entirety around him, something global,
Not just welfare of the human race
But dignity of spirit. This mean's beauty

Must be part of daily life, but I'm not talking
Just of easiness of access to magnificence
In nature, parks and woodlands, mere proximity,
But equal social access for the rich man
And the poor man, for the Negro and
The white man, for the farmer and
The city dweller. Beauty's not an easy thing
To measure on those charts we like to point to,
On a pie chart, but in any computation of
Our true wealth beauty can't be overlooked,
It's a component. We've been careless,
We've delayed, we have proceeded with abandon
Toward destruction, some catastrophe, till now,
But since the danger's been identified, I trust
That we will place ourselves to stem the tide
Of blight, the irreversible destruction of our planet.

63.

A drunken man was stumbling down the road, unshaven,
Red-eyed. In his home town. Johnson turned to me
And held his thumb a hair's breadth from his finger.
"Don't forget," he said, "the margin's only that much
Keeping you and me from being just like him."

64.

We don't have any propaganda operation running,
But we've got to get our stuff out, get on top of this.
Red Mueller planted seedlings in their head
And now they're sprouting, that the vote
Was not for me, that neither one of us was loved,

That I was chosen as the lesser of the evils,
I was lacking in rapport, that I lacked style
And seemed buffoonish, Mr. Cornpone.
Every campaign stop I made in every state--
I went to forty-four myself and counting
Lady Bird, the two girls, we touched down
In forty-nine--I had the biggest crowds
That anybody's seen, I got the biggest vote
That anybody's gotten, greatest pouring of
Affection out on any public figure, greatest
Loyalty, big business men and labor plus
The Nigras and the Jews and all the ethnic groups.
Got more of everyBODY! But these experts say
That that does not amount to much, the followers
Of Bobby are behind it, they put out this stuff,
That no one really loves old Lyndon Johnson.
By January 1st they'll have it all built up
That I received no mandate in the first place,
That the people didn't care for me at all.
Dick Daley says he thought that we'd run
Seven hundred fifty in Chicago, now it's
More like eight five oh or maybe nine,
We kept the Governor from losing.
I think someone has to quote him,
Someone has to quote Dave Lawrence,
Interject them into this, show their opinions.
And we have got to sell the fact
That different viewpoints can be
Brought together, business men and labor,
There's no necessary hatred there,
We always come together in a war,
Why not in peace time? Someone's
Got to tell *The New York Times* to back off
Just a little, give me breathing space, not try
To turn me into Warren Harding with this stuff

They've got on Baker, Walter Jenkins.
Next they'll try to have this Southern Coalition
Come together with Republicans and fix it
So no legislation passes. Even Roosevelt
In 1936 did not have people that were jumpin'
In the air and pledging loyalty the way
They were for me, we've got to call that
To the editors' attention. You have got to
Call that advertising agency we have there
In New York and haul them in. Bill Moyers
Hired them, find out who these people are...

65.

"You knew what my position was,
So why did you vote with Lyndon?"
"It was this way: Lyndon's
Grabbing my lapels, he's got his face
On top of mine and he keeps talking--
I mean TALKING--in the end I thought
It's either cast my vote with him or drown."

66.

In the country where I come from in the spring
The sun begins to come up early
And the ground is getting warmer
And the steam begins to rise, the sap is dripping,
My prize bull is in his pen, and he's the biggest,
Best-hung bull in our whole region.
In the spring he gets a hankerin' for those cows

And he begins to paw the ground
And he gets restless, so I open up the pen
And he goes down the hill, he's lookin'
For a cow, his pecker's hangin' hard
And swingin', and those cows,
They're gettin' so goddamned excited,
They're getting moister to receive him
And their asses start to quiver,
They start quiverin' all over,
Every one of them is quiverin' the moment
That my bull struts in their pasture,
That's the way I want this conference
You're arrangin'--make it quiver.
I want every goddamned delegate
To quiver with excitement at the thought
That we can really make a change in civil rights.

67.

The question was is Lyndon Johnson
Man enough to stand up to the commies.

I assured him that the differences between us
On the bombing were apparent, not substantial.
I assured him he could count upon your firmness.
I did not describe the problems
You were having keeping liberals in line,
For which his sympathy I'm sure is nonexistent.
He'd denounce us for neglecting
To extinguish raging fires
While we were seeking to attain unreal consensus.
I would wager he believes that we can never keep
The New York Times on our side

And should therefore not expend
Our strength in trying.

68.

The junta led by Duong Van Minh
Is unenthusiastic, covert raids
Upon the North seem ill-advised to them,
The use of U.S. planes
With South Viet Nam's kind of markings.
Minh told McNamara bombing
Would not get him real good military outcomes
And would only harm the local population
Which was innocent. The junta
Did not want the U.S. going into
Villages and districts--too colonial a flavor.
And the junta wished to draw the NLF
Out from their jungles into governments
Of reconciliation. That last prospect
Most of all set off alarm bells.
What the fuck would there be left
For us to do out there?
What happens to our war?

69.

Internal confusion, glaring inability, a failure
To provide clear definitions by
The "architects" themselves of our commitment,
Inability to answer basic questions like
What type of war it was that we were fighting
And therefore how we were imagining we'd end it.

Was it a civil war or was there international
Aggression as the motivating factor
And if that was so, who then was the aggressor,
Who our enemy? The Viet Cong? Hanoi?
Peking? Or Moscow? Or some subset
Of the communistic specter?
Different enemies would call for different tactics.
And the question of American objectives
Was an equally confused one,
That great overarching cry of (almost) anguish,
Our perplexity, why were we (after all) in Vietnam
Remained there sounding.
I remember my assignment from a boss
Of mine in 1964 to draft a speech for McNamara
To deliver which among its other purposes
Would put to rest the notion
(which American officialdom resisted
To the death as some canard)
That what we faced in Vietnam
Was civil war "although it was one
In a sense" I mused out loud
As I was getting this assignment.
"Don't play word games!"
Was my boss's brusque retort.

70.

For a while we were convinced we understood
Just how much strength the Viet Cong had--
And the North Vietnamese. You will remember
Rather optimistic numbers and projections
That came into us from last year, so
Quite frankly it was shocking

That the North possessed the forces
And the skill to pull the Tet offensive off.
They made strong inroads in Saigon and Hue,
Other cities. And the countryside felt impacts.
Thus the country we are trying to preserve
Has suffered quantities of damage.
It seems possible the country we are
Trying to preserve has been relying
On the USA too much and when we try
To look ahead and make our plans
We find we very well may denigrate
The power of that country to assume
Its own defense, we aren't enhancing
Their ability to do so. I am not sure
That the strategy we're presently pursuing
Is the right one, is the long-term course
This country ought to take, or that
A military victory as commonly defined
Is even possible at this point...
There's been talk of what the ARVN's
Going to do but when the crunch comes
They still look to us for more, and when
The Tet offensive came, Thieu's statement
Wasn't what more they were going to do
But that the time had come for us to send
More troops. How do we answer this?...
We seem to have a sinkhole. We put in more
And the North can always match it,
And the South's not doing everything it should
And then the Soviets and Chinese have agreed
That they will keep the North well armed
And well supplied. I see more fighting,
Greater casualties on our side
And no end in sight to action...
We can no more just rely upon

The field commander's outlook.
He will ask for troops repeatedly,
Then more troops, and then still more.
We must understand the impact
This is having overall, we have to think about
Our economic standing, other problems
In the world and what it's doing to
Our country back at home, we must consider
The example we've been setting, would
What we've been through deter some other nations
From responding to a threat? And if
Our allies do not mean it
When they say that they'll do something,
We should know that fact right now...
There is another plan that might be utilized,
Allowing us more latitude and flexibility,
And to avoid more bloodshed--
Perhaps by letting go of certain areas.
We might start to change our concept
From protecting real estate.
But are the people we'd protect
Instead of real estate prepared to help themselves?
That is the fundamental question.
I am not sure we can ever find our way out of
This mess if we continue shoveling men in.
I am sure we'd be divided every which way
If we took a vote right now
About the troop request, to send 200,000
More men in or send in no men.
But I wonder if we're really
Making progress toward our goal
If we continue with the plan
We've so far followed.

71.

"They know where they can reach me"
Is a good position. Hold it.
Hold it publicly without equivocation.
Do not qualify. "Of course
We are continuing to seek
All private channels that might lead us
To a peace" or any other kind
Of placatory statements should be left out.
"We are ready to negotiate" suffices.
"We invite, request, and welcome
U Thant's work to find a way
To end this war" is also all right.
Don't be humble. Don't apologize.
The moment calls for toughness and resolve.
Not for humility. I've always thought
That once we were committed to
A shooting sort of war we had to win it.
My position isn't winning for the sake
Of merely winning, that 110%
American gung-ho tough guy outlook,
Our side has to be on top. It is deliberate
Since we're the only nation
Or the last remaining nation
Whose existence and preparedness,
Whose willingness to fight
Deters the Communists from acting up
In Asia, seeking dominance in Asia
Or in fact in all the world. Unless we win,
Our whole psychology will suffer,
As a nation we will shrink from
Self-assertion, from participation elsewhere
On a scale that is substantial.
Self-disparagement, timidity will spread,

Affect our economic programs,
All our governmental outreach,
We'll be shaken, we'll have opened up
The pathway for a demagogue to triumph,
One who lacks de Gaulle's
Few mitigating virtues.
What do I mean of course by winning?
Please forgive me but I wonder
If we've adequately pondered...
Is it possible we'll ever reach a point
Where we could get out if the basic
Situation in the North remains the same?
I think we have to bring the war home
To the North though I'm aware of
All the dangers of a strike there.
Have we really asked the question
Just how far against the wall
We have to push North Vietnam,
How much we punish them until
For sake of mere self-preservation
They decide that it is time to discontinue?
I just don't think the further loss
Of soldiers in the South
Will be enough to make them do it,
We'd have to squeeze them far more tightly.
Was everything that anyone could think of
Done to stir our nation up and to advise
The world about the massive genocide,
The outrage of the Communist offensive?
By denunciations and by word sent out
To U.S. personnel plus broadcast pictures?
Some might argue it was *your* fault
That the Tet offensive happened
Since it's our war being waged
And it was us the Tet offensive

Tried to oust, but such an argument
Would not be very telling.
If we have the capability,
I think we ought to strike against
Hanoi and other targets in the North.
I mean all out. Discard the theory
Or the pretense of attacking just
Supply lines from the North, the means
They have for infiltration. Can't we
Instigate or strongly urge the step-up
Of activity inside North Viet Nam
By Southern soldiers, sneak raids, sabotage
And so forth? I repeat: the war must
Somehow be exported to the North.

72.

--If we're silent, nothing new is said,
The people will begin to sense a staleness.
--In itself a major peace proposal
Doesn't promise much without
Cessation of the bombing.
There are risks though to a bombing halt.
It looks bad to a segment here at home
If we halt bombing at the same time
That we're calling up reserves.
—You're aware, though, how our method
Gets depicted by our critics: they say
Our way of establishing democracy
Is to pursue the last VC until he's dead.
--Is there any way of giving the impression
We're more willing now for peace,
Of saying "This almost is it,

Conditions will get better"?
-The TET offensive took away
The element of hope. The people
Now don't see an end as very likely.
--Why are we even contemplating
Sending more troops in?
Senator Stennis said he did not favor
Sending more troops in
Without the war's also expanding
Though he did say
He'd accept some reinforcements
To protect troops there already.
--The only thing Hanoi wants is
Suspension of the bombing.
Moves toward peace must be realistic.
A suspension of the bombing
Would at least get peace talks started.
Where they'd go from there is anybody's guess.
We need to start them.
--I think bombing keeps lead out of our men's bodies.
Pour more steel in on the enemy. Don't crawl.
--Can we offer something new besides more war?
De-escalation? The beginnings of it?
Gradual approach. If you accept this,
We will have another offer.
If that other one's accepted,
We will offer yet another.
--Any major offer now will seem like weakness.
We're too sensitive to critics
And we don't like shedding blood.
Clark has lined up well the points
For sending troops in. But the framework
Must be strength and resolution.
This is not a time for making any offers.
Bobby Kennedy, McCarthy...both will see it

As a kind of empty gesture and Hanoi
Will think we're floundering around
To get a bigger piece of candy.
--How much time do we have left though
If we keep on as we have or even
Make a greater effort--the economy's involved--
We may need wage and price controls.
I think it's just too much.
--The theory of our treaties was and is
We'll stop the Hitlers of tomorrow.
If they march, then they'll be met.
I just don't think that it's the time
To offer peace except to say
That we're prepared to start to talk
At any time. It is a dismal situation.
But we must support the men we've got there now.

73.

Just the word "negotiations" was anathema to Washington
From 1961 to '65 and not till April '65 did "unconditional
Discussions" get respectable, a presidential speech
Conferred that status. Even then Dean Rusk was stressing
In his tête-à-têtes with newsmen that there really was
No change, "negotiations" weren't the same thing as
"Discussions." Some months later this whole issue
Got resolved but it took longer to obtain
A frail consensus that negotiating parties
Might include the Viet Cong as something more
Than an appendage to the Hanoi delegation.
All these games of verbal pitty-pat
Were being played by grownups.

74.

"We intend to land the first man
On the surface of the moon
And we intend to land him there
Before the present decade's out"
Or some such words I rather
Cavalierly wrote in let's say
March of '66...oh well, the mayhem
They provoked you can't conceive,
I thought for sure I'd lost my job,
That I'd be out there on the sidewalk
Monday morning with my suitcase,
Hat in hand, in deep disgrace.
I'd only written them for starters,
Sure some other aide, some higher
Up the line would tune them finer,
Make them correspond more closely
To the facts, whatever they were.
I could not have been more startled
When the President just read them
As I wrote them, never checked
The facts at all. So all the scientists
And bureaucrats at NASA went berserk
Since they were running years behind
And just assumed that they could coast.
"That's what I call a real good news lead"
Was the President's reaction to the storm
My lines had set off, calmly chuckling
At the almost blunted purpose
Which my thoughtless lines
Had brought back into focus,
Sharpened up. Just calmly smiling.
You just never know what impact
Words might have. They budge foundations.

Which the President was fond of
Seeing move I can assure you.

75.

Inertia: Lyndon Johnson understood
As no one else did how the system
Was arranged to keep it sitting,
Dove-like brooding on the throne,
The bird of Dullness staving change off,
No one else had ever both by his experience
And temperament been so supremely ready,
So equipped to mount the charge
That would unseat it, he evinced the needed
N'er punch-wearied drive. That drive
Did not conduce with gaining popularity, however,
That whole effort he expended like a drill bit,
It left bruises, he lost friends, he angered many,
His ambition to dislodge the massive system
From the ooze which it was mudded in
A never-resting engine, he kept pounding,
And by God the whole huge thing began to move.

76.

The main weight of the war of course
Came down on Lyndon Johnson, who was coming
From a wholly different background.
First Hawaii which his view of Asia turned on.
It was linked with civil rights for him.
He saw it as a model of a multi-racial
Harmony that really could exist, not just

Some pipe-dream, but a model he'd
Neglected, even spurned throughout his life.
"We looked away from the Pacific"
Was the way he once expressed it in a speech,
He knew he'd fought Hawaiian statehood
In the Congress till the evidence of history
And Jack Burns' irresistible persuasiveness
Effected his conversion at the same time
He was advocating laws for civil rights
However cautiously, or starting to.
The link between these causes was a constant
In his mind from this time on though,
One can sense it in conclusions he arrived at
On his Asian trip in May of '61
Including this the most important,
That the greatest danger Southeast Asia
Offered to the US wasn't Communism proper--
That a momentary passing sort of threat--
But rather ignorance and poverty
And hunger and disease. By '65 though,
Much politically was cropping up in Asia.
First Sukarno left the U.N. and aligned himself
With Hanoi and with Peking. Inside
Indonesia proper he worked closely with Aidit,
Who led the Communists. Sukarno launched
The confrontation tactics with Malaysia
Which the British called up eighty ships
To counter, at the same time that
The North Vietnamese had started infiltrating
Regions of the South. No future hope
Seemed to exist for anti-communists in Asia,
This impression, this conviction had an impact
In Saigon and even more it had a huge effect on us.
It seemed we had to meet this escalation
From the North and from Sukarno.

So the President reluctantly--and one should put
The greatest stress on this "reluctantly"--
Concluded. He resisted. He kept listening
To Ball. I think his heart went out to Ball.
But he had McNamara, Bundy with their famous
Memorandum--now's the moment to decide,
We've reached the fork when we could
Either send more troops in or negotiate to salvage
Some bare minimum, some margin
Which would not increase our military risk.
But they both advocated sending in more troops,
There was this vacuum in the South, Diem
And Nhu dead, it was total disarray there,
And the US was responsible, the mess was of our
Making in the world's eyes, we'd encouraged
Or connived at coup d'état, could not just
Walk out on it now, this was the wisdom
Of the moment, Johnson felt that Asia mattered,
We should fight for it, it mattered for the future
Of America, it needed to be nurtured.
At the end of '66 he went through Asia
For three weeks, he hardly spoke about the war
In Vietnam, he spoke of Asia's need to organize,
Unite, we built a barrier behind which
This could happen, we gave Southeast Asia time.
But time was running out for us.
South Vietnam had been explicitly protected
In a formalized agreement which the Soviets
Had said they'd guarantee, that no third party
Would be transited by Hanoi to guerrillas
In the South, to bring supplies. North Vietnam
Did not obey this for a minute, they simply flouted
These accords. But there was one chance which we had
To call the Soviets to task for not fulfilling obligations
Which they'd willingly agreed on in a treaty--

This one chance was when Mikoyan
Came to Washington in 1962--this was October--
One can understand John Kennedy's reluctance
To put any further pressure on the Russians
When he'd gotten them to yield to us in Cuba.
Southeast Asia seemed of minuscule significance
At that point when the world was in the balance--
Still, one lets such issues pass and then
The next time they come up you're in
"A waning situation," you negotiate from weakness.
Stennis asked the crucial question five years later:
Why did we keep on sending more men in
If we just left them at the mercy of guerrillas
Who kept getting more supplies?
We had to stomp out that supply line,
But we didn't. And the sanctuary granted
To Hanoi was incompatible with victory for us
Inside the time frame which the patience
Of our people would permit,
And all our bombing of the trails remained
Demonstrably inadequate, the flow
Of their supplies was unabated.
We could have blocked them on the ground,
Not from the air, but such a strategy
Was vetoed by the President in 1967,
He thought blocking on the ground
Would bring the Russians and the Chinese
Into battle. Bill Westmoreland
Later credited the President for keeping it
Confined, for not provoking wider war,
Provoking world war. At the time, though,
Bill believed his hands were tied.
This was the doctrine of containment
Of the communists which everyone subscribed to,
Block expansion of the communists

While minimizing threats of Armageddon,
A tricky tightrope to be crossing.
And the President courageously admitted
In his Houston speech--did anybody hear him?--
That he could not say for certain
If the communists took over Southeast Asia
We would not be drawing close to World War III--
He was concerned as he gazed back
Upon the years in which he'd lived,
He was convinced that if we saw this struggle through,
We were reducing any chance of larger war,
We had to face the danger then and not bequeath it.
He was haunted by appeasement, he was baffled
When he could not bring the war to quick conclusion.
At the same time he was heartened
By the progress he saw Southeast Asia make
Behind the barrier he'd built,
The final test of it was Tet,
Which was disaster for the communists,
The people of the South did not rise up
To join the North, but how ironic then
That this was when some nerve snapped
In our country, our resolve was sapped
Exactly when (if you can use a term like this)
We'd won, the course for Asia now was set,
The long term course, though it took many years
For all concerned to run it,
For an independent Asia to emerge.
The war was anything but pointless.

77.

A sort of paradox obtains,

The odds are even we won't have to
Send in troops if we're prepared
To do so fully. If we're not prepared,
Our program stays halfhearted,
We'll get sucked in.
This commitment is a touchstone of
Our will, and if we're willing,
We won't have to. If we're willing
In our heart of hearts that is,
Don't second guess ourselves.
It's something like believing in a god.

78.

The detachment of the bureaucrats was catching,
It was something you assumed to show your worthiness
To play upon the team, your bona fides,
I'd compare it to the callousness (as other people see it)
Of the surgeon, it was no accident perhaps
That they referred to strikes as surgical, no feelings
Were involved in drawing blood for them.
But this semantics of the military muted war's reality
For those who made the policy back home
In quiet air-conditioned offices with thick rugs
Safely distant from the mess, they were the sober-minded men,
They'd be discussing things like "systematic turmoil
And the pressure," "armed reconnaissance"—
They even talked of body counts serenely,
This strange affect-less dispassion of the games-
Theorists, they had to show that they could talk
This kind of bleached-out talk, not blinking.
This surpassed a surreality for me one time in 1964,
We were discussing future bombing, just how heavy

It should be and how far strafing should extend
As part of "systematic pressure," one decision-maker
Proffered his solution to the problem:
"The orchestration of our bombing should be
Mainly violins it seems to me, but periodically
We ought to mix in brass, sound brief brass touches."
He seemed to relish the refinement of his own metaphor,
Its precious elegance. The shock when I returned
To teaching hit me, I would walk across the campus
Feeling sickened, in a daze, it was the flesh and blood
Young men whom I was passing every day
Or who were facing me in class to whom the numbers
On the charts we'd been discussing back in Washington
Referred, they weren't abstractions, it was
Their bodies which might be counted, Cambridge
Brought me up against the war more closely
Than I'd been to it in Washington, D.C.,
I found this puzzling, it disturbed me.

79.

Mining the harbors is an altogether different
Kind of issue, much more serious and complex.
The dilemma it would force upon the Russians
Is the problem: how to keep up
Their position and prestige in such
A place of disadvantage and distress.
They might, although the chances are they might not
Want to pick a fight with us in Southeast Asia,
Force some kind of confrontation.
Their vital interests wouldn't be at stake
So clearly as were ours, say,
Back in 1961 when Russia blocked

Our way of access to Berlin,
Sealed off the corridor.
Moscow might send in some volunteers
Or pilots and provide North Viet Nam
With better weapons, they might also
Start some action in Korea or Iran,
The Middle East, or they could
Think about Berlin again, to save themselves
Some face, they can control the heat
Of crisis better there.
The Chinese on the other hand
Would seize upon the mining of the harbors
As a chance to outshine Russia in Hanoi's eyes
If the Russians took no military action,
Did not open up the ports again to vessels.
Peking might interpret mining of the harbors
As the US putting pressure on the North
To make them fold, an indication that the US
Planned eventual invasion of the North.
If so, China might believe they had to
Intervene with troops and with their air force.
And so the US would be forced to answer that,
We'd have to bomb some Chinese air fields,
Other targets too perhaps. The whole thing
Mushrooms, Hanoi meanwhile tightens belts
And simply perseveres in fighting, will not
Talk to us, continues in the course
They've been maintaining. They would
Be of course dependent on the Chinese for supplies
And so the influence of Russia is reduced.

80.

They would go down to the courthouse
And instead of going in where white folks registered
They'd get sent down to a back room
Where they stood in line from 6 A.M. till 2
Since just a few of them were let in at a time.
You'd have a person with a Ph.D. or Masters
Whom they treated like a school kid,
They would order him to sit down at a desk
And copy out some chosen section of
The U.S. Constitution, then they'd ask him
To interpret it and fill out questionnaires,
He'd leave a self-addressed, stamped envelope
To hear from them but never heard a word of course,
The silent months slipped by, then they would go back,
Start the process up again, the most determined
Did this six or seven times, some of them
Stood there in a line for three whole days
Until their turn came. The authorities
Would find some way to block them.

81.

They carried me into a room
And they was two Nigra boys in there.
The state highway patrolman
Give them boys a long wide blackjack,
He said "Take this,"
And the Nigra boy he ast him
"This what you want me to use?"
The state patrolman say "That's right,
And if you don't use it on her,

You know what I gwine use on you."
I had to get me on a bed flat on my stomach.
That boy beat me till he give out.
By me screamin'....this here plain clothes man,
He didn't have no uniform or nothin',
Just there watchin'...got so het up
He jist run and started poundin'
On the back here of my haid.
I tried to guard the licks with my hands,
But they kep' beatin' both my hands
Till they got blue, him and that Nigra boy.
That Nigra boy was beatin' till I knowed
That he was give out, then they told
The other Nigra boy to beat me,
He took over and he jest kept on to beatin'.
They whupt Anabella Ponder,
I could hear her screamin' next door, then they
Walked her by my cell, her mouf was bleedin'
And her hair was standin' straight up
On her head and it was horrifyin'.
Over in the night I heerd more screamin',
I said Lawd they's someone else
Be gettin' it too now. It was Guyot.
I could see him in the mornin'
When they cracked the door a little,
Let some air in. He weren't smilin'
Like he used to, it was gittin on my nerves.
I was half dead when they let me out of jail,
Then I found out that Medgar Evers
Got shot down in his front yard.
Now I aint lookin' for no equal rights
With white men--if I was,
I'd be a murderer and a thief.
You have to realize that the white man
Is the scaredest thing on earth,

Out in the daylight he don't do nothin'.
Come the night though he be tossin' bombs
And payin' other people off to kill.
The white man's sceerd that someone
Treat him like he's always treated Nigras,
Beat him up the way them men done beat on me.
I couldn't carry that much hate inside my soul.
It wouldn't solve none of the problems,
Just for me to hate the white man
Cause he hates me. There's so much hate.
Only God has kept the Nigra people sane.

82.

Is America prepared to pay its dues?--
Since we're not asking just for meat
And bread and jobs. A share of power's
What we really want at this point.
Will we get it by the reconciling path
Or will we take it in frustration
And display it or the need for it
In rioting and blood? We want real power.
One suspects that it's the purpose of
The system...they pass pacifiers out,
Pass out polite meaningless labels,
Tokens, phantoms of respect, seats at
The table, even simulars of being represented--
Not the thing itself though: power.
They kept telling us we had to be
Responsible, Republicans might profit
From the actions, the insistence of
The Mississippi Democratic Freedom Party
Pushing to be seated. Who's supposed to be

Responsible? Let the folks who cry "responsible"
Alleviate the causes making black folks
Take their feelings of despair out to the streets.
And no more compromises callin'
Nothin' somethin'. We refuse to see
The victory in them or to adopt it.
We are unvictorious, hungry, homeless, jobless,
Sometimes beaten. We retain the strength
To fight though, we give thanks and praise for that.
To have taken up the half loaf
Or the quarter loaf they laid upon the table
Would have made us bigger liars
Than the people who were asking us
To swallow down their lies, it would have
Sent the crazy message we were sharing
Now in power when we weren't,
Our liberal sponsors would have felt
Such great relief, a job well done,
A bill of goods sold. And the Democratic
Party could have looked down yet again
On segregationist Republicans
And smugly pointed out
That their own Negroes were content now,
In the fold, when that's a lie,
This nation's racist through and through,
We need a naked confrontation with ourselves.
And if you wonder why we aren't exactly
Singing hymns of everlasting praise
Because a civil right bill's passed...
Well, we remember all the bills
That came before and we remember
Reconstruction...

83.

If they'd seen him in those meetings
With the small groups--what he did there
Doesn't go down on TV--deploying arguments,
Tell stories, make analogies--a whirlwind--
Or a poet. It was always hard to follow
In the sense of ordered logic, presentation--
He'd touch first base, then the next thing
He'd be up there in the bleachers
Selling hot dogs, preaching sermons,
Then he'd hop back on the field
And circle bases heading home
Although you thought he'd never get there,
Never come back to his point.
But then it all came back
With overwhelming, comprehensive force,
Tremendous power--it was damned near
Irresistible, you could never figure out
Quite how he got there, how he'd knocked you
On your back. "My God, if people
Could behold him in those meetings."
I can't calculate the number of
The people I've heard say that.
I mean people of distinction
Who'd come into him suspicious to begin with,
Not susceptible to salesmanship or charms.

84.

We've looked at every program that there is,
What works the best is what you leaders
Do the best, you train them in house,

On the job. Remember this though:
What we're talking now is hard-core
Unemployed, you'll have to teach them
How to wash and how to read
And write their names, you'll have to teach them
What you got at home from mommies
And from daddies, only these folk
Don't have mommies, don't have daddies,
No one gives a damn about them,
Or their mommies and their daddies,
If they do care, just can't help them,
Don't know how to read themselves.
You'll have to wake them in the morning
Since they've never had a thing
Worth getting up for.
Then you're going to have to scrub them.
Then you'll have to teach them basics
Since they've had no education.
Then you'll have to show them
How to do your jobs, they've got no clue.
This is no bullshit kind of meeting.
I am giving you assignments to commit to
And deliver on, I didn't bring you down here
To be told how tough a job this is,
I invited you to get this tough job done
Since only men like you can do it,
You're our leaders. This economy
Has been so good to you you can afford
To give a small piece of it back,
And if you get these people working,
You'll avoid a revolution, they won't
Throw bombs at your homes
And in your plants if they've got jobs,
They won't have time to burn your cars

If they've got work, and you'll be doing
Something vital for your country,
Just as vital as Marine platoons
In Vietnam are doing.
We're going to put people to work
Who never thought that they could work,
And we will get you federal funding
To assist you with the extra costs of teaching.
But I still need your commitment.
This is basically a job to save your country.

85.

We were only middle-level in the new Administration,
We were chatting at a cocktail party somewhere,
I could sense this sort of big guy out of place
Off to my right who would have joined us
If he could have, then I realized that this guy
Who seemed to have no place to go,
Who lacked a friend, was Lyndon Johnson
Whom we didn't make an effort to include,
We rather shunned him, froze him out.
It wasn't nice. He walked away.
I was a little bit embarrassed or concerned
And so I said to Ron "I think we've just
Insulted our Vice-President." "Well fuck him,"
Ron replied. This really shocked me.
It was unkind. It was loud enough for LBJ to hear.
It was in keeping with the tenor of the in-crowd
In those early days when we thought
We were rulers of the world, could spit on losers.
Johnson whirled around as if he might confront us.

Reconsidering and looking somewhat sad I thought—
Defeated—he then turned and walked away.

86.

I was sent to see Ted Sorenson, to make peace in effect.
The way I did or tried to do this was to ask
What role Ted Sorenson envisioned Lyndon Johnson
As performing in the new administration.
Johnson's role, Ted said, should be to act
As "salesman for the Presidential program"
(LBJ as Willy Loman). But as we continued talking,
I could see that Ted envisioned no role, nothing
For the V-P in the corridors of Congress.
Various aides from HEW and Budget
Kept on entering the office with their questions,
They were always asking Ted about the legislation
They would soon be sending to the Congress.
Ted would always introduce me to these men
But in a way that seemed perfunctory,
Disparaging almost or vaguely pitying.
"With the V-P" he would put beside my name
A sort of tag, as if my being with the V-P meant
I needed some excuse, I bore some stigma—hush hush,
Don't say this too loud. But these young deputies
Reacted in the same way to a man. "Oh gee,
I wish that we could get the V-P's input on our bill,
His help would make a crucial difference."
They remembered Lyndon Johnson as he was.
But Ted would never let me make a straight response,
He came between me and these guys,
He blocked me out, denied me access.
I had this feeling when I left that I'd attended

Some strange summit conference held upon
An iceberg, two men meeting who were members
Of the same faith or who claimed to be
Though each in fact had come and more importantly
Had left with his own god to whom he clung
With strict devotion.

87.

—They're out of office now, they're not consulted,
They don't feel that weight of power on their shoulders,
You could put all three of them upon the same scale
At the same time, they'd weigh less than ninety pounds,
They have these parties out in Georgetown,
This is what Bill Moyers tells me,
They were havin' them a party there last night,
Joe Alsop calls me up this morning all excited
Said that he knew Kraft and Evans
And that crowd around the Kennedys decided
I had framed up our Armed Services Committee
In the Senate, I had had Dick Russell call up
John McCone to put the war in Vietnam
On JFK's tomb, I'd conspired to show how Kennedy
Was immature and how his faulty judgment
Got us into this and his unsure direction
Of the war had brought sheer havoc to that country,
That McCone had gone and done it,
This was my game, blamin' Kennedy
For immature bad judgment when McCone told me
He didn't even mention Vietnam so I assumed
That since Bob McNamara started out with them
In that Administration…
—And since they'll tag him for the war in any case…

—But I assumed he wasn't feeling much resentment
Toward the things that I've been saying,
He could otherwise have told me it was not true,
I told Moyers I felt liable still for Kennedy's decisions,
On the hook, and that whatever JFK did I supported,
That if anyone in Georgetown could produce a man
In Washington more loyal to his memory than I was
They should introduce me to him and that my slice
Of the Presidential pie had been much bigger,
I mean making John F. Kennedy the President
Than Evans's or Kraft's, they may have written him
Some speeches, that's the story, now I wanted you
To know what they've been sayin', I assume
That what they say is an injustice to McCone.
—I think that's right and I might help with this,
And I should probably have been there
At that party, I'll communicate with some of them
And try to cast a realistic light on what they're thinking.
Did I understand correctly it was Alsop who conveyed this?
—Called Bill Moyers up to tell him.
Alsop's charging that I'm getting John McCone
To lay the blame for Vietnam on JFK's tomb
When you know I've never blamed him.
Have you ever heard me lay the slightest bit of blame on Jack?
—Of course not, Mr. President. I've mentioned this to Jackie
Several times because your attitude's impressive in the present
As it was when JFK was still alive.
—I may not have too much in my life but I've got loyalty.
If any of this crowd is in your neighborhood just tell them
I assume responsibility for everything
And don't ask anybody else to take a part including Kennedy,
And while old Jack was still alive whatever he did I was for
And in his death I'm still responsible for that,
I do not shove it off on anybody else.

88.

"Now Lyndon you could say it's not my business.
But it's my country too and I'm concerned.
You ought to fire McNamara right away
'Cause if you don't
He's going to hang this Viet Nam around your neck.
Ask Harry Truman. He learned
Just what I'm advising you the hard way."

89.

Mobility ability of US troops is great
And they're superior in weapons
But strategically and technically
They're now completely deadlocked
Since they're forced to fight the tactics
Of our people's kind of battle,
The initiative's been taken
And the US troops must passively
React to our attacks, can't fight in their way.
The imperialists are bellicose, they're stubborn
As they escalate the war although
The fact that they must do so
Shows how isolated and defensive
The position they are in is.
Escalating war when they're at
Such a disadvantage means
They never can succeed in their expansion.
If they try to use their forces on the ground,
Against the North, it will increase
The time it takes us to defeat them.
We can draw on full resources

Of the Chinese to support us—inexhaustible—
And in war the one who has the greater pool
Which he can draw on will inevitably win.
Before it was American advisors
Who got bogged down, 20,00 more or less,
Now it's that whole enormous army
Mired in quicksand.
If they don't increase their forces,
We'll defeat them. If they do though,
We'll defeat them just the same.
Whatever the conditions we'll defeat them.
If they bring in 700,000 men,
They will encounter such confusion,
Such a conflict of conditions.
Thirty one million people from the South
And from the North who have been
Mobilized against them. Our armed forces,
Our artillery are always getting stronger.
If the enemy invades North Vietnam,
We will continue massing forces in the South
To fight him there.
He will need to use 500,000 men
Against guerrillas. Other countries
Will send in their volunteers.
If China sends in hers,
We may have one million soldiers.
The enemy increases his attacks upon the North,
But has his escalation maybe reached
The top rung of the ladder?
On the home front his position is unstable
Whereas ours is growing stronger every day.
They are well-to-do but fighting
A protracted war is arduous.
We can easily endure protracted hardships
Whereas they can't. They can maybe

Go on fighting for a short time
In their stubbornness,
But five or ten more years?
They will discover we are difficult to deal with.
They want to fight fast to avoid protracted war
But they keep sinking in the very muddy marsh
And so protraction's what they get,
Their leaders can no longer speak
Of winning in a hurry, even Johnson
Wouldn't dare to. In reality they only
Want to go fast, but the more
They try to go fast they sink deeper,
And the more men they throw in the more they sink.

90.

I wish that I could say to you
We'll soon complete this conflict
With its limited objectives
And the danger to us seemingly remote
But I cannot...in an attempt
To keep a larger war from coming
If the Communists succeed in overrunning...
We face more cost, loss, more agony.
But the U.S. *will* stand firm in Viet Nam.

It is true that West Virginia
Has amassed more casualties percentage wise
Than any other state, but we're behind you,
We want victory in 1967.
We must cease from picking nits on Viet Nam,
We must get on with it. The people
Of the U.S.A. want action.

Rusk's position
Inconsistent with the President's remarks.

George Smathers has a son
Who's just come back from Vietnam,
He has a second son who's getting set to go.
The son who's back told him dissent
Within the Senate was a damper
To morale among the troops,
That it gave comfort to our enemies.

Go in and win or get out.
We'd be better off to end the war right now
Than end it later... long before we get in trouble.
Costing too much. Its effect upon the budget.

Senator Hill says he wants Haiphong Harbor closed
With Senator Russell in agreement.

Our involvement in this war was something bad.
Step up the tempo of it.

500,000 troops would now be needed,
Bomb new targets in the North
And not just military targets...

U.S. people still behind us for the most part
But they wonder why it's taking us
So long to win this war.

We must keep applying unrelenting pressure.

No new resolution called for
From the Congress. Inadvisable.
Our support since '64 would be way down.

An unconditional cessation of the bombing,
Further efforts to negotiate.

Those civilian deaths should shock us
Just as much as did such deaths in Nagasaki.

It's a a national dilemma (read:disaster).
Richard Nixon's
Going to murder us in 1968,
He will become the biggest dove
You ever saw.

There's no reduction
Of the rate of infiltration from the North
Because of bombing
Yet
They really do believe
They'll gain a military victory by summer.

I'll destroy you and your dove friends
Every one of them politically
In six months.

Just announce that you'll stop bombing
If they'll come to the negotiating table
And be damned sure that you're ready
To negotiate if they do come.

He was shouting and he seemed to be unstable.

...If the word of the United States
Is any good at all. We don't give up,
We are not quitters. We will stay
Until the reasons we are in there for
Have fully been accomplished.

Let's get out of here. This prejudice
And propaganda airing. Whereupon
The two stood up.

I cannot tell you
How much pressure this administration's
Under to go farther militarily.

This war's against the interest of our nation
And the world.

It was unruly.

And the best thing you can say
For demonstrations of this sort
Is that they're badly misinformed.

We have to fight this war to win.

Three hundred students rushed against
The car and started banging with their fists.
What could the V.P. do but sit and smile
Though badly shaken up inside?

It was subversion.

Public polling still suggests
That increased military pressure
Is the best, perhaps the only way
To liquidate this war.

91.

He'd be in his chopper
And he would chew some sergeant out
Because the a-c wasn't on
Or wasn't working,
He was "suffocating," therefore
This poor sergeant had to suffer.
Five hours later he'd be saying
To the sergeant, "Someone told me
That your wife is very sick.
Why are you here now, you get on home,
Here's some money, you go
Over there and stay till she gets well,
Don't even think about your work here."
It might seem self-contradiction.
Well, a person who can act that way
Is not one man, he's many.

92.

—Pacification bogging. VC active in the South.
An instability of government. The DRV
Is infiltrating more. The thing
Will not collapse tomorrow
But the game is being lost.
Should we attack to boost the GVN
And weaken Viet Cong?
—How did Diem do it?
—Ran a tight ship. No cement
Among the people. Needed:
One courageous man with army backing.
Huong courageous. We are

Better off today than one month back.
—A stable government's essential.
Need to pull all groups together.
We did in the US post-assassination.
We don't want a new Diem.
It has to be their war or else.
No use in hitting North
If South is not together.
Khanh seemed good but now he's gone.
—We've given warnings.
—Why not say that this is it?
Not sending Johnson City boys out there
To fight if they're not fighting.
—Their politicos inclined to think
The VC's now our problem.
More civilians in control?
Or US taking over all?
Or should we shrink our role, get out?
And if Huong falls…
—Both getting in and getting out are easy actions.
Being patient is the hardest, for the long haul.
How much more would make good Rangers of the South?
We cannot interdict the Viet Cong with jets.
Make good guerrillas of the South?
—That's what we're doing.
—34,000 hard core Viet Cong
Against 200,000 soldiers in the South.
—So 34 can lick 200.
—But the ratio is 10 to 1
Or 20 for guerrilla situations.
—If it's dollars that they need,
Then give 'em dollars.
Don't send widow lady
Out to slap Jack Dempsey.
DRV will bomb Saigon once,

Then we'll all be off and runnin' to the races.
We perhaps have given training.
Nothing left but give more people.
Day of reckoning is near.
We must be sure that we've done
Everything we can.
There must be more things we can do.
But what are those?
We could have kept Diem in office.
—Huong plus Vien added up
May give Diem.
I think we're probably progressing,
But it's slow.
We must eliminate Hanoi.
—But don't we need to shape up first,
Pull stable government together?
Put in everything we can
Before Bus Wheeler saddles up?
Bring in third countries.
Try to get much better press.
Go sock your neighbor
If your fever's one-oh-four?
I wouldn't think so.
Get well first.
We've never been
In a position to attack.
Just socking's easy.
Taking Wayne Morse way is easy.
They'll be back one month from now though.
We will want to be prepared
To answer questions. Make
A new Diem if needed.
If we tell Bus Wheeler slap,
We'll be prepared to take the slap back.
—Hanoi slapping back seems doubtful.

—Didn't Doug MacArthur say that in Korea?
—Every measure mentioned's heeded.
Not enough. Three months
Might keep this Saigon government
Sort of fumbling. Not much time
To put new factor in except…
—Agreed. We must start under our volition,
But it's better if we have
The allies with us. Get dependents out.
We've done all that we can.
—Bob cited Westy on the need
To have a base first.
—We are undertaking some of that
Already in our plan, but give
Max Taylor one last chance.
We'll have McCone talk to the Pope,
Dean Rusk to allies.
If there's more of same in store,
Then I'll be talking to you, General.
Fulbright, Hickenlooper, Saltonstall
And Russell need a briefing
In a small group. Don't want
Word of this to spread.
I shoot the man
Who leaks a word of this at dawn.
About the House, Mahon if here
And maybe Ford.
—Backgrounder bad.
You call the press in
For a conference or you don't.

93.

In 1965 for instance Westy wanted M-16s for ARVN
Since the first thing you could do for them
Was modernize equipment.
Garands are useful things if you are
Shooting moose or something,
But they're not much good for shooting Viet Cong.
ARVN was being totally outgunned,
I mean those poor bastards...
A platoon from the North and a main line
Viet Cong group had the seven point six two
Type stuff, and they could mow down those battalions
From the South. "So they need weapons," Westy said in '65,
But nothing happened, M-16s got issued finally
In May of '68. I am not absolutely sure
Why there was such a great delay,
I think it had to do...well, the Pentagon
Just wanted Viets out of this, to arm them
Would have gone against this plan,
It would have complicated things
To have them in, but there was
Something else at work: systems analysis,
That watchword, all that horse shit.
You can bet that when the order,
That request came in from Westy for those rifles,
It was sent to some computer in the Pentagon.
Now in terms of cost effectiveness
What is the best way to provide
Your ARVN troops with greater fire
Against the North Vietnamese?
So your computer grinds this question,
Wheels are turning click click click,
Out comes your answer: air artillery.
That's fine, so every time some ARVN company

Gets pinned, they blow their horn,
The goddamned jets come and
A hundred fifty howitzers
From thirty miles away, they zero in,
It has a marvelous effect,
You say bye-bye to all your enemies,
It also blows the goddamned countryside
Sky high. This isn't war on someone else's turf
You're fighting, you're supposedly maintaining
Your own nation. So you come into a village,
You find snipers, you send soldiers in
To chase them, you don't blow the village up.
We just used ARVN as our decoys,
They were sent out there to wait
Till someone shot at them,
Then they could call for airplanes.

94.

The bureaucrats, the men who made our policy
Evinced a strange detachment, they were also
Cryptoracists. It was not that they were consciously
Contemptuous of Asian loss of life.
There was this Western sense in play though,
In the background, there were multitudes
Of Asians after all, these Asians all were fatalistic
It was thought about the loss of human life,
Were cruel, barbaric to their own kind,
They were not of our same species, they were
Different (though all Asians looked alike)
And so the upshot of this background noise,
This static of our attitude toward Asians
Was the question whether Asians, Asian peasants,

Asian communists were people, were they
Really human beings in the way that we felt
We were. I can ask it in a slightly different way:
Would all the policies and military tactics
We pursued have been the same if those
We labeled as our enemies were white?

95.

Regarding "coonskin on the wall" at Cam Rahn Bay,
What do you think he should have said,
"Go out and die there for a compromise"?
You had a basic problem, here's the President,
He's talking to the troops, his hands
Are tied behind his back, you can't go in,
Invade the North, blow up the dikes
And then obliterate Haiphong. And yet
In rallying the troops out on the battlefield
You can't exactly say "You're going to die
So that our bargaining position at the table
Will improve." You simply can't.
And so in this respect the critics of the President
Were morons. My opinion.

96.

--There is nothing on the Russian side to cause us to refrain from further
bombing

—So perhaps we ought to bomb again, then pause, then bomb again.

--I thought that we were going to pause this time for only five days.

--To achieve the proper object we should pause I'd say for seven.

--We would make *The Times* quite happy since they asked us for a week.

And I'm certain we could hold out then till Wednesday.

--I would go again on Monday, I would start then,

Then the pause would be for six days.

--We could start again on Tuesday evening our time.

--The French and the British have talked to the Russians.

They urged them to move on that meeting.

So we ought to get a telegram to Taylor.

--We do not need to settle that tonight

Except we do need to decide about the bombing.

What to say about resumption of the bombing.

--We should have had some answer from Hanoi by now

Since you informed them Tuesday.

It will be six days on Monday.

If you want to start the bombing up on Tuesday that's OK.

We can tell them in the Congress that we had to make adjustments.

We'll inform Mansfield. But we'll never manage to satisfy *The Times*.

Now if this is what you all want we will go on Tuesday evening

Our time. But I think I'd go for Monday.

What do we say then to the press though?

--I would say to Mansfield, Kennedy and Fulbright

That we notified the others--and for six days held off bombing.

Nothing happened. We were willing to be pleasantly surprised.

We cannot just throw our guns away at present.

But no one thanked us for the pause.

--And Mansfield ought to know Hanoi was spitting in our face.

--I'm afraid that if we go their way we'll wind up having no one on our side.

The public never wanted us to hold back on the bombing.

We're deferring now to Mansfield and to Fulbright.

We will lose support though if we do it their way too long.

We will go to Tuesday night to keep you happy.

I myself would favor Monday.

If you have good reasons though we'll go when you say.

We can tell them what we did, that we have used the time

To get in some reconnaissance...Respect for Buddha's birthday...

One whole week...We told Dobrynin and Gromyko.

I would call them in and tell them we are starting Monday night.

And then *The New York Times* would tell us to delay.

--Tell them we are starting to bomb on Monday night again.

Target # 29 is military barracks ten miles further north than we have ever gone.

Let's leave that in. Our generals will say that we've gone soft

If we remove it yet again. Hanoi and Peking get the message.

--You can only go so far before you bring the Russians in,

There is a flash point with Hanoi.

And Gromyko said decisively he'd help North Viet Nam out.

—But what about the SAM sites? Do we let the clock tick on?

Or do we take them out right now?

—No. Those airfields for the MIGs have got to go first.

All night long B-52s to plaster airfields.

All the bombs won't hit their targets so there may be some civilians.

Send the fighter bombers after, take the SAMs out.

--I think you ought to show them we are open and receptive to ideas.

Nothing came of this idea.

---I would like to keep the barracks off the first day's list of bombing.

--Ball will say our bombing's keyed to their aggression. He'll announce that.

Give the other side two weeks to think it over, test their mettle.

If this plan works, the rebellion may be over.

--Give these people will to fight and will to win.

97.

--We have an urgent matter to decide: how we
Instruct our representatives in Paris.
Is cessation of the bombing to be total?
--The word cessation does mean total if you use it.
--This is no time to be making any threats.
--But they are stepping forces up
Both in the South and in the North
Because the bombing's been suspended.
We should bomb between the 19th
And the 20th again to keep them honest.
--We are in a better posture though
Regarding world opinion.
We are giving out the image of a nation
Seeking peace while our opponents are inflexible.
They have given the impression of a nation
Seeking only propaganda opportunities.

We'd jeopardize advantages we've gained
From world opinion
And would not gain militarily enough
From our resumption of the bombing.
--I would hate to freeze us underneath the 19th.
We do not need any big dramatic
Publicized attack above that line
But could engage MIGs, could continue
Route reconnaissance above it.
--I agree. How long before we just get trapped
Below the 19th? It was force I think
That brought them to the table not our eloquence
On March the 31st. All we are doing now
Is let them build back up.
I think the military people feel quite strongly
We should bomb up to the 20th again.
And doesn't every day we stay out
Make it harder to go back?
--I think it does.--I don't agree.
--It is a key communications hub,
A key transshipment point.
--Just how much do we suffer from restraint?
--It's an advantage to the enemy whenever
He can put supplies down closer
To his front lines safely.
And the military price is going up for us
In Hanoi and in Haiphong
When we don't strike them.
--My approach is more pragmatic.
We decided not to go above the 19th
As our margin, to be absolutely sure
We wouldn't find ourselves
Involved above the 20th.
--But I'm against our going on with this.
Whatever we have done once isn't total.

And the North may read what we are doing now
As some strange voluntary foolishness on our part.
--I believe this very deeply, I'm not merely
Being stubborn. You can go up to the 20th
If and when conditions warrant it again.
But now the tenor of the last week
Is support for what we're doing.
Something's bound to come from Paris.
Or I hope so. With such limitations placed
Upon our military action, we have no plans,
No real way to win the war if we
Cannot invade the North or mine their harbors.
And the enemy controls the situation
In the South. We're in a war we cannot win.
Last fall the North put in their stack,
The Tet offensive, but they didn't win with that.
So they may now think that it's time
For them to settle. They can't win this
Militarily. Nor can we.
--I disagree.--I disagree to some extent.
--We have sought to keep the North
From taking over in the South by force.
To that degree we have succeeded.
--Militarily the North can't win the war.
They are aware of that.
But that fact doesn't mean that we
Have won it or are winning,
And unless we get some settlement in Paris
I do not believe that they'll give up the effort.
They're not running out of men,
They can go on ad infinitum,
That's the kind of war we're mired in.
We have lost so many of our own men.
We were having an erosion of support
Until the 31st of March when all was changed.

But we could start a new erosion.
--We will not get any settlement in Paris
Till we show them they cannot win in the South.
--They've already seen they can't win in the South,
That's why they're talking now in Paris.
--It seems worthwhile for them sending men
To Paris when it gets for them the bonus of
No bombing in the North,
--I will put it off again against my judgment,
Wait till Wednesday. But below the 20th parallel
I think we ought to hit them.

98.

The galoots are loose by God!
It is as if somewhere, a short while back,
George Wallace had been wakened
By a vision almost blinding in its brightness:
That they all hate blacks,
The whole damned country does,
They're all afraid of them and so that's it:
The whole United States is Southern.

A letter came from Rensselaer, NY
To his campaign:
"George Wallace is the only man
Outside of God who can retrieve us
From the mess and get us
Back to where we were before the trouble
For our Glorious Nation started:
FDR's inauguration."

His eyes were deep set
With exhaustion and with strain.

One thought at first that he had
Ringed them with mascara.
From his shiny blue suit's
Breast pocket poked a phalanx
Of cigars along with spectacles
He sometimes used for reading
And the handkerchief he'd pull out
And would carefully spit into.
He would cordially shake hands
With that great cohort of policeman
Which would gather to protect him,
Every man on each occasion.
A fair-sized crowd would cheer
Along the fence, and he'd salute them
Rather smartly, an ingratiating
Cocky little bantam in that gesture,
In that tribute, this would work for him
Down South and in Chicago,
He had found a way to translate
Alabama's brand of rawly racist tactics,
They had started to express
The deep-dyed discontents,
Uncertainties and hatreds of
Americans all over.
There's a belief among a segment
Of this country's population—
Many Southerners but people of the North too—
That the branches of the government have fallen
Under sway of an unscrupulous elite
Who could be counted on to rig the game against
The run of ordinary folks at the expense
Of strict construction of the U.S. Constitution.
The Northerners would try of course
To play down racist elements
Of their support for Wallace which they

Always called a populist rebellion.
It was sprouting from the sidewalks though
In all three-dollar wards as someone put it.
His supporters were the members of
The lower middle classes
Or the working class to put the matter plainly,
To dispel the nice illusion that America is classless.

Dick Smith often warmed the crowds up
With remarks that mostly fell flat
Since old Dick sure wasn't Wallace.
He was finance chairman though
So it was his job every night
To make the promise that "the Wallace girls"
Would soon come out among them.
They would carry buckets made
Of yellow plastic, they did not exactly
Work to comb the crowd for contributions,
They merely wandered out among them
Looking cute and chewing gum—
White blouses, black skirts were the mandatory
Outfit, Wallace sashes tucked in tight
Across their bosoms, Wallace boaters
Perched atop their pretty heads
Red white and blue (that is the boaters were).
Perhaps one out of three would put
Some money in the buckets and the cash
Which this indifferent haul brought in
Would always end up in a trunk
They called "the woman" since,
As Dick Smith would explain,
"We never let our hands get off her."
Revival meetings in a sense
Were what these Wallace rallies were
Which meant you had this sort of perfume

Added in that you'd distinctly call erotic,
This excitement which the girls who took collection
Represented though these Wallace girls
Were mostly at the same time what you'd call
Forbidden fruit, they all were ladylike and dainty,
Not the type that you'd find after in the bushes
Or the back seat of a car for "fornication"
As a postlude, they were sublimated
Southern belles and queens of their sororities,
They were almost all related to
Some member of the Wallace inner circle,
They were friendly and their bleached blonde hair
Was swept up into oreoles and ringlets,
Massive cotton candy beehives.
"Look what we got here" the men
They moved among would say
With admiration, keeping hands off
Since they held these gals as things enskied
And sainted, this was all just Southern flirting.
It was a mystery worth pondering perhaps
How those stiff structures on their heads
Could get configured, reconstructed
In that narrow space of time
Between the closing of the hotel night club's doors
And when the baggage call
For all campaigners came at 6 A.M.

Wallace claimed he had the whole South
And the Border States, he also had his issue
Which came down to "law'n'order" once the Democrats'
Convention had descended into chaos in Chicago—
All those beatniks, their offense to civic norms.
Was a Wallace vote the kind of vote,
Assuming it existed as one had to,
That a mill hand cast, the mean occulted vote,

The dark intention he would not confess to pollsters,
What a guy keeps kind of burning in his gut
Until he goes into the booth, starts seeing red,
And pulls the lever?
Or was the threat to vote for Wallace
Just a private form of grousing, vented steam,
Because of Vietnam, a war we were not winning,
Hippie riots and "the mess,"
But merely protest after all that most Americans
Had too much sense to waste their precious vote on?

Thus the question hung there dagger-like,
The Damoclean sword of early autumn '68.

99.

—John, I think we have a problem
With our old friend Mendel Rivers
Or perhaps a little war.
280 people I've discussed this with...
Not ten have disagreed with me.
What I would like to have if I could find
A loyal Democratic chairman or committee
Is a moderate, a reasoned understanding.
The President would be required to notify
The Congress—that's desirable or feasible.
On this I'm overriding all the lawyers
And my own Attorney General.
I think that I can live with thirty days
Like what the GSA act has,
I think I'd tolerate the weaker kind
Of President who took that,
It's been done already with the rest

Of the Departments and I see no reason why
It can't be done now with Defense,
So I agreed to what I sent you in that memo.
But I absolutely will not now agree to any more.
Mendel wants another veto
And he wants more funds impounded.
If he wants to take me on, well that
Will be OK with me, I mean if Mendel
Wants a war he sure will get one out of me.
He's been out there always playing games
With McNamara, Bob does not know how to fight him,
I can hold a good sharp knife,
I mean to use it with him. You just tell
This Mr. Mendel he's too big for his own britches.
I have served with him for years
And I don't trust him as a very good tactician,
He's near ruined me by ordering
That we should bomb Peking.
Now those in Congress need to be a bit responsible.
No matter what seniority they have they are Americans.
That damned fool is out there advocating
Bombing of Peking, he's got no business
Being head of that committee any longer,
He deserves to be removed, in fact
He ought to be expelled because he advocated
Bombing of Peking, with things as bad
As they are now you've got to talk to him,
If you can't do the job I'll have to
Call him in myself though I just talked to him
Two nights ago, how thrilled he was he said
Since I had signed his pay bill,
But they tell me they have met with him
Three times or so this morning, he just
Rants and raves and tries to throw
His weight around.

—You talked to him you say the other night.
—Yes sir, I surely did, almost the first man
I called up, I TOLD him then, I said
I have two bills before me, I'll sign one,
It's wrong to sign it, it will cost 600 million
Dollars more. Now you and Albert,
All the rest of them, should have denounced
This as an outrage, irresponsible—
We went ahead and passed it, though,
Unanimous 414 votes to none against it.
Now just you think of that, 600
Extra million, almost all of it is wasted,
It does not go to the people it should go to,
It will go to kinds of people we do not need
In the service, we need specialists
In things like electronics.
But I signed the bill, I told him.
On the other bill I told him
That I could not go along with it,
It ruins our whole set-up of Defense
And I was not prepared to ruin
Our whole country even if the House
And Senate didn't seem to know much better.
Most Senators did not know what was written
In the bill, it was that craziest committee
Running rampant, I was talking to the Senators,
Not one of them knew what was in the bill
Which is a sad fact to report but it's a true one.
I called Mendel up myself and he gets treacly,
Mr. President I'm sure that we can find some way
That we can work this problem out
To all our satisfactions. I informed him
I was saying in my message I was not opposed
To something that made sense as far as
Notifying Congress was concerned

Although my A.G. was opposed, he said
A President should not agree to that,
But I intend to do it anyway
To try and be amenable with Mendel.
McNamara says they've argued this one out
With him all day. I said to Bob just tell him
Thirty days or he can go jump
In the river, I will veto what he sends me,
I'm elected and I'm going to be
The President while I sit at this desk.
—Does he advocate the bombing of Peking?
—Yes sir, he does and he's been scarin'
All our allies. All intelligence reports
Contain his statements and the government
In England's coming close to fallin' in on this
Since they just read these statements
That a fool like Mendel Rivers or like Morse makes.
They should be more careful, our Marines
Are out there fighting every day and they don't
Understand what folks back home are saying.
Here's what one marine is saying on the ticker,
I'll just read it, it's from Hamilton, New Jersey.
"I feel sorry for those people who are saying
That the war in Viet Nam is not their war."
This is Sgt. George Deluzio who wrote this
Just three days before he died. "Just ask
The fighting men, they'll tell you that
The war in Vietnam is really needed."
This Marine wrote that if China takes
Control of Vietnam, the Indian Ocean then
Will fall to her control and she can put
Her tactics into all of Africa, Australia,
Then Japan, she keeps on moving
And unless we stop them now,
Then George and Mike in fifteen years

Will have to fight them. George is 7, Mike is 2.
"When I hear about the demonstrations back home,
All the people saying this is not their war,
I just feel sorry for them." End of letter quoted.
Here's what Rivers said last week in New York City,
Write it down. I will accept nothing
But complete and total victory as the outcome
From our war in Vietnam. Who in the hell is I?
What meat does Caesar feed on, John?
You must keep our soldiers safe there in the House.
You can't protect them with a lot of damned fool stuff
Like Rivers' comments being broadcast
Live on tickers round the world and at a time
When I am trying to negotiate agreement.
—I'm completely in support .
—You bet you are. But you and Carl
Have got to grab this guy and tell him
Thirty days and not one day more.
And if we have to fight we'll fight him.

100.

I'm convinced that in a certain sense
He didn't quite believe there was a real world
Out there. I think many of the things
He did his whole life were attempts
To break the mask and get in contact
Wit that world if it existed.
In a certain way his efforts were pathetic.
That was why he used the telephone so much,
To get in contact with that world.
And there were aspects of his character.
His genius as a mimic. He was always

Trying people on for size in an attempt
I think to see if someone else
Was Lyndon Johnson.
He was not sure who he was.
He could not bear to be alone
Unless he got completely drunk.
There really is no other explanation
For those sessions with the press
Which he would conjure up on Saturdays,
The worst time you could think of,
In the mornings—he was lonesome.
And it explains I think to some extent
His love affairs with women,
He became through them a part of
Someone else, stopped being lonesome.
So it's not correct to talk of him
As frantic with the phone,
As someone so completely hooked
He had to be in constant touch
With all his projects, checking in.
It was the other way around
With Lyndon generating projects for the sake
Of making contact. He'd come up
With things to do to be in touch.

101.

He never really understood what news was, basic stories,
Much less pressures any journalist was under..
And he never seemed to realize that reporters
Had to move on things.
He may not have had this kind of
Situation back in Texas where reporters

Didn't act on every story right away
Or from necessity. In Washington
The press was too competitive, a Washington
Reporter who declined to act at once
Upon a story could expect to get
A phone call from his editor--not happy--
Who'd inform he had read about that story
Somewhere else. But Johnson
Never seemed to look upon the press
As something there, an institution
He was going to have to deal with
On its own terms. He believed that you
Could have a situation with the White House
Only putting out what it preferred to issue.
He attempted to abolish daily briefings
For the press, he had no notion
Of the value of a basic point of contact--
As though the press might disappear
If he ignored them. He was thinking
All askew here. He thought journalists
Were critics pure and simple, either for him
Or against him. He just thought in terms
Of adjectives, was always after adjectives.
"L.B. Johnson, beaming, handsome and sincere,
And with the good of people always
In the forefront of his mind, today did so and so."
He thought stories might be written up in that way.
It was crazy. He lacked any kind of notion
Of the news as simply being there, reporters
Writing things up for their readers
Just to talk about, as basic information.

102.

…Had constructed for himself
A past in which he played the victim…
This appealed to certain sympathetic types,
A weak, despised, rejected figure,
Poor young Lyndon, when the truth was
Something different since his youthful friends
Insisted he was handicapped or crippled
Not by youthful deprivation
But from being too indulged, they said
His parents in his boyhood
Spoiled him rotten…

103.

After his thirty-ninth birthday
He began to need a lot of loving care
But he weren't gettin' any,
That was his big problem, people didn't
Seem to realize what a monumental thing
It was for him to see the big four-oh ahead.
He even had a sort of unsaid rule:
He didn't want people past forty around him,
This was all through his career,
When he was President he still preferred
His people under 30, under 35 at most.
I mean the people on his staff.

And so in 1947 he was saying
That he wasn't going to run, they had this meeting,
There was Connally of course, Jess Kellam,
Phinney, maybe Pickle and some others.

The accepted way that Connally taught us all
Was to agree with him when he would talk this way,
You had to play him like a fish, just say
Oh yes, I think you really shouldn't run
Because he'd turn around and say
"Now wait a minute." So they did that.
He had told them that he would not run for Senate.
Someone said, "Oh good, we'll get us
A campaign up now for John,"
And so a great sour look came over Johnson's face,
"Now just a minute, wait a minute,
I don't know so much about that."
And the fact was that these other guys
Were really wanting John, he was their friend
And their coëval, more approachable,
Less difficult than Johnson, much more fun
Since Johnson kept them on their toes,
He never let up. In this meeting
Connally said to him "Don't run
If you don't want to, no one's giving you an order.
But I would say, assuming you don't run,
You've turned your back on Franklin Roosevelt
Who made you what you are
And on a lot of things I'm sure
That you believe in. Just abandoning.
And you're deserting Texas too
To a direction that a lot of us
Don't want to see it go in." This speech
Had a great effect, it offered counsel
Johnson could not disregard and so
He dropped the plan he'd mooted
To announce on New Year's Day
He was withdrawing from the race,
That he was getting out of politics completely.
He went that far with this group of his advisers

And he continued playing rather hard to get,
You would have thought he was the prom queen.
"I'm not agreeing I will run."
He groused a little bit about how everyone
Was forcing him to run since after all
These other people weren't in politics themselves.
So John would ask the question
"What would make you happy?"
That may sound somewhat peculiar,
Here you had this man whose aura
Was of strength whereas in fact
Those on his staff were often dealing with a child,
We had to think of ways to make this fella happy.
You could tell when he was sulkin',
Feelin' sorry for himself. There was the time
We had to find a front man for him,
Someone running interference when
He had to mix with crowds, polite society.
"I know just who to get for him," John said,
"We'll get Hal Woodward's brother Warren,
He was Kappa Sig when he attended Rice,
He's a thousand percent personality type."
This guy was going to have to be well dressed
The way John Connally always was,
The way you looked was always high
On Johnson's list. "Well go and hire him,"
Johnson said on Connally's word
And sight unseen. And so the candidate
Was mollified at first, he thought he'd got
Another Connally in his camp.
That didn't last long, he began to sulk again,
You sensed his sulking, he would stand up
In a meeting, he would walk around the room,
He'd have his hands poked down real deep
Inside his pockets, he was jigglin' all his coins

And all his car keys. This was not a stress response,
This was a way he had of thinkin',
He would walk around a room, gaze at
The ceiling, he'd be jinglin' all the change
Inside his pocket. "Well, what else is eatin' on you?
Is there somethin' else you want?"
Was Connally's question, he was tuned
To every blip in Johnson's radar.
It took coaxin', but the candidate
Came out with it at last, what he still wanted.
"As long as I have had a job in Washington, D.C.
I have observed something: that the men
Who get ahead up there—and there is no exception
To this rule—they always have some little fellow
In the corner of their office, he does not display
Much personality or charm, he doesn't need to,
He don't need to dress too well, his tie
Aint tied right, he might have a button
Missin' off his shirt, he's got these fingers
Stained with nicotine, no coat.
But he sits back there broodin' in that corner,
Never meets the people comin' to that office.
He just reads and sits and cogitates,
Comes up with new ideas, makes the fella
He's been workin' for look smart.
I've never had one of those men
But now I want one." I know
Just what Johnson meant, his observations
Were correct, this was a thing
With the Establishment that Johnson
Got involved with, FDR had sort of grabbed him,
He had made him his lieutenant under Vinson,
You began to have investment banker types
Start comin' down, they always tended
Toward the Navy, that's the area that FDR

Put Johnson in to be his sort of lookout.
These investment types came down,
They always had good educations,
They had done a bit of traveling in the world,
We didn't have too many men back then
Who'd been abroad except to fight in World War I,
You might have people who had world views
In the cotton business—otherwise those men
Were not that common in our culture,
But you had them in the banking world,
On Wall Street, in the law firms,
They were coming down to Washington at this time
Out of patriotic spirit, they would work for you
A year, get paid one dollar, these were really
Top flight guys, old family types, aristocratic.
They remained Republicans but where their fathers
If you'd told them that the Japanese were steaming
Up the Chesapeake would not have worked for FDR,
This slightly younger generation was appearing
In executive-type jobs, they were in almost every case
Creating new things, there were massive kinds
Of planning being done to meet the needs
We knew would soon be thrust upon us
After Benelux went down in 1940,
They were studying logistics, they would study
Transportation, they were toting up our assets.
FDR knew how to use these men
In very skillful ways and he made LBJ his agent
In the House to these aristocratic upper crust
Establishment type figures, they respected LBJ,
He was a master of the Congress even then
And they preferred to work with him,
He was straightforward unlike
Many Southern chairmen of committees
Whom you'd have to do a kind of

Courtship dance with, drink their bourbon.
They weren't hell-for-leather, get-things-done
Like Johnson who was 28 years old.
He'd go and see them in their offices,
They'd have some sort of young man
At their front desks with a three-piece suit.
That kind of suit caught Johnson's eye straight off,
In later years he'd ask some aide
"Now where's your vest?"—not only his aides—
Someone else's. He reverted to this image
Of the people from his early-learning years
And he'd make some of them get livid,
Telling people how to dress. So Johnson
Jollied up this three piece type of suit guy
At the front desk, then he'd finally get inside
To have a conference with the guy
Who was in charge of some vast enterprise
Perhaps without a title, he had come
To have this banker type tell him what kind
Of purpose needed getting done for Roosevelt.
Johnson came in there persuading,
Pumping arms and winning arguments.
At some point though would come this little man
Out from the corner, he would sit down at he desk
Beside the man for whom he worked
And write out notes for him,
The man for whom he worked
Was getting smart now, Johnson noticed,
He'd have answers back for Johnson.
The dynamic of the meeting got transformed.
This was the type of little man that Johnson wanted.
He was always thinking how to seek advantage.
And I suppose that I became that little man for him
Without the tie-stains or tobacco…

104.

As it approached reform the Great Society was
Non-ideologic, strictly technical and grounded
To a high degree in deep self-satisfaction
With our economic system, it did not reflect
A vision of the Left to start to open up
The status quo to questions, or the willingness
To question all foundations. Those foundations
Of our economic system were not part of
Its agenda as they were for social democratic
Counterparts in Europe and except for Medicare,
It did not offer much substantial re-arrangement
Of our country's way of life,
It stopped well short of any plan
To start to modify the marketplace, it left alone
The way our work was organized,
Our patterns of investment,
And it left alone the business class for certain.
Capitalism was never even slightly called
In question, larger contours of our
Economic system were not called
In question either or the tools of it,
A variant of Keynes that had been worked out
For the management of macroeconomics—
Growth, employment and inflation.
The war on poverty residing at its center
Was, alas, a rather timid call to arms
In which the enemy was circumspectly named.
Just correct inequities and problems
At the margins of an economic system
Of production and consumption that was thriving
Was the governing assumption and the hope.
Above all save the systems's basic features.

105.

The authorities evinced this show of
Shock, surprise, and horror at the riots,
But apparently they just don't give a damn
About conditions, there's a lack of sanitation,
People pushing Harlem people all around
Are an affront. They send in thousands
Of policemen, they'd do better just to send
About a third as many people in
To have a look at buildings—like inspectors—
And a thousand sanitation workers too.
They'd do better to attempt some proper schooling.
What we'll probably be hearing soon instead is
"Keep the natives up there quiet so the rest of us
Can go about our business as we always have."
Riots might erupt in any other city
Where the Negro population is substantial.
I've been walking through the Harlem streets
The last few days and I have heard the Negroes saying
"We've got nothing now to lose, what more could happen?"
Can the average Negro leader ask his race
To any longer follow ways of moderation?
Our ideals lack any relevance to practice
And the Negroes start to sense this,
There's this gap that's really gotten so ingrained,
It is the gap between the promise and performance,
It's ingrained within the system
Blacks are being told to fight to have a chance in.
You might ask why should they bother
If the gap is going to stay there.
Blacks are bound to get more militant,
Resistance on the part of whites will grow.
Will the actual power follow the demands
The civil rights groups make

Or will it follow the resistance
That the white groups show to change?
And even so the power to bring about some change
Through legislation isn't equal to the power
To enforce the new consensus,
There's a tendency to sit back, to assume
The word is equal to the deed whereas
The real work's only starting with the word.
I must reluctantly conclude that even liberals
Have a somewhat tainted record in the area of race.
In the areas where liberals have the power
As in our labor unions, schools, and in our politics,
The Negro's plight is really not much better
Than it is where liberals don't maintain control.
That ingrained gap remains the problem
And thus the counsel of despair the Negroes utter,
"We've got nothing now to lose, what more could happen?"

106.

Lawson knew from hateful looks
On faces of policemen and the hate calls
He'd been getting in the night
That many white folks wished him dead.
After one late night negotiating session
He returned to where he'd parked his rather
Brightly colored car beneath a streetlight
In the open, he had feared that someone
Might have hooked a bomb
To his ignition switch, he sat down
Sideways in the car with both his feet out,
Turned the switch on, then he jumped.
The fact that it did not explode made him

Feel foolish—still, from this time forth
He put a piece of tape between his fender
And his hood—a broken seal meant
Someone tampered underneath it.
Alzada Clark had taught him this precaution.
She opposed the KKK when it had terrorized
Her union and had fought to thwart
Her organizing efforts. After all
A bomb had blown up Wharlest Jackson's car
In Natchez when he'd fought to open
Skilled jobs in the factory he worked in
Up to blacks. And Lawson knew
Of other bombings. Neither Lawson
Nor the men who worked for Martin Luther King
Felt they could ask police in Memphis
Or the FBI for help. Not only that:
You had these agents dressed in street clothes
From the US Army's hundred and eleventh M.I.D. group
Tracking King, they had been tracking him
Since 1957 as a Communist when he was still
A Morehouse College student—this was
Total violation of his First Amendment rights.
King was too involved now in opposing
Vietnam and in a panic
They considered him a menace to the Empire.

107.

In the name of Heaven can we do no better?
We have Fuchs and Hiss and Acheson
And H-bombs coming at us from the outside
And the New Deal eating meanwhile
At the innards of our nation.

108.

You could say "the Groton ethic" was their style
For whom low burdens were their backhand way
Of reigning—nothing *infra dignitatem*—
No loud saber-rattling crudeness of display,
The pricks of conscience to be honored but
The wishes of America would have to be respected
And its strength would thus be felt throughout the world.
To advocate restraint yet to despise softness.
Walking softly with one's big stick
Fully ready to crack heads with it necessity arising.

The "soft-line" men got shunted out of State off to the tropics.
"Hard-nosed" men, "tough-minded" types were at the center.
And it didn't seem to matter that indifference to the details
Of the country we'd committed so much might to
Was pandemic. Why sweat details (as for living,
Let the servants do that for us)? Viet Nam was only
Something incidental. The Establishment accepted
That we'd have to ramp the war up
If the only other outcome was to lose there.
We'd be horrified to have another Munich.
We had the doctrine of containment
Which we rigidly applied (a nice abstraction),
By its terms we saw the Communists as bloc-ish,
Viet Nam was like an afterthought, it almost
Didn't matter in the grand scheme, in itself,
And yet it did, we had to get into this war
Or else the dominoes were forfeit.
All these sages said our will was being tested.

Containment if one rightly understood it
Was an antidote to war—it meant the US

Must not panic in the face of Russian pressure
On the West's free institutions, that we must rather
With the steadiness of surgeons push back firmly,
Mount a countervailing force. This wasn't "rollback"
As conceived by Foster Dulles, it was
"Steady as she goes," a form of persevering patience
Which did work in that it kept us out of war
Without the Soviets invading Western Europe
If they ever meant to do so. This shrewd policy
Then hardened into dogma. Was the dogma
Asking Congress for a blank check
Both in military terms and in the funds
We were preparing to commit?
If we girdled the world with our treaty commitments
And established all the bases to fulfill them
Just as Dulles always argued that we had to…
Well, it seemed there was no end to this
Proliferating US supervision. Did our readiness
To fight in Viet Nam mean warfare anywhere on earth
Could, if the President so judged, be called
"Attack upon our nation," which the President
Had license to defend us from without consent
Of Congress? Was he following the logic of containment?
It became a kind of funhouse hall of mirrors,
A Lernean type of hydra, all the threats we saw pop up.

You can talk of Lyndon Johnson as the culprit all you want,
But the Establishment was wedded to this doctrine
Up till 1964, it was our right and I suppose some thought
Our duty (sacred honor): intervention
With whatever means we needed not excluding military,
Covert action or avowed throughout the world
To limit communist expansion or the rise
Of any radical regimes which we thought
Threatened US interests, any group which our electorate

Disliked. To stand for this
Would raise your Presidential ratings.

A Western coalition with the U.S. as the "balance wheel"
That Britain once had been, to hold the infidel at bay,
We were the military/economic guarantor,
The "free world's" moral leader. It was our grand cause
To rush into a power vacuum
Any time we thought one had arisen.

109.

Rhetorical escalation—there's the need
To sell the people, press, and Congress
On this costly war that no one really cares for,
Wants to own (which makes the selling
That much harder)—the objectives
Of the war are all in flux as all the difficulties
Of it and the costs continue mounting,
So the definition of the stakes has mounted too,
It's all inflated. This has not been, though,
An orderly progression since the prose
Of leaders comes from many writers.
But there is an upward spiral nonetheless
And once you've said that the American
Experiment depends on how things end
In Vietnam, that it's the crux, it's very hard
To tune the rhetoric back down, you can't go back.
"A fundamental test of America's will":
That phrase was often sounded, often bandied,
With a rather pompous clearing of the throat
Of any statesman who invoked it,
This was Colonel Stimson's doctrine,

And the Colonel was the holiest of holies,
Some dim figurehead whose memory was sacred
And absolved all present arguments to boot.
Ours was not to reason why, our only task
Was always follow in the Colonel's sacred footsteps.
Such a view struck me as strange though:
Did the Asians not have wills too?
In a contest must the wills of Anglo-Saxons
Automatically prevail? And this belief
That our wills always must prevail
Was tied in somehow with obsessing
Over power which the USA possessed
In such a magnitude as history could not
Depict the likes of. Any man who called in doubt
Our sacred role in Vietnam was called a shrinker
From the burdens of that power we possessed,
The burdens power thrust upon us, power's
Awesome obligations. And by implication
Doubters were effete, soft-headed men.
In fact there was some hint they were not
Real men in any sense that mattered
As when LBJ declared that Bowles
Was yellow-bellied, had to be cashiered.

110.

...Resulting from the long war then
The enemy gets weary and discouraged,
Suffers torments of nostalgia for his home,
The French economy's exhausted.
It's more difficult to keep the troops supplied,
And France's soldiers have to suffer great privations.
The sentiment at home is for the war

To be abandoned, diehard sentiment
In favor of the war becomes untenable
As protests get more fierce, the French
Colonials rise up against their rulers,
World opinion starts to isolate
The French in condemnation,
Peace proposals score successes.
During this stage then the enemy surrenders
His position in the field, takes up
Entrenchment in the cities.
He may enter into false negotiations
With us hoping to delay his own erosion
Or to receive some great assistance from his allies.
As for us our aim's consistent,
That the country rise up *en masse*,
On the offense and annihilate the enemy,
Achieve true independence, re-unite.
Our troops will always come together quickly
And will launch planned lightning strikes
Against the cities and will circle round
The enemies, annihilating all of them.
In brief we throw our forces through
The country into battle, crush
The enemy completely, win our land back.
The machinery of conquest that the enemy
Sets up will be removed
By being smashed and at the bottom
Of that scrap heap lie the corpses
Of the puppet-traitors slowly decomposing.
This the third stage of our warfare
Is the shortest, but the valiance
And the victory are greatest.

111.

Was Israel the aggressor in the Six Day War,
Was its attack unjustified? McCloskey
Told reporters our position in the war was strictly neutral.
If the President should really set neutrality in motion,
It might well prevent Israelis selling war bonds in this country.
A position of neutrality might also mean
The US wouldn't ship supplies to Israel.
Even Fortas called, expressed deep reservations
To the President about our being neutral.
So the President gave orders to his spokesmen
They should back off from McCloskey.
Still, reports of LBJ displeased with Israel
For precipitating war against the Arabs
Prompted further angst for Jews.
He had me call up certain friends of his
To offer reassurance and to urge them:
Get the US friends of Israel off his back,
He was behind them. He was nettled
Being drawn into this crisis. And he had problems
In his own Administration: Larry Levinson,
Ben Wattenberg had written him a memo:
If the President would offer reassurance
To a Jewish rally scheduled for the next day,
He might neutralize the Sate Department's
Statement of neutrality, might even turn
A lot of Jews around on Vietnam,
Gain their support again from gratitude,
Convert the Six Day War into a great
Domestic bonus. But the President
Was mightily displeased with what the message
Urged upon him, he called Levinson who happened
To be sitting in my office, and he told him
He could not see why the Jews would not evince

Some basic trust in him.
They were far from being through though
When this conversation ended,
He and Levinson soon met out in the hall.
The President in coming
From the Oval Office spotted Larry exiting my office
And he jutted out his fist at him in anger,
And he shouted, "You're a patsy of the Zionists,
A dupe, and I've got two of them, Ben Wattenberg
And you inside the White House writing speeches.
Goddamned dupes. I'm doing all I can
For Israel, that's the message you should relay
To your rally. Can't you see that?"
Then he turned abruptly, stormed off
To the mansion, leaving Levinson
To "tremble to the marrow of his bones"
As he described it to me later.

112.

A Democratic rally in New York the night of June 4.
I had gotten final word that afternoon
That war with Egypt was beginning.
He was sitting on the dais, I went up to him
And whispered "It cannot be held back longer,
Mr. President." But still he made a speech that night
That I'd say brought the house down. No prepared text.
He just drew upon the feelings of a lifetime
In support of Jewish causes back to New Deal days,
Discussed the need for Israel to survive.
At some point Bobby Kennedy and Steve Smith
And their retinue walked in, it was a cohort
Like the gangsters in the movies—

Always traveling in a pack of snap brim flunkies.
I knew Bobby was resentful
That the President had been so damned impressive
And he said to me "Tomorrow have the leaders
Meet at your place." I said "Bobby,
It's the President who runs this operation."
He said "Maybe I should go above your head,
Convene the leaders on my own."
"And you can also go and fuck yourself," I told him,
"I am looking to the President to lead this."

113.

There are two sets of problems both related
With respect to Negro issues. Number one
Is life conditions and behavior of the Negro
Underclass that has arisen in the cities
Of the North, they are disorganized and angry,
They're a hurt group, they are given over easily
To self-destructive violent behavior.
Number two, you have another group
Of radical and nihilistic youth who are not
Members of this underclass themselves
But are identifying with it, and communicating
With it and determined to employ it
As an instrument of violent apocalyptic
Conflict, confrontation with a ruling class
Of whites whom they disparage as
The racist and the military axis or they
Vilify them rather: irredeemable.
I don't think we appreciate the depth
And the intensity of feelings as they fuel
This second group or the extent to which

They've managed to politicize the torment
Which the urban masses suffer,
How they've managed to persuade
These urban masses that the nihilistic
Outcome is not only to be wished
But that it cannot be avoided.
And the violence is far from being over.
It may get worse, may become
More terroristic. Now for liberals
This is very hard to deal with in a sense
Because we're just so goddamned decent,
Our intention is to show these people kindness
And to help them, we have gotten in the habit
Of denying the reality of life the Negro masses
Have to deal with, this has paralyzed
Capacities we might have had to help change
These conditions, we have somehow
Blamed ourselves for the deficiencies
Of poor folks and we've let the matter
Rest there, so when Coleman says their schools
Are not to blame for this disastrous
Low attainment level Negroes have achieved
As much as who they went to school with
And the matrix of their families,
We dismiss him as a racist, and we go
Our merry masochistic way
Deploring slum schools, play the blame game
With ourselves, we wring our hands,
We say it's Lyndon Johnson's fault
Or put John Lindsay in the dock,
We cannot entertain the thought
That our stability may hinge

On something hard-boiled, something
Not nice which will have to be applied,
A tough solution. What I'm saying's
Rather simple, there is nothing we can do
To change the minds of Negro nihilists
Or white folks who support them
Since the course they have embarked on
Is determined. What we can do
Is deprive them of the underclass
They feed on for their strength,
We must face up to those realities of life
That many liberals are too damned nice
To acknowledge, I'm convinced
That our reluctance—though our motives
May be good—has been a factor feeding rage
That we've seen roaring through our cities
This past summer since the Negro's
Situation looks a lot like that of Yank,
That surly, a-politic, proletarian stoker
In O'Neill's play, Yank's determined
That the world of first class passengers
Acknowledge his existence at the least,
So at Fifth Avenue and maybe 59th Street
He starts jostling men in top hats,
He insults bejeweled ladies in their furs.
What he elicits is politeness,
All these people he's accosting in a rude way
Are refusing to acknowledge Yank's existence,
What Yank knows himself to be.
"I beg your pardon" drives him mad
As their response, so Yank turns violent
And in the end he gets destroyed.

114.

A group of young black men
Accosted Martin Luther King
As he was walking through the streets of Watts
Surveying riot damage. They said "We won,"
This boast tantamount to taunting.
"How can you say you won?"
The Nobel laureate replied.
"Thirty-four Negroes have died in these riots,
This whole neighborhood's in ruins, and the white folks
Now can say they have excuses not to help us."
"Well, we won because we made them pay attention."

115.

Our aims in Viet Nam as I perceive them (being honest):
70% avoid a big humiliating rout (to reputation
As the guarantor of…everything).
20% to keep South Vietnam turf (and adjacent)
Out of grasping hands of China.
10% to let South Vietnam enjoy
A better way of life. And also:
Come out from the crisis not too tainted
By the methods we've employed.
I would not say that we were there
To "help a friend" though I'm not sure
How we would stay if asked to leave.

Our stakes in Vietnam
Are buffer real estate near Thailand
And Malaysia and (the big thing)
Our prestige.

116.

They all agreed the US
Had enough for guns *and* butter
Since our economic system had the strength
And it could generate the funds
To fix society at home
And to resist the spread of communism
Everywhere, to propagate our gospel
To the world: we had the duty and
The privilege to undertake these burdens
And "forever" was the answer
Robert McNamara gave
When asked by senators how long
We could afford to fight the war:
"Many prices must be paid to fight this war,
Some of them heavy, but in my opinion
Straining our economy is not among those prices."

The economy in fact could have afforded
Guns and butter but the federal budget could not—
Not unless we raised our taxes.
The dilemma Johnson faced was how
To carry on with both the guns and butter
In the absence of a tax raise—
Quite a juggling act. He tried
To hide the cost of war from people.
How to talk the Congress into raising taxes
When he'd only just persuaded them
To make the taxes lower was an interesting question.
In the end the Great Society would have to be postponed
So to a great extent the poor paid for the war.

In 1965 you would have thought the New Economists
Had found the famous stone that can convert

All things to gold since they asserted:
If you put the fiscal levers into their hands
They could manage our economy
According to the principles the late
Lord Keynes had outlined so that
Everyone could have his cake and eat it,
By the proper use of tax codes
They would stimulate the aggregate demand,
They would accomplish full employment—
Damn the risk of budget deficits—
They would foster steady economic growth.
What no one noticed when their paradoxic doctrines
Were announced was that they represented Keynes
Without the necessary discipline or pain,
Were Keynes transformed to get the votes for him
In Congress—could one really count
On economic growth all by itself
To meet our pressing social needs?
Well, no, but tax cuts by themselves
Might squeak past Congress, let the "public squalor"
Fester for a while, and tax reform was going to come
With each reduction of the tax rate
And it would pay for social needs.
Of course it did not come, the loopholes stayed in place.
You had investment credit first in '62,
Which bolstered profits.
But the increase in investment which was promised
Did not happen, fancy that.
The cut in income tax looked broader-based on paper,
But again the boys in Congress did not tighten up
The loopholes, S.O. Hermansen laconically predicted
That the changes in the tax laws would by 1968
Have been in favor "overwhelmingly"
Of "higher income groups," and so
This radical reform had as its practical effect

Redistribution of its benefits
Toward those already well off.
Rest in peace o vaunted era of reform.

With simple trust they really did believe in growth-religion.
Seek ye first the kingdom of the GNP and all the rest,
As if by magic, will be added unto you.
The full employment policies, the economic surge
That followed from them really raised
The living standards of the people, the majority,
And it wasn't just by paying higher wages—
Better houses, better pensions, better health
Insurance came with this same package
In the private sector—in the public
Greater governmental revenue resulted
Since although the rates of tax were low,
You had them levied on a greater income-volume,
This big "dividend" made possible at first
The Great Society. But cutting taxes surely
Was the easy way of bringing in the sheaves,
This kind of economic stimulus.
The price that would eventually be paid though
Was this rate drop on a grievously
Eroded base of taxes—how could they
Reverse this drop then? Had the US
Only taxed itself at European rates,
It would have brought in 50 billion dollars more
By '69, or if they'd just maintained Ike's tax rates
From the Fifties, they'd have brought in
25 more billion dollars for expenses,
In itself almost enough to fight the war
In Vietnam by '69, and half that sum
Just handed out in cash to every family
Underneath the line of poverty
Would have brought them all above it.

We did not even moot redistribution
Since prosperity alone was going to do it—
We would bake a bigger pie, we'd blow one up
From which each slice however small
Would be enough, our New Economists
Were claiming they could unlock our economy's
Unutilized potential, open sesames of some sort
And in 1965 it seemed they'd done that,
They'd expanded the economy,
Reduced our unemployment
And had somehow kept stability of prices.

Was it Vietnam alone, increased expenditures for it,
That brought this idyll to an end?
Well, the economists would like to have you think so,
Thus absolving all their policies of blame
Or hocus-pocus. Would inflation
Have caught up with us regardless
In an economy approaching full employment?
Well, perhaps. Or is it possible
Deflationary action by the government
As part of central planning for the war
From the beginning…Who can say,
One keeps on spinning all these what-ifs.
Just how bad the situation had become
May not have dawned yet on economists
By year's end '65 although they must have known
Inflation was in play by then.
But they issued blandly reassuring statements
Like "our vigorous economy
Is in a very strong position
To sustain the further burdens
Of our national defense,"
And it was not until the end of '66
That overoptimistic estimates of war costs

Were admitted and an error of about
10 billion dollars in the forecast was acknowledged.
Then a tax surcharge was asked for, then it wasn't,
Then it was again in August '67. Budget-fudging.
Wilbur Mills said that a surcharge wouldn't pass
Unless accompanied by deep cuts
In the social welfare programs.
Mills kept whittling billions off domestic spending
As the price for his support and Lyndon Johnson
Thus essentially was cornered.
He not only faced inflation on the home front,
He might also have to put the price of gold up,
Thus effectively devaluing the dollar
If he didn't get the surcharge.
Never mind the need for spending
On our cities lest another round of rioting begin.
The Great Society was forfeit—all but forfeit—
Three years after it had started.
LBJ became a character impaled.

Logically of course the Keynes-spawned gospel
Had implied that you would have to raise
The taxes sometimes too as part of fiddling
With the dials but understandably
Proponents of it never put much emphasis
On this side of the balance.

The true cost of labor had remained stable—
Remarkably so in the face of rising wages—
Through the early 1960s—productivity increased
From better training, education,
Higher capital investment, automation—
Labor cost per output unit rose
By only one percent each year for seven years,
Which was a notable achievement.

Then suddenly from 1965 to '69
The cost per output unit shot up
17 percentage points. Up prices went,
And wages went up too, but then their value
Was eroded by the rising prices first of all—
Inflated money-wages notched the workers
Into higher income tax brackets too
And so their economic wheels were in effect
Spinning, they were mud-stuck, they achieved
No forward progress, they weren't really
Playing catch-up ball with higher costs of living.
All the businessmen were making higher profits
From the war boom; doctors, lawyers and accountants,
The "professions" saw their incomes going up,
Stock prices surged, these were the go-go years indeed,
And you could read about what government
Was doing for the poor and in particular
The black poor, but production workers
Out there in the middle of the country
With their kids were marking time and so resentment
Started gnawing, ill-defined, inchoate, quick-
To-be-suppressed stuff since the war was at
The root of all their problems but they'd always say,
Felt forced to say we had to stand up to the Commies,
Back our President. They therefore had to swallow down
The gorge of their resentment as it rose, it was
Their patriotic duty.

117.

Once an area got designated SLAM,
It would be neutralized by air strikes.
Such an action would be followed by

Reconnaissance patrols and if appropriate
By exploitation force teams
(Special Force teams). When withdrawing
They'd leave booby traps and mines behind
In place and then the Air Force followed up
With other air-delivered land mines.
Reconnaissance patrols would sometimes
Stay upon the scene if they were needed.

118.

As far as the press goes, I feel like
A hound bitch in heat in the country.
If you run, they chew your tail off.
If you stand still they will surely slip it to ya.

119.

Every time I stop the bombing of the North
They run their trucks right up my ass.

120.

I got earphones in Moscow and Manila.
I got earphones in Rangoon and Hanoi
And on any of them all the time the only thing
I ever hear is Fuck you, Lyndon Johnson.

121.

You are getting unjust criticism now, but just remember
That the men who've gotten criticized the most
Are those whose names have shone the brightest
In the annals of our country: Lincoln, Roosevelt and Wilson.
And you might remember Jesus' crucifixion
Only three years after he'd begun his ministry of healing,
That analogy. In the long run it's what God thinks of
Our actions and what history will say a hundred
Years from now that matter. Thus I'm praying
That you'll face the somber choices of this hour
With faith and courage since the Communists
Are moving very quickly toward their goal
Of revolution for the world, and I think God
May well have brought you to the Kingdom
For a moment such as this one just to stop them.
Christian civilization's hanging in the balance.
You might be the man to save it.

122.

You can tell your boss we Southerners love bombs in Vietnam
But we hate registrars for voting here at home.

123.

"Hell, if I'd stayed in there any longer,
I'd uv come out preaching civil rights myself
To Alabama."

124.

—A wise man folds a losing hand and quits

—But what about American prestige?

—You put that in your pocket and you walk.

125.

It may be that the Poles in good faith thought
They could deliver us a live Vietnamese,
You had this whole worldwide campaign
To get negotiations started, bring the US
To the table—it was all agitprop,
They did the whole thing very well,
They'd line themselves a patsy up
Like Norman Cousins, they would
Introduce him to some U.N. guy who said
He knew a Pole, the Pole had said
He thought the war in Vietnam
Could end quite quickly, there were people
In our government however who were vested in
Continuing the war—so there goes Cousins
Or whoever was the designated patsy
Of the week, since there were others
Whom they lined up, down to Washington,
He gallops on his mission of salvation
And the President would say to him
"Well go ahead and see what you can do."
Of course the rest of us who know
How these things work were getting ready
To repair the coming damage.

You always had these trails that someone said
He wished to follow, we were set up
For a knockout punch each time,
There was some Indian who promised,
There was Kissinger who had this pal in Paris
Jean Santigny, Jean Santigny knew a guy
Who knew a guy so if we just would stop
The bombing, then the talks toward peace
Could start. I am convinced
This was the KGB at work, you always
End up looking bad because you cannot prove
A negative, you cannot prove these guys
Did not intend to really start negotiations,
That they were playing games with you,
These were maneuvers.
The one that came from India
Was a real hoax, Cousins picked it up
And ran with it. I brought him
To my office with the President's permission,
I broke out the secret cable file untouched,
He got no summaries, we hadn't doctored
Anything, and Cousins read them all
And even he said that this clearly was
A frame-up when he left but then
He wrote an editorial the next week,
Said he still was not convinced that we
Had made a good faith effort, met these
People in the middle. There was nothing
We could do with such intransigence on his part.
What he would not see was we had our position
Which Hanoi could not accept, it was
That simple, we insisted on a basically
Korean type of settlement—now there
Were many types of ornaments
That people tried to tie to this one tree,

But there was one thing we were not prepared
To give which was a coalition government,
A guarantee of that, we weren't prepared
To let them rev up that salami slicer
Used for years in Europe.
Did this mean we were holding out
For military victory? It certainly did not.
But we were not prepared to suffer a defeat.
They're not the same thing.
Now the bombing as an issue
Was the most goddamned irrelevant—
I mean a real red herring and I wrote this
In a memo to the President in 1967,
Ho Chi Minh I said would sit down
At the table to negotiate if we
Were raining bombs down through his chimney
If negotiations seemed in his best interest.
World opinion is a wholly different matter
And the bombing had been blown up
Till Americans could think of nothing else
But it in terms of ways to stop the war
And so I think it needed stopping.
This was known as my pneumonia memorandum.
The military men who were advising us
Reminded me of doctors—and I'd said this—
Who could treat you for pneumonia
But were clueless when you had the common cold,
It was in their vested interest for the patient
With the cold to get pneumonia.
McNamara was not happy with this memo.
You see, the President would hear you out
When you brought up the bombing,
Then he would send you down to Walt
And Walt would break out all his charts,
The charts were marvelous,

But they were always proving something else,
They were in reference to another war,
They cured you for pneumonia.
I never thought the US could be beaten
In a military sense except we weren't allowed
To fight that kind of war as we conceived it
Since the North was fighting something
Altogether different. Every day we sent out
Bombers chasing bridges in the North
Or something like that while the one thing
That was needful we neglected,
We did not create a South Vietnam state
That had a military working to defend it.

126.

As Mr. Sam once said to me,
I would like to go back down and make them
One more truly Democratic speech.
That poor old state:
They haven't heard a Democratic speech
In thirty years, you get election time come round
And all they ever hear is "Nigger, nigger, nigger."

127.

Mills meant to limit the number of children—
Those abandoned, illegitimate—who would receive welfare.
Johnson thought this kind of policy
Would savage little innocents,
But Mills remained unmoved.
The two men took the gloves off

During much of their exchange
But there was impasse at the end
Of their discussion, two men fighting
To a bloody kind of draw:
"Now Mr. President across town
From my mother back in Arkansas
There is this Nigra woman having her
A baby every year. Now I go home
When we're in recess and I hear about
This woman from my mother every time,
This same complaint. That Nigra woman's
Got eleven children now, but my proposal's
Gonna stop this. Let the states pay
If they want to for a woman having
Multitudes of babies, having more than
Some small number we can countenance perhaps."
When Mills left, Johnson turned to me
And said "You hear that good now.
That's exactly what we're facing in the Congress,
That's the way most members feel.
They're just afraid to say it publicly, out loud,
Unless they come from redneck districts."

128.

For the past month we've been moving with increased strength,
The ability to get things done is present, and the confidence,
The people think you're doing what you do because it's right,
You have no axe to grind in their view. This remarkable accretion
Could be lost if Wilbur Mills succeeds in rolling us on taxes.
If we end up getting no tax bill at all or if we get one
Larded up with Mills provisions, then the ball game may be over
On the Hill for us this year, indeed you may find

It's more difficult to even run your own branch of the government,
Control of that may slip. I would suggest you come out fighting
For our tax bill when you face the press tomorrow,
And I think we need to take control of Ways and Means from Mills.

129.

An independent think tank we'd created
To evaluate our programs…April 26 its board
Met for the first time…he came in
With his prepared remarks in hand
But never read them, he sat down
And laid prepared remarks aside,
Spoke from the heart:
"My intellectual liberal advisors
Wrote this speech but I would like
To tell you what's been on my mind
More plain and simply. We've assembled you
To think about the future.
I'll describe to you your problem number one
If you intend to help your country:
You have got to raise the taxes
Which can pay for social programs,
Which will educate our children, re-build cities.
You're all smart enough to tell us
Which of all our many programs
Seem to work and which ones don't,
But what we really need is someone
Who'll be smart enough to tell us
How we possibly convince our fellow
Countrymen they've got to ante up
And pay for programs. Find a formula for that
And you'll have really served your country."

130.

You got Wilbur Mills down there,
He might precipitate a world financial crisis
Just because his momma happens not
To like our welfare programs.

131.

"My name is shit to liberals, to the red hots,
Always has been, always will be.
Sure, they need me when it's time
To pass their goddamned legislation,
But they never give me credit.
I cannot unite the country."
He walked round and round
The White House grounds
Reiterating this, this was the night before
Atlantic City started, he assured me
That the next day he'd withdraw.

132.

"If we withdrew from Vietnam,
The balance of the power in the world
Would shift completely, you'd have
Asia going red and our prestige
And our integrity would suffer
Massive damage, allies everywhere
Would feel that they'd been shaken,
Even those who ask us publicly
To call a halt to bombing.

The effect on our economy at home
Would be disastrous and political
Disputes could freeze American debate
And maybe even limit freedom.
But by contrast if in Vietnam
We manage to achieve the goals
The President set forth in his
Johns Hopkins speech, great gains,
Substantial progress would accrue in many areas,
Political and economic questions
And security, the way would then be open
To combine techniques of birth control,
Techniques to make economies expand
In a gigantic arc from Vietnam
Across Iran as far as to the Middle East
And bring in unimagined new developments
And thereby clearly demonstrate the worth
Of democratic ways of growth
For all societies." How easy is it then.

133.

I never understood how Lyndon Johnson
Who was always for the little people, colored people,
Disadvantaged people, could consent to blowing
Vietnam to bits since it was full
Of all the people he had always meant to help.
Did he believe you had to help them
By destroying them to start with?

134.

I came into a room where men
I'd worked with in the past were now conferring.
I was met by stony silence when they saw me.
Doan Thanh Liem of all the group
Seemed pained the most although he spoke to me:
"When you must use these tactics
[he meant dropping bombs and napalm
And recourse to heavy fire
From our artillery in cities],
Then I know that we are losing.
4000 homes have been destroyed
Because of raids, 200 citizens are dead,
1000 wounded. Only 20 Viet Cong
Have gotten killed, 200 homes
Have been destroyed for every Viet Cong
Who's killed, in District 6 it's even worse."
When we went out to look around,
He put a press sign on my windshield—
Not protection from the Viet Cong he told me—
From the local population which is bitterly
Resentful toward the U.S. During Tet
It was the VNAF airplanes flying raids
But the Americans have taken over now.
The local population's bitter.
They can't understand the bombing
Of their homes when there are
So few Viet Cong around. Liem said:
"Someone ought to go on trial, I mean
To answer for this murder and destruction."

135.

Some symptoms of the virus of
The year of '66 as it was spreading:

"There's a haziness of purpose, an uneasiness
Of vision, it's a troubling of the spirit of
Our presence awesome armor notwithstanding,
There's a fatal flaw, ideas like--
Misguidedly--this notion that we have
Some special gift for bringing forth
A new and independent nation. It's not likely,
Though there is now some debate,
That we are stretched thin militarily--too far--
Since we could soldier on in some sense
Staying unscathed many decades.
But politically the recklessness...
Extravagant...appallingly abandoned...
This commitment...there's no analog to this
In any country we've defended in the past
That you can name, Korea, Greece,
To take examples, for the undertaking here
Implies a purpose unlike any we've professed
In other places since behind the shield
Our military poses we must educate
A people who are unschooled as to
Governing themselves--they've never done that--
It is our job to identify, to conjure up almost
A corps of democratic leaders where one never
Has existed, writing laws, combating poverty,
Creating institutions. We must inculcate
A sturdy sense of nationhood
In people who have never been a nation.
This experiment (delirious design) requires
Above all else a vast amount of time--

Which we don't have of course.
Our time is running out in Vietnam.
Our choices seem to be dissolving down to one.
A statesman versed in Southeast Asian ways
Expressed it simply: you are going to have
To leave South Vietnam--you won't be routed
Or humiliated quite, you are the power
In the region, your armada and your bombers
Make that certain--still you're going to have
To leave, your airborne cavalry is no match
For this country's very earth-bound set of problems.

136.

At the usual cocktail party of the great ones he approached me,
He spoke fiercely as he poked me in the chest:
"The American journalists all think thy can win
Pulitzer Prizes for reporting, but remember,
They will ask you someday just which side you're on,
And I can't think of how you fellows, you reporters, will reply."

137.

There is a genuine element of pathos—we must pray God
That it not turn into tragedy full-blown—
To have to watch this most extraordinary man
Inside the White House asked to struggle
With the war in Vietnam, which is distasteful to him,
All the while he's simply longing to return
To what he loves and what he's best at:
Making miracles at home.

138.

What would Eastland say if I was entertaining niggers
At the White House, those ambassadors from…..

It's those damned Kennedy ambassadors, they're
Scattered through the world, they're out to get me.

Here's Reston's column on Kennedy's speech.
You make sure that we don't say a goddamned thing
That he says Bobby said. I won't.

Initiatives toward arms control were cancelled
With the only reason being Bobby Kennedy
Had made some puny speech and mentioned topics.

You know I never let myself go free
Because I don't know where I'll stop.

Tell Bundy that the President
Would be extremely pleased if he resigned
Since he's disloyal. Or on second thought
Perhaps I ought to tell him so myself.
No, you go do it.

That's the trouble with my own staff,
They're all sleeping with the Kennedys.

Moyers just called me to talk about Johnson.
He told me he was feeling very worried,
Very weird whenever he would have to talk to him,
He almost felt he wasn't even talking
To a human being at all.

Did you get back to Bundy?
No I didn't, Mr. President.
He just grunted, kept on reading memoranda.

He won't act on his words but he believes them,
This erratic flow of unconnected thoughts,
But they're connected in his mind somehow.

I won't have any more to do with liberals,
They won't have a goddamned thing to do with me.
They're following the communistic line,
They're all the same, the U.N.'s tried
To make a fool of me, they're set against me.
I will not make any overtures to Russians.
They will have to come to me.
In Paris Gargarin wouldn't shake hands
With our astronauts. I sent those men myself
And so the insult was to me.
I can't trust anybody anymore.
I'll take a tougher line and I'll get rid of anyone
Who is against my policies, I'll put Abe Fortas
Or Clark Clifford in the Bundy job.
I'm not going to go in the liberal direction,
There's no future going that way
Since the liberals are simply out to get me,
Always have been.

He asked if we thought Wicker
Was conspiring to destroy us,
We said no, he writes some good things,
Then some bad things, but
We couldn't change his mind.
He changed the subject.
It was true he'd said that he'd make
Harland Cleland number two man at the UN

But because he'd leaked the UN speech to Reston,
Now he wouldn't name that man to run
The DC dog pound. Ed Clark's flaying
In the media had Kennedy behind it,
Little Bobby—Little Bobby had assassinated Ed.

You know, Dick, that the communists...

They'll know me as the President
Who gave up Southeast Asia,
As the President who lost it.
I'm the one who lost that governmental form.
You know the communists control
Our major networks and the forty major outlets
Of our news communications.
Walter Lippman is a communist
And so is Teddy White, you'd all be shocked
At what the FBI reports reveal about them.

I want to talk with you in confidence,
I don't want anyone—don't even
Tell your wife—to know we've talked,
But I was out there on the boat
With your boy Fulbright.
They are really getting to him.
And *The New York Times* is out to prove
That we went off the deep end.
You've got two or three young Jewish boys up there,
Our wire taps tell us, other sources,
That they're in on this with communists.
Colluding.
Herbert Matthews says
This hemisphere would be much better off
If every nation to the South of us
Put in the Castro system. They're agreed

And we have got them on the record,
They've been calling us imperialistic plunderers.

How would you feel with these secrets treaties
Threatening to blow up in your face in case
The US overstepped specific limits,
Then the Russians and the Chinese would be
Coming in to help North Vietnam.
I never know when I'll be sitting there
Approving certain targets one two three
If maybe one of those I've marked down
Might be triggering provisions of the treaties.
Every day I have to ask myself that question.

139.

Historians may some day see the Sixties as the decade
When the West—I mean post-Reformation West,
That massive civilizing force—had reached its end.
A nuclear disaster will not end it
But a new polarization of the world,
The restless poor nonwhites led on by China
As opposed to North American and Europe,
Which will find themselves besieged.
The West can still politically survive,
And as a culture, and our military power
Will continue overwhelming every nation,
Could at any time reduce the Asian land mass
And the African to ashes. This does not provide
Much comfort. Thus the West
Must somehow hold onto (or at the least
It must not willingly default on or surrender)
All its access to, communication with,

And its benignity of influence over Africa and Asia.
We have much of worth to offer, much to gain.
Our society and theirs can be enriched
And both be nourished by the two-way flow:
Ideas, goods, and people. China closes down
Its doors at least at present.
But every door that closes picks the pace up
Of the rich-poor, colored-white,
North-South division of the world.

140.

Three factors made our confidence o'erweening.
#1 was all our military might, no other
Country could surpass it. #2
Was technological supremacy,
No doubts about it worth the entertaining.
#3 was our benevolence, our altruism,
Affluence, we weren't in this
For territorial grabs, for grabs of land,
We had that innocence, that purity of motive,
This was like some kind of three-ply
Suit of armor we came wrapped in.
Thus above the sceptered sway (of baser nations)
We were offered opportunity,
And with a kind of obligation we could make
The poorer nations of the world modern,
We could usher in stability and peace,
We'd have a Pax Americana Technocratica,
How easy was it then, this bright new day.
Along the primrose path to reach this goal
There was a last and crucial test in Vietnam.
Once we'd succeeded there, the way ahead was clear.

141.

McClellan wouldn't let me in to see him,
I discussed this with the President, I told him
My frustration, he suggested that I try
A bit of off-the-record leaking, say that
Senator McClellan kept on holding up the bill
Because he wants the Army Corps of Engineers
To build a dam on land he owns
So that he'll get a lot of money
When the government is forced to buy
The land from him to build it.
I asked him if this story he proposed I leak
Was true. He simply leaned back,
Slyly smiling, in his chair and told another.
"The first time Mr. Kleberg ran for Congress,
He was back home thumping tubs
With this campaign speech, this attack
On his opponent. 'It's not easy,' Kleberg said,
'but I can understand these fine Hill Country folk
Consenting maybe when the man
Who represents them up in Washington, D.C.
Does too much drinking, I can see why
They might vote for him regardless.
It's not easy but I guess that I
Can even understand it when these fine
Hill Country folk might let themselves
Be represented by a man up there
In Washington, D.C. who goes carousin'
With the women of that city while his wife
Back here at home and his poor children
Have to toil and work his land,
But for the life of me as God above's my witness,
I will never understand it, why these good
Hill Country folk would let themselves

Be represented by a man who goes alone
Into the hills at night and takes as his companion
Female sheep.' When Mr. Kleberg
Had completed that strange speech, I raised
Some protest, 'Mr. Kleberg, that's not true.'
And can you guess what Mr. Kleberg said at that point?"
Johnson asked me leaning forward with that way
He had of peering in your eyes. I said I couldn't.
"Let the son of a bitch deny what I've just said then,"
Johnson said.

142.

He was a bully and an egoist, a sadist and a lout.
He had no sense of loyalty at all
Despite protesting it was loyalty he prized
Above all else and he enjoyed tormenting those
Who'd done the most for him. It was
The custom of his staff to make excuses
For his manners and his barnyard way of speaking,
Crude behavior, burping, farting through
Innumerable discussions, as the simple ways
Of someone who was earthy, of the earth,
A man still rooted in his native soil of Texas.
This was pure and simple nonsense.
He'd spent all his life, or most of it,
His adult life, in Washington D.C., not quite
Your hookworm and pellagra belt.
His lapses from acceptable behavior
Were deliberate, their purpose was
Subordinating others to his will.
A man in turmoil. A tormented man.
I'm not quite sure what the torment was about though.

"I'm like an animal, a wild one on a leash,"
He once admitted, "and you know
I keep that leash reined in real tight,
My instinct's always for the jugular
Of anyone I meet." It was perhaps
The kinds of goals he kept on setting
For himself, he knew no rest, he had
His mother watching, father watching,
FDR was watching, God was watching,
He was always being graded.
Horace Busby said that LBJ believed
He was expected to be versed in every issue
Of importance to the nation, this the standard
Any President was held to. Heavy burden!

143.

Of particular importance is the struggle Johnson had
Achieving any independence from his mother,
An ambitious, highly domineering woman
Who believed that she had married far beneath her.
She was totally determined that her boy
Would be successful, and she pushed him
To the nth degree. Such pushing puts the son
Into a conflict situation. On the one hand
There's a tendency to simply buckle under
To his mother's domination. On the other hand
Rebellion rears its head to reassert his independence,
"Be a man." So he was ver much concerned
Throughout his life about a kind of self-assertion,
He could not brook any outside interference.
His political career with his demands
To make his own decisions always, to control

A situation, seems deep-rooted
In this conflict with his mother.

144.

"Well, we killed some of them as they came storming over,"
Said the Green Beret the next day as they rebuilt Loc Ninh's
Mine field and repaired the foot trap breaches.
They felt shaken, they had never known the Viet Cong
To press with an attack for more than four hours
In a firestorm. Therefore Westy had responded.
He had lost a Special Forces camp in 1966 at A Shau
To the north, near Laos, lots of factors came together,
Like the weather, tough terrain—a foggy valley—
Rising panic of the native troops that turned that place's
Desperate defense into retreat, a real disaster,
And the loss of it still rankled. He would not allow
A repeat, he moved combat troops, artillery
To Loc Ninh, he brought mercenary troops
To reinforce the Green Beret camp.
B-52s and fighter bombers were diverted.
The Viet Cong the next night tried
To take the Special Forces camp again.
But down at one end of the air strip six artillery pieces
Kept on firing beehive rounds into the flank
Of the attacking force, each special-purpose shell
Contained 8000 wingèd steel darts called flechettes.
The shells hummed, sang insanely as they sped.
Here was a true whiff of the grape.
When the artillery men ran out of beehive rounds,
They lowered barrels of their guns and skipped
Their high explosive shells right off the runway,
Scythed the Viet Cong with shrapnel.

The sacrifice of forces by the Viet Cong was awesome.
They were feeding men like cordwood to a furnace
Into battle, it was thought they lost about 2000 troops
In weeks of fighting at Loc Ninh. What did it mean?
They launched division-sized attacks when six weeks earlier
The word was Cong incapable of military action
Much above battalion level. "One of the most
Important actions of the war" was Westy's verdict
On Loc Ninh, "I am delighted, and you only made
One very small mistake, you made it all look somewhat easy."
Brownfield added "Situation getting better,
I have doubts the Viet Cong can hang on longer."
Dok To next. An army sergeant from the North
Who had deserted told of plans for an attack
Against Dok To. Here Westy really poured it on.
"There are certain bells you ring and Westy
Comes out of his corner like a pug, one bell's A Shau.
Another bell's the Central Highlands."
Helicopters flocked in such great numbers to Dok To
They had to bring in special fuel to slake their thirst,
About 800,000 gallons, and by dynamiting tops off
Of a dozen local mountains engineers built level platforms
For artillery, our "chemists" bathed the slopes all round
With herbicides to strip them of their foliage—
Under pounding from artillery shells, attacks from
Fighter bombers and the stuff B-52s dropped
Jungle canopy split open, in the end it simply
Hung in blackened tatters. This the closest thing
To Big War Westy knew of. Still the battle
Wasn't nearly so one-sided as Loc Ninh had been
Despite our knowing enemy positions and intentions.
A rocket regiment fired missiles at our airfield,
Two big cargo planes got burned up on the runway
And a thousand tons of ammunition blew up
In a blast that rolled its shockwaves all the way

Across the valley. "Jesus, Charlie
Must have got himself some nukes," said one lieutenant.
And Charlie mousetrapped one battalion of the airborne
On the slopes of Hill Eight hundred seven five,
They were unable to advance or to retreat, cut off
From water and from early reinforcements,
Deeply shaken by an errant bomb that weighed 500 pounds
And landed squarely in the middle of their station.
They were caught and fought alone for 50 hours,
124 got killed, 347 wounded.
"The success of US arms was overwhelming,
We're superior in firepower and maneuver,
15 U.S. and Vietnamese battalions beat the enemy
And sent survivors limping back to scattered sanctuaries
Somewhere." But some journalist remarked in sage demurral
That the NVA was sucking US troops away
From population centers, that the US troops
Were bogged down by this fighting in the mountains,
That the Viet Cong were free to take control back
In the lowlands. Oh, but Westy knew these battles
Near the border weren't diversions but defeats,
He'd used both fists against the enemy but hadn't
Let his guard down in the lowlands, he'd depleted
His opponent. "We've begun to see the end come into view."
He said the reason that the Viet Cong and NVA
Had gone on with their fighting in this war
Was sheer delusion, they had banked on opposition from
The home front and defeat of one big U.S. army unit
To precipitate American surrender. They were wrong,
They'd lost their gamble. In October LBJ received a letter.
Men and women, 49 of them, who worked as volunteers
In Vietnam filed their objection to the US style of war,
The use of napalm and the herbicides, forced relocation
Of the rural populations—an atrocity of overwhelming
Magnitude. And Robert McNamara had resigned,

The war "too dangerous and costly to the nation."
"We just drop a $20,000 bomb each time we see
Four Viet Cong behind a bush or think we see them,"
Tip O'Neill said. "That's not working."
Twenty five hundred casualties on our side
Back in 1965, but 80,000 now in 1967.
The long face of the President spoke volumes.
He told Westy he was thinking of retiring.
Westy still maintained his inner resolution,
Showing confidence did not involve an act,
It really mirrored what he felt, but as commander
He was sure he had to demonstrate this feeling
For the men. He really wanted some great battle.
Dienbienphu in reverse.

145.

You never knew what signals he'd be sending
Or the signals contradicted one another.
The speech he gave at Howard University
Ranks up there with the most inspiring speeches
Of my life in its compassion for the Negroes
And the total comprehension of their plight
Which it displayed and yet the accent of the man
Who was delivering that speech, that long-drawn
Southern preacher's face with those big ears,
That sort of white high collar shirt,
That sort of luminescent suit he used to wear—
It didn't seem that such a man could be delivering
Those words, there was a dissonance at play
Although the problem may have risen more in me,
A lot of prejudicial thinking, condescension
Toward the South of which the President

Was all too well aware, it made him act out
In the presence of those Eastern types he thought of
As disparaging his Southernness the most,
He'd so offend to make offensiveness a skill
If such offense was what he thought they were
Expecting, it was self-defeating pride
And deep resentment that would drive him
In the presence of the Ivy League type minions,
Native crudity came bubbling to the surface,
Strange delight to be disgusting in their sight.

146.

Sometime in the middle of the night
He came and crawled in bed with me.
This morning, worn and haggard,
He just looked at me and mentioned
What an awful thing had happened,
Five of Bosch's friends had been returning
And the key one...there was fighting
In the street and he got killed.
Lyndon said he'd only slept two hours
Monday night and almost hadn't slept
At all last night. If there were some way
I could reach him, ease his mind...

147.

—What's the story on that colonel getting killed?
—We have an FBI report that says
It was Americans who shot him.
Accidentally. They shot him in the back.

—And what about our planes?
Are any back in Vietnam?
—No planes are back yet, sir. No word's come in.
—I sure am anxious on those ones
That we've sent flying close to Hánoi.
You be sure to let me know if we lose any.
At whatever time of night the word comes in,
It doesn't matter.

148.

Then the balance of our payments was another problem
Lyndon Johnson faced as things turned bad for him in 1965.
We had been sitting pretty once—late 1940s—
Like a poker player feeling no great need
To reach down deep into his own roll and indeed
Without much focus on the game somehow
The other players' chips had all accrued to us,
Were sitting in a big stack on the table
Right before us, it had seemed to work like magic,
Half the monetary gold of all the world was in Fort Knox
Or in New York at the Reserve Bank,
And at Bretton Woods they'd formalized
Predominance of dollars, they had made them
Fundamental to the monetary system.
In the IMF the US quota set at 41, which was
An underestimation of the real strength of the dollar.
One quarter of the imports of the other nations worldwide
Came from us—those other nations
Would have bought more US goods
If they'd been able to afford them.
From 1950 on the US started showing overall
A deficit, a small one, in the balance of its payments,

It arose from our "imperial" decision, we advanced
From '45 to '64 a sum of 27 billion dollars, loans and grants
To Western Europe, reconstruction and development.
We spent 21 billion more on foreign military aid,
Including NATO, and on maintenance supply
Of troops in Europe we spent 21 billion more
Plus some spare change. In twenty years
The total spending bent the mind, we'd put out
67 billion meant for military aid and on
Expenditures for military might and then
For economic aid we added 77 billion to the grand sum,
144 billion sent abroad. Defending interests.
US deficits amounted to a quarter of the sum we'd sent abroad:
35 billion dollars not covered by exports.
The deficits we ran up were regarded as a sign
Of our benevolence and strength, we were
The bankers of the world, outflow of dollars
From American reserves made liquid capital
Available to meet the desperate need
For reconstruction and development.
The "dollar gap," a problem for the world,
Was something we were bent on closing.
But we closed it too successfully perhaps.
In twenty years our gold reserves had melted
To a third of what they'd been, the German government
Alone amassed more dollars than what Fort Knox
Held in gold, and liabilities which foreigners
Were holding far exceeded our reserves.
The cause of US deficits was changing over time
So that the dollar couldn't really stand the strain
Of escalation of the war in Vietnam.
The gold reserves declined by almost 9 billion dollars
In the last three years of Ike's administration.
The Kennedy administration set in motion
Measures to correct unbalanced payments

When it came in. Our government spending overseas
Would be curtailed, US commercial exports
Heartily encouraged and by 1964
The measures worked because our trade accounts
Improved by more than 5 billion dollars.
Yet the deficit remained there overall
At more than 3 billion dollars. Two new trends
Had made an ominous appearance.
First the tendency of US corporations
To export capital as they established operations
Where the labor costs were lower overseas.
The capital required for these new set-ups all flowed out
Through the exchanges so instead of US exports
You had capital that moved in this direction,
Flowing outwards through exchanges,
Thus replacing US exports. In the second place
The "Eurodollar" market was increasing,
An enormous sum was mostly held in dollars
As a pool which could be drawn on out of
European banks which were affiliates new-formed
Of US banks in many instances, the higher interest rates
These European banks could offer were attractive
To our U.S. corporations, they liked leaving
Larger balances to grow within this Eurodollar pool,
And then the rates of growth in Europe were increasing
As enticement for investment of the money.
Thus the capital outflow item in our
Payments balance grew, it got cut back,
Constraints came, voluntary first, then tougher, tighter.
These new measures "worked," they dealt with one
Specific sort of problem. Still the deficit remained there
Overall, would not respond, gross foreign exchange costs
Of the military based in other lands almost accounted
By themselves for our whole payment balance deficit.
And imports kept increasing, foreign manufacturers beat us

At our own game, we began to lose our edge, the world
Caught up with us and we were caught flat-footed,
Productivity declined as did investment,
U.S. shares of world trade too.
Imports of oil were expanding, we were far less self-sufficient.

To pay any price in our defense of so-called freedom
As John F. Kennedy had promised we would do?
We hadn't thought we'd ever have to, that we would ever
Feel the pinch, that soaring rhetoric was hollow,
And when we did begin to feel it…

149.

I can't sell this proposal to Russell or Dirksen
Or to Ford or to the George Mahons
For one damned dollar bill, I simply cannot.
I'll be getting all this pressure if the government
We put in is the least bit sympathetic
To the Communists or soft or even kind.
And even so I won't be getting
Arthur Schlesinger's support or any liberal's
If the plan's to let the Communists remain
In some back room and then go underground
On Sunday for the church meeting,
Then come back out on the weekdays,
Run the show, we can't have that,
It's got to be both anti-Communist and liberal.
To have them start to think we lost prestige
And that we went in there to get us up
Some satellite would be a big mistake,
A tragic error. God Almighty knows
I don't just want my brand put on

This satellite, I do not know a one of them,
I never heard of one of them, I'm doubtful
Of them all and I do not intend to put
The LBJ brand onto every goddamned country
In this Hemisphere. Already
They're demanding that we hold investigations,
ADA is, Arthur Schlesinger and his bunch
Have been calling for a full investigation
As of yesterday. They'll get one.
Bosch's bunch has damned near made a mess
In Europe, with the liberals abroad
And all the articles from here say
What we're doing's unilateral, they're taking
The position that this man Johnson
Is another Führer. I don't want a new
Dominican Republic with the LBJ brand
Stamped on it. But Bobby Kennedy will act
As if I do and so will Schlesinger.
And while I'm taking them on on the left,
The right will rear up like the Russells
And the Riverses that run the big committees,
I know just what they'll be sayin',
That I ran in with Marines and that I marched them
Up the hill and then I marched them
Right back down and all for what?
And as you know I don't go all the way with Bundy,
And it wasn't my idea that he go there.
You remember every time you called
He'd grab the phone away from me,
You always started off by saying "Bundy"
And we wound up getting Bundy.
If we get him back I'd say and haven't wrecked him,
And if I'm not wrecked,
Then I'll be sure to say a good prayer to the Lord
Because I think that Bundy's brilliant,

I'm attached to him, he's almost indispensable,
But he's precise and pretty positive, inflexible I guess.
And he gets pretty nervous too,
I tried to talk to him right after Bay of Pigs,
But then the President requested I not do so,
Stay away from him he said,
Don't mention anything to him,
He's just so *nervous*. Now I know
We'll have to live with him a long time,
I'm prepared to, I have nothing in the world
I want to do except the right as I believe it.
I don't always know what's right,
Sometimes I have to lean on other people's judgments,
I get mis-led. Like this sending in our troops
To the Dominican Republic. But the man
I got mis-led by in this instance
Was myself, was Lyndon Johnson. No one else.
I was the fellow who decided, I can't blame
Another goddamned human being.
And I also don't want any of them
Taking any credit, I will ride this crisis out
And I'm aware of how it looks,
It looks the opposite of how I want it lookin',
It is not my wish to be an intervener,
I think Castro intervened there pretty good
When he kicked Reid out, Reid was not
Your dictatorial type of person,
He was genuine and honest when you think
About the rest of them I met there.
His agenda was to clean up all those
Goddamned crooked generals and set him up
A government that worked and would sustain itself.
Those crackpots overthrew him in the midst
Of this attempt and I would say the same
Is happening to me, I think they're making me

The Reid of North America,
I try to get my system up and moving,
To support this thing with jobs and the economy,
And that's when all these experts in
The London Times, the Kurzmans and the Szulcs
And Arthur Schlesinger start giving me the works,
So you may see me in the same place soon as Reid.
"Move over next week, Reid"
Is what you'll start to hear me holler…

150.

The members of the Far East Asian Bureau were committed
To a single party line in '61: the close containment
Of the Chinese, mainland China; the harassment
Of those nations that were seeking neutral status,
Un-aligned with either Washington or Peking;
The establishment and maintenance of a network
Of alliances, of client states "on our side,"
Anti-communist, "chain-linked" on the periphery
Of China. The McCarthy scare had exorcised
All subtlety from their consideration of the problems.
McCarthy era memories continued very sharp
And then the margin of the Democratic victory
Had been exceeding thin in 1960, it was perilous
To "think fresh" or to move too fast on Asia.
And the new Administration seemed to swallow down
Without a whole lot of reflection a perception of
"Great China on the march," a sense of vastness,
Almost unimagined numbers, much belligerence,
And even a revived sense of the Golden Horde perhaps.
China's having intervened in the Korean War
Helped fuel this apprehension of their

Overbearing might despite the fact that
Their involvement in the war had been an offshoot
Of appallingly inept communications and of gross
Miscalculations both on our part and on theirs.
And the new Administration seemed at first
To have accepted some idea of the Communists
As bloc-like, monolithic, thus the Sino-Soviet split
As something real and maybe final didn't seem
To dent their heads till circa 1962, they never
Gave much thought at all to how much two
Competing outlooks might corrode Communism.
The theory that the dominoes might fall
In swift succession if the first one fell bespoke
A kind of ignorance of Asia almost too deep
To conceive of, of the differences of nations
And societies in Asia. It may also have resulted
From a sense that since "all Asians look alike,"
All Asian nations would react alike to pressures.
Such a theory in its condescending outlook
Was an insult yet it long continued reigning.

151.

China's just like Germany in 1917,
Or it's like the 1930s, you had
Germany again and in the East you had Japan,
Or it's like 1947 when the USSR loomed,
A threat to Europe—China undercuts
Our impact and effectiveness right now
And in the long term they might organize
The Asian world against us—all of Asia.
We cannot achieve our ends
Nor can we play the role of leadership

We need to if some virulent
And overwhelming nation is allowed
To group its segment of the world
Along the lines of some philosophy
Inimical to ours.

152.

If the threat of Chinese coming in disturbs you,
Just relax—the escalation of the air war
In the North and added pressure put on Ho
Will not be rape but just seduction.
If the Chinese should react to escalation
Like a woman, say, who slaps you in the face
When you seduce her, then we'd still have time
To ease off in the bombing, diplomatically retreat.
If we suddenly assault the North all out,
That is we rape her, there could be no turning back,
Chinese reaction might be total.
I'm pursuing this one carefully, believe me.
I'm proceeding inch by inch along her leg
And I'll be getting to the snatch
Before she even knows what hit her.

153.

This shabby business mocks all our professions
In the case of Indochina. It might represent
Improvement over earlier colonial regimes,
That brutal stuff, but it's preposterous
To settle for the price of some cheap substitute
At this late date: to think that Viet Nam

Can be fubbed off by so much less
Than what the Dutch gave Indochina.
For Americans to stand behind the French
In their attempt will cost our standing
And prestige in Southeast Asia. Sure,
A lot of that prestige went down the drain
With Chang Kai-shek, the rest will go down
With the Bao Dai regime if we support it.
It is not too much to speak of our relationship
To this regime as shameful. I just heard
That Ev Case argued it's too late
For getting out, we must continue
Our support for Bao Dai now.
I'd contest that. I would say there's no
Such thing as being too late if a policy's
Mistaken and we think we ought to change it.
Why now tie ourselves to France's battered kite?

154.

What price shall we pay for the glory of marching
Through defoliated countrysides and streets
Of burning ruins in our triumph, strutting
Monarchs of the scene that we survey?
We'll have achieved nothing
But destruction of a culture not our own.
And then we'll face the long, hard task
Of doing penance at enormous cost for havoc
We've created in the name
Of some vague notion of the honor of our nation
And to fight the holy war against
The "atheistic Commies."
We'll be ridden by this hag for many years.

155.

I cannot go to the President and tell him that
In contrast to reports that I and other chiefs have made
As to the progress of the war in which we've
Laid stress on the thesis that the seizing of
Initiative is crucial, we have reached a situation
When we're not sure where initiative now lies,
That there are many more attacks on us
Than previously stated--a discrepancy.
At least we must explain it. If the news of this
Got out, though, to the public,
It would surely blow the lid off.

156.

The jungle thinned out slightly and we reached some huts--
The hamlet. They were all completely empty.
Household animals, even barnyard fowl, all gone.
Behind the huts a hole containing filthy water festered.
Mud sides. Mud slides. And surrounding this
Like wheel spokes there were thirty bloated corpses
In their governmental uniforms--the Army.
The decomposition process had been hastened by
The hot sun. The intestines forced their way out
Of the gaping belly wounds, they seemed alive
As they extruded, yellow piles atop each body.
The tracks showed that the bodies
All got towed there by their buffaloes with ropes.

157.

A burly red-faced captain with his paratrooper cohort.
"Ask these people where the fucking Viet Cong went,"
Burly bellows. His interpreter was shaking, but he asked
As he was told to. Some old man, the village elder,
Starts to gabble. "Shut up, loudmouth," Burly says
And makes him sit down. Speaking English. Reconsiders.
"Take him down the road a hundred yards or so,
Since if they think we're going to blow his fucking
Head off, then they'll talk." They did not talk,
Although the women and the children sobbed and wailed.
The captain's cohort was embarrassed.
The paratroopers started loading peasants on a truck
To drive them off for further questioning.
The soldiers were as gentle as they could be
In the present situation, making up
For how their captain had performed, but still
The villagers kept wailing, being packed off to
Imprisonment or exile, execution they supposed.
A lieutenant felt compunction, even doubt about
Such tactics, then dismissed his hesitations.
"If they're not the Viet Cong, what are they doing
Way out here? Why aren't they living in some city?"

158.

We sure do have a lot to thank
Those backroom boys at Dow for.
That first stuff they made for us was not so hot—
It didn't work—if they were quick enough,
The gooks could scrape it off.
Dow started adding polystyrene.

Now the stuff sticks just like shit sticks
To a blanket, 'cept the gooks
If they jumped under water quick
Could stop the burning. So they added
Willie Peter so's to make it burn
Much better. It'll even keep on burning
Under water, just one drop of it's enough
So that it burns down to the bone,
The gooks will die no matter what
Because the phosphorous is poison.

159.

By 1967 social scientists were flooding Vietnam,
They made reports to U.S. colonels:
"Send out German shepherd dogs on night patrols
Instead of soldiers." "Build a moat around Saigon
To shore defenses." "Great success of the elections
And the drive against corruption." "Build a bridge
Between the legislature newly coming in now
And elected village councils to eliminate
The military bureaucrats' autonomy"—
As if the generals would tolerate such power
Being handed to a group of unarmed legislators,
Creatures of the latest US whim.
In the third year of a war that made Vietnamese
Civilians mere survivors hanging on,
Young men from RAND and Simulmatics,
Solely sovereign in their sway and imperturbable
In masterdom would float around the countryside
In Land Rovers doing esoteric research
On a topic such as how much recent land reform
Would increase the motivation of the peasants.

"Of course," they'd say with great panache,
And with a hint perhaps of swagger as they emptied
Clips from Swedish K machine guns,
"If the GVN just brought to bear the PF's
Full potential at the village level, hierarchies
Set up by the NFL would melt away in no time."
Whereat long time Viet staffers rolled their eyes.

160.

I just don't know how anyone can stop
What they've been doin' with that Freedom Party problem,
I know I've tried but I couldn't,
I think Bobby may have been the one
To start it. I could not get
Any sleep last night, I waked
At half past two, I tried to figure
What I'd do if I was running for the V.P.
And the boss man said no you cannot be it,
You cause me trouble in the South.
What I would do I think is try
To make the South be worthless for us both.
That's what he's doing. Rauh and Martin Luther King
And folks that run with that crowd normally
Are leading them. Old Hubert's tried to stop 'em
But he hasn't had much luck,
It will be difficult for you or any other
Politician from the South who's got
Substantial Negro numbers just to sit by,
Let their sister states be thrown out
When their delegates were chosen by the rules
But at the same time how can Dick Hughes,
Lawrence, Daley, go back home and tell their people

They approved of seating groups from Alabama,
Mississippi, who would not say they'd support
The nominee. You've split the party
Even worse than the Republicans are split,
They've got those Rockefeller factions goin' off.
We've got such forces in our party
That would do that, I don't doubt it.
Now they claim they got a Texas millionaire,
Some Texas oil man poking into things in Harlem.
I'm not sure who such a Texas man could be
Unless old Hunt got him some money.
Hoover's after it and they know all the Communists
Involved in this but I think both sides
Are involved in all these riots—hell,
Those rioters have got them walkie talkies,
That takes finance. One night Brooklyn,
One night Harlem, it'll be some other part
Of New York City in a minute.
He went out to Illinois last night,
I got some kind of memo, a reliable observer
Someone really in the know reports
Mayor Daley favors RFK for number 2 man
On the ticket but he might not press that matter
In an open opposition to the Presidential wishes.
I've concluded just as sure as you and I
Are here now talkin' on this phone that Bobby's
Going to force a roll call on his name in nomination
For the first place or the other,
They're going to force some big emotion with this film
And with Miz Kennedy. He's gonna make a pitch,
My main advisors here are saying
That I ought to call him in a month ahead of time
And spell the whole thing out, tell him exactly how I feel,
And if these people don't want me, why that's all right,
Let them take him because if I don't get the party's

Nomination I'm sure he will and I think that I'll give
Daley till tomorrow, he had said that he'd call back
By Thursday morning or by Friday.
If I haven't heard from him, I'll have to call
This fellow in, he'll want to argue, I have heard say
He's opposed to our man Hubert,
He told Clifford he'd consider him an insult
Since he ran against his brother.
Most of them are sure that what he really wants
Is this job, he'll do anything to get it.
If he has to cause a fight at our convention.
That may mean that I'll be throwing the election.
He would even like to see me get defeated.
When this fellow looks at me, it's like he means
To look a hole right through my chest and out the back end,
It's as if I were a spy. If we just go down there
And fight, somehow the aura of the office,
Its prestige will pull me through,
And it'll be like Daley says, I've got to wait
Till I get up there. On the other hand there's Clifford
And some others, they keep saying
If I think to do it that way I'll be too late,
They think Bobby's group would be in charge
By then, he says I've got to tell him now.
If I can't stop him…
He believes that he would probably resign
And then we'll simply have to see which one can win,
I have the office but I don't have much to fight with.
But I didn't even sleep two hours last night.
It may be I can get out this way easy.
Save some face by just resigning, getting beat.
I got Goldwater in here tomorrow for a meetin'.
Not one damned thing good can come from meeting him.
He wants to use it as a forum
To promote some kind of backlash,

Stirring backlash up is where his future is,
Since peace and harmony would hurt him.
I do not see any any answer to this damned
Convention thing though, to this seating.
If they have a hundred thousand nigras up there
And they picket Mississippi being seated,
If the convention kicks the Mississippi delegation out,
Then this whole country's going to think the niggers
Wanted them kicked out and got their way.
That won't do much for my standing in the Deep South.
If I could push a button for the nominee,
I'd go for McNamara, he's by the far the biggest help
To me of any damned body you can think of.
There's not one of them that's got
A delegation would approve though.
If we haven't got a man from our own party
I can't do that. So old McNamara's out.
If I decide to go in on the Catholic thing…
You don't have anybody being strongly for McCarthy.
Clifford still thinks we may be compelled to take him
So the Catholics can't say their man got cut down
Because the Protestants took over,
And that the men who worked for Kennedy's defeat
While he was living have defeated him in death.
I'm talkin' LBJ and Humphrey.
You can see how I'm fenced in here.
All the labor people, nigra people,
Folks that do the work and have the votes
And put up money wouldn't leave if I took Humphrey.
Now I need a good debater, someone looks good on TV,
Can take 'em on because I'm tied down in this job,
I wouldn't say it but I wish I knew some decent way
To let 'em fight it out, whoever thinks he wants this job
Can damned well have it, I've got more problems
Than a man like me can handle. Khrushchev, Castro,

Say they're gonna shoot your planes down.
I've got old enough and flabby, I cannot surmount
The obstacles, and I don't have all the help
And the advice and all the counselors
And the loved ones gathered round me,
Every man in my whole Cabinet's
A hand-me-down from Kennedy you know,
I had no way that I could change 'em and supposing
That I could, where would I get the personnel?
San Marcos Teachers College isn't listed on the resumé
Of these folks, it's just agony, believe me,
And I shudder thinking what if you had
That guy, the Republican in office?
He's had two nervous breakdowns, he's not stable.
How to handle it's beyond me.
If I win it seems I lose because I want the South for me.
If I can't even take the South, what do I offer
That the Democrats would want?
I have no standing in Chicago.
Now my judgment is we're going to lose the South,
I just don't think that it can take this nigra stuff.
And the Republicans are gonna pour it on.
I think I'll have that conversation though with Bobby.
We'll just have to make a deep pitch to
The governors and leaders, will they stand firm
With their President? I think I have to say
That if they won't…let's put it this way…
I can't have some man in bed that's gonna murder me,
I can't be President on those terms.
That's exactly what he wants because if he has
Such support for number two man on the ticket
And with me out, he would have it
More than anybody else has.

I don't think my self respect
Could suffer this kind of defeat
Among the delegates, then turn around
And take their nomination to the top spot.
So I simply have to say it, I can't play
The crying baby any longer.
If this fight against the South gets up..
The Northerners aint for me on the grounds
That I'm a Southerner, I have no real rapport
With people up there, all I've got
Is my possession of the office at the moment.
But the South will not be for me either no how.
I think Ribicoff won't do as number two man.
It will have to be Humphrey, McCarthy, or Bobby.
I would not take Bobby.
I think Humphrey causes trouble in the South,
He's not much better there than Bobby.
But McCarthy gets you smear too
Since he votes with oil and gas,
And he would get unshirted hell from old Drew Pearson,
All that crowd, they have as much as told me that,
He's kind of thought of as a renegade, he's a liberal.
Too flighty...

161.

—Does Bobby feel that he's entitled to it?
Does he feel he wants to fight for it or what?
—It's not the latter.

162.

I had a real nice meetin' with your boy just now,
He says to me you're lookin' mighty fine,
I tell him never felt so good in all my life,
You know these people will not let me have a drink,
They got policemen posted everywhere,
Around at every gate so you can't slip out
For a date with pretty gals, you can't play poker.
Only one thing's left to do at night, you read
These damned reports, the FBI's and those
Intelligence reports that they pile on you.
There's no reason in the world I can't look good.
He said I wanted you to know I won't get
Personal as this campaign heats up.
As for conservatives, you know I can't
Control 'em, there are lots of them around.
But I will do the best I can to keep down riots.
It would hurt me to the quick if someone died
Because of something I had said.
I thought the more I talked the greater danger
I'd be in and so I said here's what I'm thinking
I might say about our meetin' once you've left.
I had this little one page statement all typed up.
He said that statement's fine by me,
But I am going out the back way.
So I walked out that way with him.
"What's the name of that new plane
You just announced, I'd like to ride in it," he said.
I replied I did not like to hear
That he was flying planes still
Over San Francisco Bay, it wasn't safe.
He said, "Oh no, you won't get me to give up flyin'."

163.

The commitment we supposedly have made
To let the South Vietnamese become
The masters of their future is absolved
If they refuse to help themselves.
We might hope for certain outcomes,
But it's not in our commitment
To expel the regroupees (who may be
South Vietnamese) though we dislike them.
It is not in our commitment to ensure
That certain people, certain groups
Retain control or that their power
Is pervasive to the far ends of the land
(though there are types that we prefer,
For whom we're rooting).
To guarantee non-Communist results
To their elections is (whatever we may
Hope for or expect) beyond the scope
Of our commitment. To insist
The South stay separate from the North
Is (once again) beyond our call
Or what we think we may have promised.
We are not obliged to pour our effort in
Out of proportion to the effort
Which they're making in the South
Or in the face of coups, corruption,
Increased apathy or other indications
Of a failure in Saigon to make
Some valid contribution,
To cooperate effectively.
The United States already
Has fulfilled its main commitments.

Has achieved what could be called
A real success once the elections
In September have been held.

164.

It surely is a fact that in
The early part of 1965 South Vietnam
Thought it was headed for defeat,
That was the sense, whereas today
There is the sense that with a lot of US help
The country's headed in the opposite direction,
That the country has a present chance
To learn to run itself and that
The North Vietnamese will be expelled
However far off in the future that may be.
We must maintain and strongly fortify
This underlying confidence, this sense
That it is worth our while
To run this country properly and well.
There are of course observers who report—
And the performance of the South Vietnamese
May well confirm—that massive US intervention
Is achieving bad effects, has made
The South think Uncle Sam
Will do their job for them forever.
When we say the South must "do the job themselves"
We have in mind specific functions while
The war is going on, but we're referring to
A country of the future at the same time
That can stand on its own feet whenever
North Vietnam calls the whole war off,
Concedes defeat. It is at that point,

If our victory unravels, that the effort
Which we've made would look ridiculous,
We'd undermine the gains in southeast Asia
Which we've made, destroy the confidence
And compromise American resolve
To shoulder burdens in the future
Here in Asia and in fact throughout the world.
In Asian eyes the struggle is a test case,
It is far more black and white
Than even we ourselves imagine,
For the Asians there's no beating of their breasts
Like what you see back in the US or in Europe.
All the Asians would quite simply be appalled
If we withdrew from Vietnam
Or if the peace for which we settled
Were delusive, let the North take over
Quickly, did not give the South a chance
To run its own show in the aftermath.
The question is to what extent we tolerate
The present imperfections while the war
Keeps grinding on. Are we to walk away
And leave South Vietnam because it failed
In what we knew from the beginning
Was a task exceeding almost any other nation's
Lasting reservoirs of courage: while guerrilla war
Was raging to become a true democracy?
We can all see how they've failed to use
The opportunity we've offered them.
That failure wouldn't mitigate the impact
Of our giving up the fight in Asian eyes though.
I would say we have to stiffen our resolve
And stay the course.

165.

When O'Daniel ran the first time, that was 1938,
And I went out once in the yard—
We had this old, this ancient black man
Who would come and keep our lawn for us,
And he would not keep anybody else's lawn,
You couldn't hire him, he had put my father
Up there on a pedestal, he'd come out
In his own car every week to keep our lawn
Because he knew that Brother Busby
Often had to be away from his own home.
This man was known as Nigger Will,
He called himself that. When he came
And knocked each week, he would
Announce himself, he'd say "it's Nigger Will."
And it was dangerous, provocative in those days,
Quite a bad thing to address a black
Or let one hear you speak of him as being black—
Real fightin' words—and that was true
Up to the era of the Sixties, there was some speech
Johnson made, I don't remember now
Which one, he used the term "blacks" for the first time,
It was nigh unto a wrestling match
Since brought up as I was you could refer
To blacks as colored people only.
I'd have had my mouth washed out with soap for sure
If I had called somebody black.
But this one time that I'm remembering
I went out in the yard, I was excited,
All I talked about was politics to anyone
At this point, Nigger Will…well, I considered him
A friend, one of my best friends—
"Are you really for O'Daniel?" was a question
That was always on my mind when I

Would talk to folks, small wonder that it came out
In my talk with Nigger Will, and he was handlin' me
All right, but I could tell he wasn't feelin' very easy.
But my sister called me from the door almost at once,
"Now Horace Jr., come inside." So I came in
And I got taken to the kitchen, both my sister
And my mother now rebuked me,
"Don't go askin' Nigger Will about how
He intends to vote since they don't vote."
I did not understand who they were.

166.

Now I hate to bring this up
Since it casts Alvin in a bad light
But it shows the kind of thinking at the time.
I remember Alvin, Lyndon and the rest of them
All sitting down at our house,
I got talking on the right to vote, my big cause.
Alvin said, "Now if you do push that stuff through,
You'd have the colored people voting,
That would really mess things up."
"Well, why shouldn't colored people get to vote?"
I asked him back and I remember now
Exactly what he said. He said
"Now look, I sure like mules,
But you don't bring them in the parlor."
This was the thinking of the people
In the South then, they put Negroes
On a level with the mules. They weren't
Unkind to them, unkind I mean
To Negroes. But equality!
I think that what made Lyndon so amazing

Was he overcame that attitude
The same way Cliff and I did.
We were all raised Southern racists,
Segregationists.

167.

He explained to me some ugly racial epithets
He'd spotted scrawled on signs as we'd been
Riding in the motorcade that afternoon in Memphis:
"I can tell you what's behind it: just convince
The lowest white man that he's better than the best
Of any colored, he won't notice that you're
Cleaning out his pockets. Hell, just give him
Someone lower down than he is, just convince him,
And he'll empty out his pockets' contents for you."

168.

Before I went to Saigon I had heard and read that napalm
Melts the flesh. I thought: that's nonsense.
I can put a roast into the oven
And the meat remains there though the fat melts.
But I found out when I went that it was true,
I saw these children burned by napalm
Melted down, that is the chemical reaction
Of the napalm melts the flesh, the flesh
Runs down along their faces to their chests
And sits and grows there.
No longer can these children turn their heads
Because they've grown so thick with flesh.
And when the gangrene sets in,

They can cut their hands or fingers or their feet off
But the only thing they can't cut off's their head.

169.

At the weekly luncheon meeting of the people
Who are planning your campaign
It seemed we startled Marvin Watson
With the force of our opinions in regard
To Vietnam—the unanimity—
I don't think he was ready.
I am writing now to follow up on that
And with the frankness that has always held
Between us. At the same time
I've expressed my views to Clark
Although I recognize that politics at home
Are only one of many factors
That the President and he have got to
"crank into computers of decision."
Still this factor of the politics at home
Must be considered, it can certainly
Affect your power to act.
I recognize that Marvin might dissent
About the views I'm writing down here
Since he said that of 400 politicians he's
Consulted since Bob said that he was running
All but one said he was still for LBJ.
But the rest of us, your whole
Campaign committee, are disturbed.
We make suggestions. That the President
Must take dramatic action sometime soon,
Before Wisconsin. We don't have in mind
Some gimmick. This is point one

We've been hearing from the politicians
Talking to the people in the streets.
The image of the President who'd walk
As many miles as he was asked to
In his desperate search for peace
Has gotten lost. He's now
The candidate of war. It's all the others
Who are candidates for peace. So that
The President has got to change his tactics
On the hard line. I've been shocked
By all the phone calls I've received
About the speech in Minneapolis you made.
Our people on the front line in Wisconsin
Say that speech has hurt us badly.
Many "doves" have called to say
They'd been "respectful opposition"
Up until that speech was made
But in the speech you called them traitors.
Now they're bitter and resentful,
They are saying that the President
Should face facts, that the country
Is divided, that it's not non-patriotic
To express their opposition.
Even people who support you on the war
Have called me up to say that speech
Has done a lot to "hurt our side."
The message of that speech was "win the war."
I think the ads Bob Burchardt's running
In Wisconsin state your point of view much better
And the fact is "win the war"
Has few adherents any longer.
Almost everyone wants out,
The only question now is how
We might achieve that. Burchardt's
News spots ask that people help the President

Win peace for us with honor. Peace
With honor shapes debate for us much better,
That is from having only those two stated
Candidates for peace against the President
Who's advocating war we now will have
Another candidate for peace possessed of
Knowhow, more responsible, the President,
Against a pair of fuzzy-minded do-goods
Who don't care much for the war
But don't quite know what they
Should do about it either.
The Tet offensive gave a massive shock,
We have to face that. Most (including
You I'd wager) thought our troops
Were doing well, that they were making
Steady progress in the field though maybe not
On civil matters, but the number of the people
In the middle on the war (including you again
I'd guess) has dropped alarmingly since then.
There are perhaps a few more hawks
But more significant than that is that
The dove camp's grown enormously.
The polls may say the hawks outnumber doves,
But I insist as do the men I've asked
Who've asked around the country
That the hawks are down to one or two
At random in a sampling, diehard holdouts,
True believers. Everyone's become a dove now.
You must face such dismal facts.
It is incredible to me that though you won
Both Minnesota and New Hampshire,
People speak of these results as big defeats.
It makes no sense.
What will the verdict be if we should lose
Wisconsin which we might?

170.

War of attrition—such a bland term
But its meaning for the people
And the country hadn't registered quite yet
At least for me. The Viet Cong
And NVA would move back in,
They'd just re-occupy those hamlets
We'd cleared out. What then would we do
In response? I put that question to the General.
"We go back in and we kill
More sons of bitches," he replied.

171.

I think you have to take into account first
How Americans have saturated life there
Since at 1500 feet in any Huey on a given afternoon
You might look out and there are eagles, flights
Of choppers going in to chase VC, air strikes
In progress, our artillery is "prepping" other regions;
A division camp in one place, a battalion
Forward area someplace else, our trucks in motion.
Flying north above the highway in Danang
You understand why it's "secure" since every five miles
We've stripped off great swathes of land
Now ringed with 105s and covered by our tents.
And yet it's really not secure, you can't go down
That country road that looks so peaceful
Not to mention spend the night there.
When we take off from a paddy, we have guns trained
On the peasants who are standing there impassive
On a dike to watch us leave, the whole thing

Really seems quite crazy if you step back to consider.
This first struck me when I saw a wounded soldier,
One of ours, a 23 year old I'd say, hit in the stomach,
Two big packs soaked red were balanced on
His stomach, he was pale, his eyes were open,
He was scared but holding on, a wave of grief
Just overwhelmed me, what if all we'd tried
To do out there, what if this suffering and waste
Which we'd engendered wasn't worth it,
To have built a line of defense in a bog?
I couldn't stand to even think about that question.

172.

…You would have called it total bankruptcy,
An urgent need to liquidate was sensed.
Hanoi ignored the red ink, though, and went on with
The fighting. it was stiffening of national resolve
Which U.S. bombing brought about.
They were not bowed or beaten down,
They were prepared to fight
Indefinitely on, and even Westy had admitted
That the movement of the Northern reinforcements
Toward the South had gotten greater during bombing.
It was absolutely senseless, paradoxic.
They agreed with what the Peking Marxists thought,
That if the U.S. got bogged down around the world,
Its engines grinding to no end, we would be bled.
With us tied down they thought that China
Would prevail, this was a tactic for the long term
Which the U.S. in the midst of all its flailing
In the mud of Southeast Asia was unable to
Consider—Baby Dumb Dumb—we were

Being made great fools of in successive
Small engagements which the Communists
Of Asia would be choosing. But Hanoi
Could have been thought of as atop
A sort of tiger in its dealings with Peking.
If Hanoi showed the slightest willingness
To talk with us, to moot peace,
Peking probably would forcibly react,
Close its frontier, cut off supplies
And interfere by introducing "volunteers"
To shift the balance back toward war.
They weren't above replacing Ho
If they decided he was siding
With the Soviets, they weren't above
Subverting his regime. And if
Negotiations failed, how could they pick up
With the fighting where they'd left off
Sans supplies and with a government
Subverted from within. And if they talked
With us, untuned the will to fight
Among their people, let the people think
That peace might be in prospect,
They could never get that fighting spirit back—
Untune that string and slackness followed.
Hanoi would have to see some sort of
Light at tunnel's end, some light for sure
Before they ever stepped inside that
Risky passageway of peace talks.

173.

He took me to the family plot
To show me where it was, it was

A carefully taken care of little
Tree-protected graveyard by the river
Which contained his father's headstone
And a few other relatives of his
Were also buried there
And "I'll be buried here," he said
And then the next thing that I knew
He pulls his fly down and he urinates
A stream that for the strength of it,
The sound, you would have thought
A horse produced it all the while
That he continued calmly talking.

174.

I heard him speak once to a group of Negro leaders:

Just a year ago I got signed into law
One of the landmark bills this century
Has seen, the Voting Rights Act.
Now its purpose was to make sure every registrar
In every little hamlet of the USA
Was color blind from then on
And the bill is surely working
If you read the figures, more than double
For the Negro citizens registered to vote
In Alabama in a year, in Mississippi
It is more than a quadrupling.
That's real good but if these backlash types
Get voted in in Congress many programs
That mean everything to your people
Are in danger since these backlash types
Aren't aiming just to put the Negro down,

They want to plunge a dagger deep
Into the heart of any social welfare program.
When I came in in January 1964 I said
I want a program fighting poverty
And I need 800 million—which is more
Than Franklin Roosevelt received
On several programs lumped together,
He'd turn over in his grave to think
We'd ever get that much—
That's what I got though
And the next year it was 7 million higher,
And the next year up 250
Million dollars more than that.
Now I'd have really liked to double it
Or triple it, quadruple, but I can't
Hold back my money
From the boys out in the rice fields.

So he'd finally out and said it:
We could not have guns and butter.

175.

Martin Luther King is now the crown prince
Of Vietnicks, in alliance with the ADA
He blames the war for our not having
Remedied the social ills we're plagued by.
This interpretation won't stand up
To scrutiny in time but it will gain
A certain currency the more it is repeated
And it's easier to make the war in Vietnam
The villain than to face the many problems
Of the management of our new social programs

And the failure of the Negroes to achieve
Substantial gains and the reluctance of
The Congress and the voters to support
New legislation or to adequately
Fund existing programs.

176.

In Durmont they've attracted some new industry
That uses lots of water. They need money for
The new wells, for the pipes, the pumps,
The storage tanks. They've issued bonds
To pay for this in part. Then they approached
The EDA to pay the rest. But they've been told
The money's tight, the war's the reason.
Then they want to build a new wing to extend
Their aging medical facility. Hill-Burton funds
For this may just not be there.
War's the cause again, they're told.
And then they need a new defoliant
To help them with their cotton crop,
For weeds, but it's in short supply they're told,
It's being used in Viet Nam.
Then there's the casualty. The whole town
Knows the boy who's gotten killed.
Mount Tree got word it was the captain
Of the Mount Tree High School
Football team from 1965.
The football coach, the president of the bank
And several teachers said
That they now had real doubts about the war.
His mother still defended it,
But then you'd say she simply had to

Or she might have lost her mind.
A lot of combat soldiers come
From places like Mount Tree.

177.

The specific case of Greece
Now that the British could no longer
Hold the line in '48 was taken partly
At the urging of that convert Arthur Vandenberg,
The erstwhile isolationist, as putting to the test
A lavish principle that had no working limits:
We were duty bound to interfere where "freedom"
Was at risk throughout the world—
The Truman Doctrine. This commitment
May have looked good at a certain heady moment
When the USA alone possessed the Bomb,
Before Japan and Europe got back on their feet,
Before the Russians reconstructed all their plants
And with the world's gold for the most part
Safely stowed inside Fort Knox,
Symbolic trophy of our triumph.
By the Sixties, though, this superhuman dominance
Was over, and yet the USA was stuck in its commitment
As the norm, the expectation for its leaders
And its people, this great margin
Of an effortless supremacy devolved
Into a dangerous delusion
To surrender which was poison.
The great disparity between the threat to Greece
In '48 and the Miltonic kind of language
Which Dean Acheson was using to describe it
Was a problem. Three whole continents

Were swinging in the balance he averred
Though just exactly what the threat to them
Consisted of was not completely clear—
Some vague infection, creeping menace
From the foul fiend, red stain spreading.
There was no time for appraisal he assured us,
We must act, and yet the policy he whipped us up
To follow lasted more than twenty years.
Rien ne dure, as any diplomat will tell you,
Comme le provisoire, but this was Armageddon
We were facing, what you did there
Was to battle for the Lord.

178.

—Now about this guy McKee though.
I'm aware that there's a bunch of them,
These chickenshits, they're pilots,
They don't understand this business.
I have problems if the strongest pro-
Administration men I've got, that I rely on,
My best friends are up and chasing after him
And say I oughtn't to appoint him.
—But they've got 89 of them in F.A.A right now,
I mean the military people, Mr President,
And that's contrary to the concept.
—I don't give a shit about the concept.
Why in the hell won't you people allow me
To have the best people I need?
I want you to have the best damned
Human you can get. I just don't
Have a civil service man can do
This kind of job or some fat

Businessman from Texas.
They don't understand this stuff,
I'll have another T.F.X.
And they'll be testifying all day to committees.
—I don't mean to make you trouble.
—I'm aware of that, I know how much
You help me or I wouldn't call you up.
I don't call enemies to help me.
I just let them go to hell, I chuck them out.
But you don't want to be defending me some day
When they've brought up impeachment charges.
Don't go after him, just tear that damned thing up
And put the pieces of it left in your ass pocket.
Tear it up and then you go tell Martha that by God
You want to kiss her, spend some time with her
And less time on minority reports
Because I've got to have this man to handle
Hundreds of millions of dollars.
—I wouldn't know this guy from Adam's apple.
He is probably terrific but this isn't
Any ordinary case.
—My brother in law from Texas,
I would like to bring him up here
And install him in that job if I appointed them
Like Kennedy and that bunch,
Take that damned thing, that minority report
And you can use it when you need
Some toilet paper, go on, tear that damned thing up
And don't you cause me any trouble,
I've got troubles up my ass in Vietnam
And the Dominican Republic
And every other goddamned thing
Throughout the world.
If you could hear what some of those
Joint Chiefs were recommending,

You would want to drop that phone you got
Right quick to go and spend time
With your grandchild…

179.

He couldn't tell the truth, it was an act against his nature.
He would only tell what fit with his immediate designs.
If you, more than your legislative rival, know
Which six votes coming up are going to sway which way
And for what reason, then you win.
To honestly disclose such information was equivalent
To giving up the chest of family silver,
Back in Texas somewhere he had learned that truth
Would not be advantageous for you if you gave it up
Too freely. Lyndon Johnson's view of truth
Was like a Boston trustee's angst concerning capital
Which he guarded: it was far too precious
A commodity for him to ever use it.
A riverboat gambler won't give away his hand,
He's got those cards clamped very closely
To his chest, he keeps his counsel.
JFK once said that that's what Lyndon was,
That kind of gambler, with a kind of admiration
And affection I would say, I think the insight
Was profound, but I know Lyndon would have
Really been upset since he was mortally afraid
Of being found out, being recognized,
It amounted to a mania almost, an aide
Who worked for him was not supposed
To have the slightest inkling what the President
Was thinking, much less tell him, any member
Of his staff who'd had the gall to have discovered

What the President was thinking when the President
Was focusing his efforts on pretending
He was thinking something else would be regarded
As a nuisance, he was terrified of being understood
In some way better than he understood himself.

180.

There wasn't much of any ideology in Johnson,
That's why people didn't trust him, he was
Utterly pragmatic, he was oriented only
Toward objectives, ideology was meaningless
To him. He would cooperate
With racists, white supremacists,
If they could help him get to some objective.
He didn't buy their kind of outlook in the least.
Although some people thought he did
Because he'd work with them,
Let's say some liberals didn't trust him.
But the racists would suspect that he was liberal
When he worked the liberal side
To pick up votes there too.
Some aura of suspicion clung to Johnson
Who was centrist through and through.
It was not that he said one thing
To the liberals and another to
The Southern racist mossbacks.
He in fact was saying nothing,
Kept his counsel, he was subtle, he was cunning.
He would let one person think
That he meant something, do the same thing
With a person of the opposite persuasion.
Southern racists had the feeling

They could count on him to not let
Civil righters go too far while civil righters
Were convinced he wouldn't ever let the racists
Hold things back too much,
But if you looked at what he said--
Well, he'd Houdinied them, there wasn't
Any way you could confine him to a statement.
This was one on one since sometimes
In a public speech he'd say things
That he shouldn't have, that got him
Into trouble--the excitement of the moment
Would derail him, he'd get worked up,
On the record...

181.

As V-P Johnson had this way, he'd vanish from his office
In the EOB...well, maybe not quite vanish...
He was gone, though, and you knew
Where he'd be gone to, he'd gone over
To the White House, he'd go over there
And wander through the halls like your
Obliged, obedient servant scaring work up
For himself, like someone waiting for instructions,
"Lyndon, why don't you go down
And get the President an apple," it was sad
And sort of funny and these guys who worked
For Kennedy were mostly from the Hill
Where they had known him as the Leader
Of the Senate, someone powerful and awesome,
They might still be deferential, yet they
Didn't want him messing up their work
That they were presently concerned with.

Quite a big change. He'd go over there
And take this huge reduction in his status,
Serving notice he would always be on call
In case you needed someone jetting off to Greenland,
He was there. And so he came back
To the EOB one afternoon and said
"So that's the way they're gonna play it,"
He was having this huge paranoid reaction
To the way the White House planned to set him up now
As he saw it, it played out that we were
Heading to Dakar and then the word came
We would stop in Spain en route
And meet some government officials at
A military base. Well, he went up the wall
On this one, he said Henry Cabot Lodge's
Brother's out there as ambassador—
Which was true, his brother hadn't been replaced
When the Republicans went out—and LBJ said
"I can see what they're concocting, they'll have me
Come flyin' in there, dime to dollar they'll have
Franco there to greet me." He envisioned this
As some plot to embarrass him, you sent him
On a foreign trip, he runs off very first thing
And he links arms with a person who was
Naturally allied to him, this LBJ's a fascist type
From Texas, ultra right-wing, he was storming through
The office, he was helpless, LBJ the former
Potentate and powerhouse of Congress now was helpless.

182.

Hanoi makes use of time the way the Russians
Used terrain before Napoleon's advance,

They keep retreating, losing battles, but in due course
They're creating those conditions which the enemy
Can't function in. For Napoleon
The problem was the length of his supply lines
And the coldness of the winter. Hanoi hopes
That it will be for us the increase of dissension
On the home front, our impatience with
A war that has no lines and no successes
And a growing need to make a choice
For either guns or butter—and increasingly
American repugnance at the casting of our country
As the heavy in a war in which we beat up
On this tiny Asian nation and for what?
Or here's the question: can the tortoise
Of the progress that we make in Vietnam
Outpace the hare dissent at home is turning into?

183.

I think my admiration for the President was greatest
When he said about the Bay of Pigs "the blame is mine alone."
I knew that statement wasn't true, but still he said it,
That took courage…

184.

We went into Rome at night and we could
Very well have faced two million Reds
Who'd massed to demonstrate against us.
Then the Pope made his appeal,
We had no differences, no quarrel,
He simply said that he'd do anything for peace

And could I hold on to the truce one extra day.
Now I had General Westmoreland,
He had given me the number of our soldiers
It would cost, but we did give the Pope
His extra day of truce and it is hard
Not to regret those boys of mine
Who then got killed and it is now
A great deal worse since we've had Tet,
And Westy cancelled his Tet truce
Because the house had caught on fire,
Just look at Pueblo, look at Khe Sanh,
Look at Saigon and you see them,
They're a part of one big effort
To defeat us, we can dodge it
Being weak-kneed if we want to.
What I said at San Antonio
Was as far as I could go
And it went farther than my military wanted,
We have made it fully clear how much our wishes
Are for talking, not for bombing
Just as long as some response
That seems productive comes from them.
But if you sneak around at night and hit
Our bases, hit our cities, we cannot hold back
From bombing, we have gotten our response
From this offensive, it should satisfy
The dove who prays for peace
As much as any mother does.

185.

I worked very hard on the State of the Union,
My whole Christmas, then the other night

I tuned in on TV when they discussed it
For an hour and when they finished
It amazed me, fifteen men and not one sentence,
One damned sentence from the whole
4000 words that they called good.
I just don't get it. Am I that far off the mark?
Am I that wrong? Has something happened
To my head that I don't know about?
Then Bird said yes, I think so.
You don't seem to know what year
This is you're living in. It's 1968

186.

Gene McCarthy spent a big day bringing sheaves in
Through the state of Massachusetts, he was
Greeted with a kind of adulation, jubilation,
By a mob one third of whom were Californians,
One third more was from New York,
Another third was Japanese or Upper Voltan,
And the last third simply thought that he was Joe.
The only action that occurred--if you can call it that--
Consisted of the Brookline Town Committee
Voting twenty-one to eight or thereabouts
With their endorsement of the upstart
And proposing Mike Dukakis for the national
Convention as a delegate this summer.
At the meeting Mike declared he was for Gene
So I called Tipper up this morning to inform him
Of this breaking, this disturbing bit of news
And he went roaring off to Boston, said he
Soon would straighten out that "silly kid,"
But Lester Hyman in the meantime

Just got back from touring cities south of here
In Massachusetts' nether regions--
In that section of the state they want
To blow up all of Asia he reported,
LBJ would beat McCarthy eight to one.

187.

He was caught up in the actions
Of his predecessors surely
But as much I'd say by Texas's traditions,
It was not in him to back out,
"We must not tuck tail and run
When we're attacked" was like a credo
Or a reflex he projected on the nation.
Texans always stand and fight,
Cry babies, yellow bellies have no place
Among them, can't be tolerated by them.
To a weird extent he thought of Vietnam
As some grave challenge to his courage,
To his manhood, not to show the slightest
Cowardly behavior was a personal
Imperative but also foreign policy
Perversely. Judgment, justice
Were reduced to terms of manhood,
People trying to consider what was wise
Were being pummeled with
The Presidential question
What was brave or who was brave.

188.

The students at Columbia were the children of the bourgeoisie,
Their fathers were employers of the cops to put it one way
Since the cops were to protect them and their kids
And to protect their sacred property from "proles."
Cops would do what they were told, or so the expectation went,
But at Columbia the cops opposed the kids, told pampered kids
What they must do. A cop may argue, plead or menace,
But at some point saying "Get out, move along"
Becomes his duty when he has to put his hand on any arm
That may resist him, grips it hard and twists its muscle.
If you've been brought up as a Spockie, if a cop grips you
In this way, it's the first time in your life a person's
Grabbed you out of anger, you get frightened,
Then you jerk, you bite, you spit—these were
The upper middle class kids who had found themselves
Confronted with the hired hands revolting, but the shock
Was maybe greater for the cops, they couldn't understand
The problem they were facing, the rejection of society
By those meant to inherit it, the cops were not prepared
For this reversal, this revolt, it made them angry.
And the students didn't recognize the law,
They had no knowledge of the consequence of breaking it,
When the law imposed its penalties by reflex
They were outraged, how could this devolve on them?
But they had raised important questions in acute form—
What's the duty of the citizen to law, what is the duty
Of the law to every citizen?—
To ensure domestic tranquillity was a fundamental reason
Why we'd made a Constitution, rights of protest
And assembly had been added to the Constitution later,
As an afterthought almost. Now that the latter
Called the former into question, which would win out
Wasn't clear. You could have asked about the violence

Of blacks too, but their case was not as puzzling
As the students', they'd been brought to the Americas,
Or their forebears had, in chains, without consent,
They'd made no compact with the codes
That forged their shackles, other groups had come here
Willingly in search of opportunities they'd sensed,
They had consented to be governed by the laws
That they'd helped make. And it was Lincoln
Who'd expressed the black dilemma
And the menace blacks embodied: "You've succeeded
In dehumanizing Negroes, you have rendered it
Impossible to be but as the beasts
Which plow the fields for them, you have placed them
Where the ray of hope is blown out
In the darkness like what broods above the spirits
Of the damned, now are you sure the demon you
Yourselves have roused won't turn and rend you?"
And it had throughout the Sixties.
As for the students, though, the group to whom society
Was offering the most, they had repudiated what
Was being offered as a stultifying trap—increasing wealth,
Food, shelter, leisure—they would let the working class
Aspire to have those paltry things while they,
The higher types, went off to change the world
And live on air in their ecstatic self-fulfillment.

189.

Debbie would say to people "I am a witch,"
Her face expressionless, her eyes would get
All narrow like a reptile's, weird and evil,
Only whites would show through slits and she
Would freak the other girls out, they'd start screaming.

But her mother said "She never had a boyfriend--
Not boy crazy, she was too shy."
"She had lots of men up with her,"
Said the desk clerk, "off-the-street types,
Foulest bearded beatnik hippies you could find."
She was a drop-out. Robert Kennedy discovered
That the students at a Catholic female college
To a man almost thought massive carpet bombing
Of the North would end the war in Vietnam
More expeditiously. He shouted at them:
"Don't you know what massive carpet bombing means?"
"Steep escalation just as long as you leave me out,"
Seemed to him to be the answer they'd have given
If they hadn't just remained politely smiling,
Such nice girls, no drop-outs they, most well-behaved,
Reflecting well upon their parents and their church.
And in between these two extremes the slyly smiling
Richard Nixon, who could play or could exploit
This garbled music like a master, re-arrange it,
Make it work to his advantage, tap ambivalence.
"Please make this endless nightmare go away,
Restore our country to us, help us
To pretend the world's still stable."

190.

The need we have to pass this legislation's very clear
You have these beatniks and these so-called
"Campus cults" which burn their draft cards.
This is how they mean to demonstrate contempt
For their own country and to undermine resistance
To the communists and all they represent.
These harmful actions are suggested, have been

Led by their professors in the colleges
Whose salaries are paid for by our citizens
Through taxes. That's an outrage. We've just seen
This very week a mob attacking our own country
While it praised the Viet Cong attempt to storm
The inner citadels of Congress. At the head of them
You saw a Yale professor. It in general
Was a filthy, sleazy, beatnik sort of gang
But still the questions which they raised
Must cause concern because the Communists
Have planned to use the Judas goats to lead those
Who are free in mass defection, these so-called students
And the stooges of the Communists at home
And overseas by belittling and by vilifying
Downgrade our great country in the eyes
Of all the world and try to shake faith
In the democratic way of life our soldiers
Are defending. They will aim to vanquish freedom
By subversion and erosion of the pride
We ought to take in our great nation
And its heritage of serving as a beacon to the world.

191.

Humphrey came back from his conference with the President
Dejected, looking ravaged. He at first denied they'd even had
A meeting. "I did not get in to see him. He had visitors."
I knew that wasn't true and so I pressed him. "What just happened?"
"I was warned that if I argued for a peace plank,
He'd denounce me. That the blood of his two sons-in-law
Would be upon my hands." A long pause followed,
Then the V-P made this final observation:
"You know I've eaten so much shit the last few years

The stuff is almost tasting good."

192.

Lord Birkenhead once said
There was a Lord of Derby who
Was like a cushion with the bum-print of
The last man who had sat upon it on it.
Hubert Humphrey was in this way dented in
Except the bum-print which defined him
Never altered—LBJ
Kept Hubert squashed on Vietnam.

193.

I was sitting on my suitcase in the airport dozing off,
I had an early morning flight to catch back home
When someone tapped me on the shoulder,
I looked up and there was Kennedy who asked me
How I was, was I OK. He said "I see you're for McCarthy,
Could we talk for just a minute? Would you like
To have some breakfast?" Though the coffee shop
Was closed, they talked to someone, got it open.
We were sitting there till 3 or 4 AM, this was surreal,
He asked us why we weren't supporting his campaign,
He was concerned he had attracted only students
That were C grade, all the best were for McCarthy.
Did we not see that McCarthy couldn't win?
I was thinking, this guy's just campaigned his ass off,
He has won here very big in Indiana, he has probably
Not slept for four days running, now he's staying up
All night to talk to us, two twenty-one year olds.

We asked him why he hadn't been a candidate before,
Why he had only jumped in after Gene had done well
In New Hampshire, we were calling him a kind
Of opportunist to his face but he just took it.
I was facing being drafted, my draft physical
Was coming up quite soon and if I passed it,
It was Canada for me and so I told him.
He encouraged me to serve if I was drafted,
Then he added, "I am every bit as much against
This evil war as you are." I was thinking but I did not say,
"Well sure, but you don't have to go and fight it."
I was in this race because of civil rights
And I'd been canvassing for Gene among the blacks
But getting nowhere, RFK possessed "the name."
And he agreed that his advantage was enormous.
But then he asked "Why can't McCarthy enter ghettoes?"
"McCarthy has no feel for either poverty or black folks,
Civil rights" was how he answered his own question,
He had gotten there ahead of me. He said that he did,
Had that feel, that he could win, that I should back him,
He was that blunt. Pat and I were both bowled over
Just by being in his presence, I was proud of us
For sticking to our guns, supporting Gene.
He didn't like that. He was giving us a sort of
Johnson treatment, his attempt to win us over,
Pushing his side. Still we parted ways in very
Friendly fashion. Pat and I now stayed awake
And we produced for him a kind of manifesto
Of the topics we'd discussed, we pushed it
Underneath the door of some campaign aide.
I remained with Gene but later on decided
I would never speak again in opposition to
The Kennedy campaign, I'd gotten neutralized somewhat
But more than that I'd been attracted by
The passion RFK had shown for blacks.

Gene had seemed to be indifferent to the power side
Of politics equations, I'd admired that for a while.
There was a limit, though to how far
You could float above the fray as I was learning.

194.

A President responsible to no one out of blind pride,
Willful stubbornness and misplaced sense of
National prestige now meant to press the war
Beyond the bounds of reason.

Are we really winning the war
Or is it possible to ever really win it
In a military sense?—those were the questions
Which you couldn't just dismiss.
Our senior officers, the men who ran the war,
Those men of honor all had marshaled
Mildly optimistic arguments
With force and some coherence, but….

Several hundred thousand people in the North
Had been diverted by the bombing
From their economic tasks, this was undoubtedly
A strain but still the primitive economy
Left great room for maneuver, they had China
Meeting many of their food needs.
In a tough authoritarian regime a coolie
Labor force in wartime could be moved
From place to place for scarcely more
That what it took to feed them rice.
Chinese labor troops were stationed in the North
And doing certain engineering and supply tasks.

Since the call for greater bombing in the North
Had come from Stennis's committee,
55,000 sorties had been flown, a hundred
Thousand tons of ordnance in addition
Had been dropped and yet no drop in the ability
Of Hanoi to supply its operations in the South
Could be detected, enemy forces in the South
Were four times larger than they had been
When the bombing had begun in '65
And they possessed a greater quantity
Of weapons that were better thanks to Russia
And their transportation system in response
To all the bombing had if anything become
A lot more versatile, new roads and added bridges,
Better barge routes and the number
Of the depots for supplies had gotten greater,
And their size. And all the evidence suggested
That the bombing had created in Hanoi
A sort of spirit like to London's in the Blitz,
The social fabric in the North had gotten stronger.
Manpower in the North was inexhaustible.
Old Westy said that we were in at least for two
More years of large scale battles, maybe more,
Plus several years of mopping up and no
Negotiated settlement was mentioned,
Westy's plan envisioned victory alone
And it assumed that we the people were prepared
To stay the course and pay the price
Whatever that turned out to be,
That this was in the nation's interest.
To the question "Were we winning?"
His reply was "Yes, but slowly."
Still another question "Can we win?"
Was hanging there unanswered.
Would Peking and Moscow let the North's

Insurgency be totally defeated?
They might not like the roles that they'd been
Thrust into—defenders of the North—
And Peking said each country had to fight
Its wars of liberation on its own, but they
Could not ignore the "cutting edge of Communism"-
Look North Vietnam had now dramatically assumed.
If the kind of special warfare the Americans
Were testing in the South of Vietnam
Could be defeated, that would mean
It could be vanquished through the world.
They were compelled to give support to Ho Chi Minh.
Not that they had to meet the USA head-on,
There were a hundred little knife cuts
They could give us that would bleed us,
That would frustrate our objectives, bog us down,
Achieve the dreaded state of stalemate
Which the people of the US
Would not tolerate much longer.

The President it seemed could not by temperament admit
To any error. Not that he was getting "error" in analyses
Advisors were supplying. Even so, he seemed to relish
Being cast in some Lone Ranger role, embattled
In the quest for peace and freedom as he saw it,
Not allowing timid men to circumvent
His lofty vision which he saw as being vindicated
Some day. Stubborn, bellicose, he simply plunged ahead,
Lashed out at critics whom he likened to appeasers.
"We will not be pudding-headed, we will not say
We'll stop our half of the war and hope and pray
That they'll stop their half. We have tried
On some occasions to begin negotiations—
They always escalate their efforts, kill our soldiers."
He flew around the world at Christmas time

To buck the soldiers up—the clenched fist there,
The note of suffering and bravery, of resolute endurance
(not in anger but in sorrow). He consulted with
The Pope as man of peace, the unclenched fist
Extended then, the noble offer to negotiate
Held foremost in a masterly performance,
He had turned the wheel full circle geographically
And every other way, but he had left our U.S. policy
Exactly where it had been bent on military victory
Whatever it might cost though always open to
A settlement at any time on our terms
If Hanoi would just admit that it was beaten.

195.

The master politician Lyndon Johnson now was gone,
The man who'd reconciled all conflicts,
Who had always found or always forged consensus.
In his place you saw some huddled paranoiac.
What had happened? I remember one time
Seventy or so of us were called in
To the White House for a briefing.
I had heard the kind of boilerplate or b.s.
Rusk and McNamara handed out this day
One time too often, something snapped in me,
So I stood up and said "When can we start
To hear the truth on Viet Nam?"
The President was standing to the side
Against the wall, he rushed right toward me,
He came over and he grabbed me by the arm
And said "I don't want you remaining
In my house, you're going to leave"
And never eased up on his grip, he led me out

And he escorted me the whole length
Of the hall down to the door and as I left I said
"You know, sir, you cannot call this your house."
He called me up a few days later.
"I was right to make you leave," he said,
"But you were also right to say
That this is not my house." And so we left it.
More in sorrow. And we haven't spoken since
Though we were colleagues in the Congress.
It was strange you know, I'm taller than the President,
I'm taller by an inch I think, but that day
He impressed me as so big, so overwhelming.
It was frightening to have him throw me out
This way, he seemed a scary man. And rather sad.
Or disappointing. Or embarrassing.
Some part of me still wanted to protect him.
He was acting in a way that was beneath him.

196.

Some part of me can see when even Westy says
This war could last forever if we can't get Hanoi out
That this is no time to be pouring more men in
And yet there has to be a breaking point for them
Although I'll grant you that there seems to be no end
To hordes of soldiers, willing soldiers they keep
Calling up and sending down the trail, so why not
Do what Aiken says, just say we won and start
Withdrawing, say we've reached our main objectives.
Can't the South take up its own defense by now?
Or say what McNamara says, that we've forestalled
The intervention of the North, set new elections
In the South for next September, let a coalition

Surface from results of those elections not excluding
Viet Cong, and if it crumbles under Communist attacks,
We could encourage the creation of another new
Non-Communist regime for keeping order which
Would take three years at least or maybe five
Before the Communists controlled it.
Five years hence would this conversion
Be considered a defeat for us? Who knows?
But that's just McNamara talking, he's gone
Yellow-bellied on me, he's not what I'd call a man now.
After one more round of U.S. escalation,
And a national election in the South
Come next September, we'd declare South Vietnam
Somewhat secure and start withdrawing U.S. forces.
If they start to howl in Saigon, we could threaten
To cut off the aid the government requires
For its survival, we'd just get tough. If they fell
A few years later, who would care back here by then
About how Vietnam was lost, I mean speak out?
You'd have a few. I'd say we've sacrificed enough,
And there's a weariness, exhaustion, a revulsion
In our country, who'd complain about a leader
Who was wise enough and resolute enough
To put the plug back in the drain, this war's
Depleting us for sure, and yet it's right there
At the center of my four years, I can't say now
How it got there since I wanted so much else,
And if I have to say it's bankrupt, if I say
That our commitment was mistaken,
Our commitment which I had us ante up,
I shoved the stack in, what's the verdict on
My judgment then? I'm in this thing too deep now,
I cannot admit defeat and I'd sink faster
If I struggled to withdraw. The North keeps getting
Their supplies in, bombing doesn't seem to stop them,

Bombing doesn't even seem to slow them down a little,
And some C.I.A. report says that at seventy per cent
Diminished transport capability they'd cut out inessentials
And still eke out what they need to run the war,
Still get it through, they just don't know
When they're defeated, and the sacrifice accepted
By civilians...I keep thinking if we turn it up
One notch more they'll surrender, but they don't,
They never do, and you have got to ask the question
Are we ever going to win this goddamned war?
And I've got demonstrations here
That sap the willingness of ordinary people
When we need a steadfast spirit to sustain us,
This encourages the Communists
And makes them persevere--one more election
And the U.S.A. will crumple, this thought
Shores their spirits up. Yet you've got Rostow
Who's been talking to some Soviet official
Who assures him that the bombing
Of the North has had an impact,
That the Soviets might cut aid to Hanoi
And that the North is in a kind of desperation,
Their economy's exhausted, and they've used up
All the old stocks of their war matériel
And don't know how to use the new stuff
That the Soviets might give them. And we've heard
That they've got no men in the countryside
To call up any more, at least no young ones,
They're resorting to the D team, men from
Thirty six to fifty. One more little shove might do it.
We've got cause and will and strength and means
To do it I'm convinced, there is a core out there
That still supports this war, of decent people.
They get restless in the face of opposition,
They et anxious. You've got Komer saying Westy's

Been too cautious in assessing what momentum
We've achieved in Vietnam, and there's a coalition
Government would come out of elections in November.
I've said go ahead with all existing programs
For development. Militarily we've made
Substantial progress. The reporters are the problem.
Negativity among that group is rampant.
They're in search of some big story
That will win Pulitzer prizes. This guy Apple,
Johnnie Apple is a Communist and ought to be expelled.
And I have thought of maybe censoring the news there
To maintain morale back home, but my advisors say
The price I'd have to pay would be too great.
We've got to muzzle them in some way though
In case they might be on to something out there.
And I don't know what to make of Clifford's
Saying he was troubled by refusal of our allies
In the region to support us--if our cause
Is so important, why don't they feel
Some compulsion to send forces of their own in,
Help themselves? Why should they do so I suppose
When they've got us to do the heavy lifting
For them, we've encouraged this dependence,
It's a nightmare, we keep getting pulled in deeper,
Something's got us by the ankle--still
I don't see why if we exert more pressure,
If we escalate the bombing--we're not
Doing much to win the war at present.
It's the only way to bring them to the table--
Step up bombing. I know McNamara says
It has no impact on supplies that they get through
Or on their conduct of the war, but I just
Feel it in my bones, they must be hurting.
We've simply got to hit them harder, pour more
Steel in every place except Hanoi.

Hanoi's still weaseling on us though
As Dean Rusk says about the way talks
Might get started, it's…

197.

"This is the clearest lesson of our lifetime,
Munich taught us that by yielding to
Aggression we encourage greater threats."

Quoth suave Prince Arthur: "That is shit
And Hubert knows it." Though of course
It wasn't shit when he signed off on it
For Camelot when he was of the court.
But thus the Democrats were at each other's throats
As Tricky Dicky, slyly smiling, had predicted
And had counted on their being.
In comes Lowenstein demanding
That Americans for Democratic Action
Must on principal repudiate their leader,
Dump the President, that Vietnam
Had canceled every bet and in the bargain
Rendered all the rules of power--
Old corrupt rules--obsolete,
That sweeping power out
Was part of something larger,
Re-possessing pure democracy let's call it.

Old-style labor leaders thought such talk
Was crazy, give and take was what they lived by,
Storing power up by slow negotiations,
Endless increments and patience. They had made
The world's first middle class for masses

By this method--their accomplishment, their glory.
Lyndon Johnson understood them,
He played their game of the trade-offs,
By the rules. But now these hare-brained,
Long-haired kids were going to piss it
All away with their blithe arty-farty talk
About ideals and revolution, LBJ
As something evil. Liberal politics
Had swerved from economics to aesthetics,
To morality and culture. Nice ideas but
What happened to the poor then?
The Republicans were waiting to devour them.
LBJ might be the greatest s.o.b.
At least he's ours though.
When had labor had a champion
Like him since FDR? Just answer that one.

Well: a Democratic house built on
A Southern white foundation in an age
That's seen the Voting Rights Act passed...
There's something out of tune and joint there,
That time's over, no more labor movement
Arguing for the Cold War status quo--
That's too stand-pat--and for their
Economic interest (what they've got,
Hold on to that)--Depression mind-set in an age
Of new abundance, full employment.
Old fart thinking has to go.

And in the wings the great pretender,
Little Bobby wearing love beads,
Languid listener to arguments for running
As his aides and his admirers set them forth:
You have a lame duck leader growing
That much lamer by the day, who might

Withdraw, this was the moment for
Decisive pouncing action, any commandant
Could see that. "But they'd say
That I was splitting up the party
From ambition, out of envy,
They would not see me as doing it
From outrage at the war in Vietnam
And at the poor's plight. I think Al
Is doing well to float these feelers,
And the moment may arrive
When I'd consider getting in,
But someone else must be the first."

So you can sweep in, reap the fruits
Of someone's risk? What kind of seeking
Of a newer world is that, to throw
Some sacrificial lamb up to the power brokers,
Wait to see how they'd react to it,
Just watch the blood spurt as they tear it limb to limb?
The hell with power brokers!
People who are anguished
At the honor of this country being trampled
By the war in Vietnam don't give a shit
About Mayor Daley and his Robert's rules
Of precedence for running, who's allowed
To make his move and who must wait
His turn in line. The moment's now.

As George C. Wallace might have told him,
Man of existential daring.

198.

Why should I listen to all those student peaceniks
Marching up and down the pavement?
They were barely in their cradles in the days of World War II,
They never knew the ravages of Adolf Hitler.
When China fell, they were just beginning nursery school,
They were sitting in their grammar schools when we had
That Korean War to fight, they wouldn't recognize
A Communist from Adam, they don't understand
The world as well as I do.

199.

Ken Galbraith once suggested
That he make some kind of economic speech.
To which the President replied: "Well Ken,
A President who makes that kind of speech
Is like a fellow who starts peein' down his own leg.
Peein' makes him feel all warm,
But no one else can figure out what that man's doin'."

200.

You have to be a demagogue on little things
Throughout your life in office if
You want to be around to have your way,
Your say in big things.

201.

Another reason staffers may have found
That they could take it when they worked for Lyndon Johnson
Was that they had Lady Bird, the ever gracious Lady Bird
Who walked behind her husband always saying thank you.
Our First Couple came together as a matched set.

202.

True, you can bear any burden, you can pay any price--
If you know for sure that what you're doing's right.
But Viet Nam was like a thorn stuck in his throat,
Would not come up, would not go down,
Was just pure hell. He lacked
That reassuring feeling that sustained him
Through the crunch with civil rights or education
Of the rightness of his effort win or lose—
"We'll make it through this one some way"—
And early on he wanted out,
But couldn't find the place to get out.
It devoured him.

203.

Viet Nam was not the war he wanted.
The one he always wanted was on poverty
And ignorance and illness, that was worth
A whole man's life, but if you took that
To the people, if you spoke of civil rights let's say,
Your audience would start to shift its feet
And seem embarrassed, even hostile.

Speak of liberty, of bearing any burden
To defend it to the far ends of the earth though,
They would all stand up and cheer.

204.

You goddamned old bastards.
You're a bunch of buzzards sitting on a fence.
You'd sit and watch and let the young men die.
And die for what? You speak
Your speeches irresponsibly
And urge that we press on.
You come in here and talk to us
Like Wise Men. You may be wise.
But you haven't got a depth grasp
Of the issues Viet Nam presents us now,
You simply haven't done your homework,
You expect us just to genuflect
And swallow what you say
Because of who you may have been once...
With complexities before us which you cannot
Just finesse in quickie consults,
Grave pronouncements.

205.

All right, bomb it if you want, one more or less
Won't make a goddamned bit of difference
From the Air Force with its goddamned
Carpet bombing, dropping more on Viet Nam
Than all the bombs they dropped on Europe
In the whole of World War II and yet

We haven't got a goddamn thing
To show for it, we don't.

206.

What the sam hell does it take for us
To win this thing, he asked, what do we have to do
To beat them. He had watched that day
The helicopters bringing back green body bags,
The crewmen laid the bags out side by side
Along the airstrip, they were lumpy.
There were ARVN soldiers nearby in a billet,
You could hear the sounds, the roughhouse and
The laughter from their compound, they were
Evidently unimpressed by death, by theirs
Or others'. Thus the jawbones of that general
Who'd asked that peevish question ground
His molars down to sawdust when he heard them.
As he stood there for a minute, I was sure
He'd break the door down, kill our allies.
Then he seemed to reconsider, choke that rage back
As he turned and stormed off bilious toward his chopper.

207.

Apprehension, arrogance, misguided military expertise.
In a strange way like the Germans and the Austrians
Who sleepwalked into World War I Americans believed
A certain minor local shift of power might unhinge
The whole world's balance, therefore Hanoi,
Just as Belgrade did before the First World War,
Required a super power's challenge and chastisement

Lest the damage it could do get out of hand.
And then the USA's self-confidence was not unlike
The Germans' in the run-up to the Great War,
National "greatness" on the lookout for a challenge
That would let its strength be shown, a proper
Proving ground, refusal to believe that any problem
Was too great for it to overcome and master.
You had statesmen who might well have harbored
Doubts in their own minds (like LBJ as he
Expressed himself in talks with Richard Russell)
Who were conscious of a groundswell of opinion
From the populace, a national consensus
That conveyed them irresistibly along.

208.

"The VC tell the peasants that our spray
Is deadly poison. I can show you that it isn't."
And with that he stuck his fingers
In the spigot of a drum, they got all oily,
Then he licked them. "You could say
It tastes like kerosene," he said. "It's got
Some overtones of chemicals--not good--
Unless you drink it, though, it's not
A deadly poison. I'll assure you
No one down there's going to drink it.
The boys who do these runs are volunteers,
They'd almost have to be, you couldn't
Do this job for very long...you have to dig it.
We fly these C-123s at only ten
To fifteen knots above the speed
At which they stall although the engine's
Running smoothly since the air quits

Rushing tightly past the wings to give them lift.
The airplane drives straight downwards
When it stalls, there's not much leeway,
Ten or fifteen knots, no more, the thinnest margins,
Since these planes are making steep banks
At a hundred feet or so above the ground,
And a plane that's banking sixty as its angle needs
A lot more lift than one that's flying level,
It's what pilots call the last edge
Of their planes' performance envelope.
The ground fire when it starts up
Sounds like popcorn when it's cooking.
These defoliation planes are known as
Ranch Hands--that's their code name.
Ranch Hands' motto has been nailed
For all to read above the door inside
The Ready Room at Tan Son Nuht
Lest we forget our mission:
REMEMBER ONLY YOU
CAN PREVENT FORESTS."

209.

From 1965 to '67 it was McNamara's baby.
Bob began to wobble then in 1967.
His condition really had become quite bad,
I mean like hanging on by only fingernails.
He had started out as cocky as could be
With these computerized projections,
After two years we'd be out,
McNaughton figured out the odds.
I had immense respect for Bob
Despite the fact that he did everything

In Vietnam all wrong, he was a
Dedicated guy and a sincere guy,
But he'd deceived himself quite badly.
By the middle of the year in '67…
Well, his wife was being treated
For an ulcer, Bob himself looked very bad
And all his schemes were getting knocked back
On their ass in Vietnam. He had believed
That what emerged from some computer
When you asked it was the truth.
That wasn't working.
It was about now that the references
To Forrestal got floated, there was one time
He just sat there in the room with us,
Said nothing, and his jaw quivered.
He was broken.

210.

I was with him in the bedroom once, one morning.
He would have these certain periods of time
When he would sit there, he would read
And hand you stuff, there might be conversation sometimes.
He just really wanted someone there beside him.
Any business of your own might get discussed,
From time to time these opportunities arose.
This day I sensed one to discuss the touchy topic:
Vietnam. I said I knew he didn't think much of
George Aiken's new proposal in the Senate,
But I thought we might adopt it.
We could say now that elections
Had been held in Vietnam
And they'd elected every level

Of the government in democratic fashion,
We'd achieved our main objectives,
We could now withdraw our troop support
But keep on giving military help with arms and money.
Having said my piece, I waited.
He just glared at me. He had, you know,
This strange spell-casting power,
He could look you down or stare you down
Until you started jittering, felt nervous and impatient.
I just finally had to ask him what he thought.
He said "Get out."
Now I had known this man since 1948
And we had never had a run-in,
No cross words, we'd disagreed at times,
But still we'd had as solid a relationship
As any in my whole life, any friendship I'd enjoyed.
This day I picked my papers up and left though.
For several weeks I knew my only place
Was in the doghouse, I no longer got invited
To the meetings I attended, NSC or to the Cabinet.
Completely frozen out. Or to those family
Get-togethers at the White House
Where such useful information was
Informally exchanged. I was *non grata*.
Till one afternoon I got a call from Lady Bird.
She was planning to surprise him with some kind
Of little party, she wished both me and my wife
To be available. The two of us attended.
He was just as warm and friendly
As he'd ever been, the incident we'd had
Was never mentioned, you'd have thought
It hadn't happened. Sometime after
When he'd gone back to the ranch,
Had left the White House, I was sitting
With him once again together doing business

In the living room, the two of us
Were sitting there alone, he'd read
And hand me certain papers,
I just finally had to ask him, I recalled
That time I'd made him get so mad,
I said I couldn't understand
Why he had turned on me that way
And thrown me out.
He simply looked at me and said
"Because I knew down in my gut
That you and Aiken both were right,
But I was helpless, there was
Absolutely nothing I could do."

211

He was essentially a populist at heart
And was concerned about the Biblical injunction
That you had to honor parents. Just examine
His relationships, he had a father and a mother
Image complex, and he honored both his father
And his mother, you can see how he respected them
And talked about their values, he was worried
All the time about the average run of people
Who got old and sick and indigent, disabled,
And he meant to tackle problems they were facing.
I don't think that he was devious in any sense
You'd give that term, he thought that every person
Had some kind of weak spot, some Achilles heel
Or tendon you could analyze or find out.
What's the element in any person's background
That will bring him out so you can start to bargain?
He was like a shrewd psychiatrist, he'd always find

Some element upon which he could work with you,
It was an outgrowth of his years with Speaker Rayburn
Who would work some kind of compromise,
Establish some relationship with people
If he found out what it was that they related to.
You didn't just in toto do what A said,
B and C might disagree with that,
But if A and B and C agreed on one thing,
That could be your point of contact,
And it got to be if I was A in any situation,
Since I knew how we would work,
I'd go and talk to B and C myself
Before we started, long before I saw
The Boss Man. If you understood his methods
And aligned yourself with them, you got results.

Now people talk about his language.
It was rough, no doubt about it.
Yet he also could be the most sensitive person,
I've been with him on the ranch
And we'd be passing by the livestock
And he'd refer to all their reproductive functions—
Barnyard sex—five minutes later
He'd be standing on a hillside, he'd be sounding
Like a poet when he talked about the sunset
And the land and people's aspirations for it,
Their relationships. And so this earthy man
Could be the most amazingly complex man, Keats,
Boccaccio and the murderous Machiavelli all in one.
Too many of his critics think of monotone
And monochrome—consistency.
But human beings aren't like that.
He was bigger, more intense, and had a lot more
Human qualities than most, he was a Whitman sort
Of man containing multitudes—abounding.

As for the charge of pettiness: well, he could spend
As much time fretting over picayune appointments
To advisory committees as he would on some
Gigantic sort of issue. In fact I've known him
To accept what I advised on some gigantic kind
Of issue in an instant—no discussion—
Then spend hours disagreeing over some name
For some twenty member task force if he thought
The man or woman wasn't right, "not one of ours."
Even after the election, I mean 1968
When you would think he might be
Somewhat philosophic, more inclined to say
"What difference does it make now?"
He would still be in there fighting
Since his stock in trade remained appointing people
Who related well to him. So at the same time
He would deal with what you'd call
Inconsequential little things and things of massive
Pitch and moment and he'd be watching ticker tapes
And telling people that they had to follow up
On every issue. His capacity for work defied belief,
His range of interests was titanic, from the smallest
To the largest, it was difficult for him to pick out
One thing, save his energies for it as most essential.
He was not what you would call a close technician
Of the details, he left that to other people
Whom he trusted. He could focus on a question though,
He'd really barrel in on it. But he tried to manage
Too much stuff I think although to hear him talk
He delegated huge concerns to others.
He desired to leave his imprint on the world,
The way to do this was appointments,
Putting people in whose vision of the government
Was noble, broad and sweeping,
And he wanted you to bring them to the office

For a talk so he could know what they were thinking,
He believed in some profound sense in bureaucracy,
He'd been in government so long, you needed good people,
He understood their long term impact. So in this sense
He would recognize he couldn't do it all,
But fundamentally…the man was too hardworking,
Never took time off in terms of sheer relaxing,
I'd be with him at the ranch and we'd be swimming
In the pool, but there were people swimming with him,
His assistants, he'd be reading things and issuing
Directives in the water! He worked 24 hour days.
His aspirations were too big, the average person
Could not comprehend what he was throwing at him,
Yet the President could not do otherwise, necessity,
A sense of history devoured him, he didn't want
To be just any ordinary President, and yet
He knew that what he meant to do was going
To lose him his support, he even told us so directly
At the start of 1965, he'd called together people
In the various departments, said now look,
I've just been re-elected as the President,
An overwhelming margin, but you must realize
That my power's going to seep away right soon,
I'm going to lose votes, I will offend someone.
He then took twenty minutes and he lectured us
On history, he showed us how the power leaked away
For other Presidents, for Wilson, FDR,
And so he said about himself,
"I know that something's going to get me,
Vietnam or something else and so
I've got to do this legislation very fast, I'm on
My honeymoon with Congressmen right now."
He understood exactly what his tactics had to be
And he offended certain people with what seemed
To be a rush job, but he knew

That if he didn't get his legislation then,
He probably wouldn't get it ever.
On a day when we'd passed several bills,
This was in April '65 or thereabouts,
We got a call in Mansfield's office
From the President who asked us
"Can't you get another one or two today?"
And if you said you thought you couldn't,
He'd refer to certain bills with all the details,
He would urge them. He was not just setting records
For the sake of setting records, he was conscious
Of the moment which he needed to exploit.

212.

The West possesses military power that cannot be answered.
It projects upon the Asians its own values:
That when threatened with destruction, Asians must be
"men of reason" and surrender. When the "puny little Asians"
Show a readiness to struggle and to die beyond our power
To conceive of, show they are not men of reason…
Well, we could proceed to pummel them, insensate
In our helplessness and rage, make rubble of them.
That's exactly what we hesitate to do of course,
We cannot go quite that far, thus we can't defeat the Asians
Who dispassionately mock us with their apathetic
Persevering natures, thus in Vietnam, both we and they
Are prone to claim we've won a given battle,
This is not mere propaganda, each side's fighting
In the context of opposing expectations, of
A different set of values. We use military might,
We use our wealth to reach impersonal objectives
Like democracy, containment of the Communists.

The enemy is stoically accepting our destruction
Of what wealth he has, the loss of many lives,
He visits violence defiantly upon us, we assume
That he will compromise, capitulate if only we inflict
Sufficient suffering upon him, we assume that pain
And death for him are things to be avoided,
Such assumptions seem self-evident to us
Because we're rich, because we love life,
Want to shun pain. Expectations, though,
Of happiness and wealth don't jibe with Asian
Understanding of the nature of existence.
Death seems different, not so fearsome
When your suffering in this life's unrelieved.
Fulfilling duties in this world and death with honor
Are the passports to a greater share of comfort
When one next returns to earth. The soul advances
Slowly through the trials it undergoes
To longed-for unity with God. This is an attitude
We cannot enter into. Ill-fed, naked Viet Cong
Have gone on record when we've asked them
What will happen if the US heaps on even more
Destruction—bombs, artillery and soldiers.
"We will all die," is their answer. Fatalistic.
Unimpassioned It's an outlook every Westerner
Finds mad. It drives us crazy.

213.

We'd arrived there at the White House very late,
Like at the last minute. He was going from
The White House to the State Department,
Right before he went in for his surgery,
He just grabbed the two of us and sort of

Shoved us in the back seat of his car
With Frederic March and Florence Eldredge.
On the way he kept on telling Frederic March
That over Labor Day I'd visited the ranch,
I'd had a girlfriend, not Mathilde,
As my companion, I had brought another blonde,
Mathilde did not know. This was wild.

214

I had asked to be included in
An "escapade of Johnson" when one happened
Sometime, of the legendary kind,
I had complained to Moyers that I never
Got to see one, that I only heard about them
Sometime after. Moyers called me one day
To the Presidential bedroom, let's say
Summoned me, fulfilling my request,
Told me to hurry. I think Linda Bird
Was in there, I'm sure Lady Bird was present,
And Marie Fehmer who was there
To take dictation in the midst of all this chaos.
Now the President was lying on his side
Up on the bed and he was facing
Toward the group and on the other side
There was a nurse or a masseuse I thought at first.
The three TVs were blaring
And the President was going snap snap snap
With his dictation, he was always switching channels,
He kept yelling things to Bill, and there were others
In the room, there were some network people there
And White House staff and he was yelling
At them too. And every person in that group

Was acting normal, taking all this in their stride.
But I was walking round a little, I was puzzled
By the presence of the nurse. "But can't you see?"
Bill said to me. "I can't see anything," I said,
Which was a slight exaggeration
Since the scene was so damned crowded.
It was dawning on me slowly.
"You had asked to see a good one," Bill continued
In a whisper, "now you've got one,
This is how the man you work for
Has his enemas administered.
He prefers to have a crowd around him always."

215.

In his conduct of the war
He proved the poorest politician
That we've had in modern times
And as the leader of the nation
He could not lead—unlike Wilson,
Unlike Roosevelt and Truman who,
When faced with some reality abroad,
Explained these matters to Americans at home
And led a nation that was unified to war.
To call on the people to offer up their lives,
That is their sons' lives for the nation
Is the ultimate in Presidential genius,
Asking eloquence and wisdom,
Even poetry or magic personality,
But Lyndon Johnson lacked it,
He abysmally mismanaged Vietnam
Which was a cause that no American
Had need to be ashamed of:

The frustration of aggression in a world
Where change by violence was outlawed.
Johnson never could explain this cause
To anyone. The valor of Americans
In Vietnam, denounced as immorality
At home, was not defended by
The President himself, thus it got squandered,
Lyndon Johnson lacked the skill
To give it meaning.

216.

The President (September 26) met with
The Harvard group, 5:46 to 7:10 PM.
He began by saying that he welcomed the chance
To confer with all these people, that their feeling for
The problems "we" were facing was identical to his.
Their spokesman (unidentified) began:
"Our principal concern is that we find
A stable Vietnam solution. We're afraid
That the intensifying air war may be closing
Doors that otherwise we'd see remaining open
While a common slogan circulates: let's simply
Get it over with. But we do not believe
That there's a military way to get it over with.
We believe we must contract what we've been doing
In the North by measured steps along with
Diplomatic offers. Some restriction of the bombing
Is required. What we would like to know is this:
Is there some way that we could help
In thinking through some kind of rational solution
To this conflict?" Which the President replied to
Somewhat lengthily: " There is a great deal

You can do, there's never been a time
When you could help me more
Because your President and the nation need support.
I have stopped the bombing six times.
I have gotten no responses from the North.
We are in touch with Ho Chi Minh this very day.
The problem's not one of conviction.
Ho Chi Minh wants to possess South Vietnam,
He isn't going to give it up.
He doesn't want to talk about it.
We do not want to invade North Vietnam,
We never thought we'd gain a military victory
By doing so. I have recently told Ho
That we would stop all air bombardment
If he'd start negotiations. All this bombing's
A deterrent, it might motivate the North
To start to talk, make them inclined to talk.
But there are two important handicaps I see.
The first I'd call an overzealousness on my part,
Overzealousness for peace. The second handicap's
The enemy who listens to our Senators.
Our dissent makes it appear
That we are forcing our own government
To bow down. When we debate the war's morality,
Hanoi thinks it can win again in Washington
Exactly what it won before in Paris
Back in 1954. So we're the ones who mislead Ho.
I just don't think the North can hold out
Too much longer since they've had
Such heavy losses. We believe the time will come
When they won't have the power to make war
Any longer, when the price will be enough
To make them talk." The spokesman answered
That the group was worried too about dissent,
About the country holding on.

Then the president of Radcliffe (and a lecturer
At Harvard) Mary Bunting said that
Having heard the President and McNamara speak,
She found the whole thing more perplexing,
The alternatives more difficult, the solutions
Being mooted far less promising indeed.
But then she wondered was there some way
They could help. To which the President replied:
"It would help if you could somehow
Put the throttle on extremist types of sentiments.
Your President's in trouble. What this group
Can try to do is somehow cool it for him.
At this moment we have people being used
And they don't know it, people hurting
Their own country." At the end he asked
Some questions: "Is their anyone
Who'd have us just pull out of Vietnam?
Please raise your hands." And no one did.
There was a comment: "Not this group.
We think our interest means we stay there,
Mr. President, we're unanimous on this one,
Not to pull out." "Is there anyone for bombing
Haiphong harbor or Hanoi?" No hand was raised.
Nor was a peep. "Which one of you
Would stop the bombing of the DMZ
Along the line of the position of our men?"
None said they would. One man suggested
That we might move our men back
And out of range and then bomb only
Certain segments of the North.

John Roche wrote a memorandum
To the President the next day:
"Your performance was extraordinary last night.
I almost had to carry them away laid out

On stretchers. Talcott Parsons grabbed my shoulders.
'This has been the greatest experience of my life'
Was all that he could find to say. He looked
Quite stunned. And I must say you shot the gun
Right out of Mary Bunting's hand."

217.

The CIA report said that the peaceniks
Did not constitute one movement, there was
No simple formula, their leaders might have
Communist connections but they are not
Under communist direction.
Since it did not have the evidence he wanted
And expected LBJ refused release of this report
Or any public kind of statement. Gerry Ford
Continued urging him to make one
Since he'd gone out on climb and on the record
In October on the basis of a Presidential briefing
That the march against the Pentagon
Was cranked up in Hanoi.

218.

On Sunday morning he attended church
And then he drove around the demonstration scene.
He wanted to see what the hippies who were left
Looked like—their dress, their sex, their ages,
Bed rolls, blankets, flags and flight bags
And their flowers. A reaction rose
Against the marchers on the Pentagon,
The picketing of government officials

And the clashes with police by draft protestors.
Support has gotten firmer for the President it seems
And for the war in Vietnam.
76 % of the people polled
Felt that the recent demonstrations
Gave encouragement to Communists,
Encouraged Communists to fight harder.
70 % believed the demonstrations
Hurt the cause of opposition to the war.
68% believed the demonstrations
Were disloyal to the boys in Vietnam.

219.

"I'm concerned about the handling of the draft card burners
And the people who are handing in their draft cards."
Rusk responded: "Why not just enforce the law?"
And Wheeler added: "Not enforcing it might lead
To more unrest among the people who obey it."

220.

Of the 256 who have burned their draft cards,
A substantial number were crazy, they had
Histories with mental institutions,
This was proven by the FBI reports.
I don't want to start to sound like Joe McCarthy,
But I'd say the country's in some kind of trouble.

221.

I will not let the Commies take this government.
They're doing it right now, the movement's
Communist-controlled and so 200,000
Trouble makers ruin it for all the other people.
Let me say I've got my belly full of seeing them
On Commie planes and shipped across this country.
I have got to know what people leave this country,
Where they go and if they're going to Hanoi
How do we keep them from returning.

222.

I began to ask around, I made inquiries of people,
In the State Department sometimes, I would ask
Assistant secretaries their views, there was Shoup
Of the Marines, one night I asked him
At the Army Engineers Club, we were down there
Playing poker, I said "General, this war in Vietnam
Has got me bitterly upset, I wonder
Am I on the right side of the arguments about it?"
He surprised me with his answer:
"I have just resigned, my book is coming out,
It tells you why we shouldn't be in Vietnam."
A few nights later we had supper
And he told me all his reasons.
I received a phone call one time, it's a fellow,
From the CIA, he tells me
"I would like to have you come
And meet some friends of mine,
They're bitterly opposed to this damned war."
I went for supper, he had seven guys

Or eight guys there, I asked them
Why they'd sent for me. The CIA guy said
"We hear you're studying the war
From every angle, that you might just change
The ground on which you stand."
"That's very interesting. How do you guys know that?"
Was my answer. "We have methods," he replied.
"OK then, tell me why you think you want to see me."
"We take Presidential messages, Administration
Viewpoints to the CIA agents all around
The world. Those agents give us back reports,
Like who's against the war, just why
They are opposed. We know our messages
Don't ever reach the Presidential desk,
He never hears us." "I just simply
Can't believe that," was my first response,
"But even if it's true, why talk to me?"
"Because you're closer than the rest to John McCormack."
"I'm as close to John McCormack as is anybody maybe.
I can say I think we understand each other
Since the districts that we represent abut.
But to bring your opposition to the war
To John McCormack—it's ridiculous,
He wouldn't even entertain such talk,
I might as well go bang my head against a wall."
I think I probably told John about my supper
With these agents for the record. What a waste of time.
The agents, though, had gotten through to me,
My mind was changing. Then in June of '67
We were visiting our daughter, she was in
The Foreign Service based on Malta,
We were eating in a restaurant, this place
Was really swarming with Marines who filled
The cocktail bar, these guys came from
The naval base we had there, one came over

To our table, "You're a Congressman
From my state, I'm from Woods Hole."
I agreed with that for starters, then I grilled
This guy since he and all his buddies
Were returning from the war and they
Were totally disgusted. "We can't shoot
Until we're shot at, I've been there for 19 months
And I'll be damned if I can tell you why we're fighting,
What we're fighting." That was his view.
Malta then was in the Commonwealth,
The governor from Britain threw a party
And the admiral of the US fleet was there.
He kicked the hell out of the war:
"We shouldn't be in it, there's no attempt
To win, the only way that we can win
Is by invasion of the North and all the power plants
In Hanoi have to go and we should also mine the coast.
You've got to shut the Chinese railroad off.
Supply lines. This is crazy, we will never
Win the war, we ought to get out."
This stuff gnawed at me, I finally
Sent a letter to the people of my district
Who were pretty much divided,
I announced to them the change in my position,
Nothing wild-eyed, get the UN more involved
And stop the bombing. It was strange,
No Boston paper ever picked up on the story,
It went under all the radars, then
A *Washington Star* reporter just was cruising
Through the room where they were printing up
The letters to my district, picked an old one
Off the floor that had my new position in it.
"Gee, has no one ever used this stuff?" he asked.
That afternoon there was a story on the front page
Of the *Star*. That night I went out for my poker game

The way I went out almost every night when I was here
In Washington, it kept me out of trouble.
So I came back home at maybe 1 AM,
I parked my car in our garage, I came upstairs
And Eddie Boland, whom I shared the house with,
Asked me where the hell I'd been, he'd called
All over. I said "What for?"
"Well, the White House must have called here
Twenty times and there's a Secret Service agent
Downstairs sitting in the office, how did you
Come in the house?" I said I came through the garage,
Then Eddie said, "The Secret Service guy is waiting,
You're supposed to call the White House,
And it doesn't matter how late you've come home."
"Yeah, what about?" I said. "You mean you didn't see
The Star? My God, the President is wild."
I called the White House and they told me
That the President would see me in the morning,
9 o'clock, so I went down there, 9 o'clock
And then the President began:
"You know I've known you since the first day
You arrived here, you've been friends with
John McCormack, I made sure that you
Were also friends with Rayburn, introduced you
To the Board of Education. John McCormack
Brought you there too. I expect this kind of talk
Of opposition from the Ryans and a few like them—
The assholes—but when someone who has been as close
As you have starts to leave me..."
"Hey, Mr. President," I told him, "I've been studying
The problem. I just think you're wrong, I feel
I have to change." "And so you think that you know more
About this war than I do, I get briefed six times a day.
You think that I don't roll and toss all night
And think about the kids that I've sent over there,

Their lives?" "Hey, Mr President, I've studied this
Completely, I have talked to different people
Who advise you, they may even go along with you,
But they also tell me that you're wrong, what is a man
Supposed to do?" "So you believe it in your heart,
You think I'm wrong." I said I did believe it deeply,
In my heart. He said that answer made him glad,
'cause if he thought that I was doing this for politics,
To please the academics in my district...
"Hey, Mr. President," I said, "you've got the wrong guy.
Academics in my district don't support me,
I'm elected in the back street. I'm just feeling
In my heart and in my mind that we can't win
This war we're fighting, we're not aiming for a win,
Why are we over there and no one gives us help,
There's loss of life..." and I went on
Along the whole route in discussion. He assured me
He'd be studying those CIA reports when they came in
Since I had told him what those agents
Had complained of. Then he said
That he was happy that I did it, but he asked me
For a favor: "Make no statements to the press
Because you know that I think I'm right,
You think you're right. I'm afraid
We have a snowball getting started,
I don't want this thing to gather much momentum.
You're a part of the establishment,
When you leave everyone may start to leave,
And you are wrong." And I said
"Gee, I'm only speaking for myself, not any others."
I met later with a member of the White House staff
For liaison with Congress, I assured him,
Was at great pains to assure him as a Democrat
That if I'd known how much importance
My announcement in that letter to constituents would have,

I would have never let it out because the President to me
Was like a brother that I loved...

223.

If my first trip there convinced me
We were doing what was right,
I'd say my second trip unsettled me profoundly.
Americanization of the war was now complete,
We had taken over everything, their whole economy,
The conduct of the war. And Thieu's
Inaugural address was largely written by our embassy,
The puppeteering string pulls went that far,
It was a joke.

I see reasons for our feeling very satisfied
And even optimistic, we must find some way
To publicize the picture for the people
Back at home and help them better understand it.
I am certain that our country can be mobilized
To get behind the U.S. efforts here
Because we're winning. I see evidence
Of slow but steady progress, more than ever
I'm convinced that what we're dong here is right
And that the only choice we have is perseverance.
We must see our efforts through till they're successful.

From what I know and what I see here
I would say we're in the very deepest trouble,
We are throwing lives and money
Down a rat hole—a corrupt one.

I just hope these people know what they've been up to,

I'm damned certain we're not doing anybody
Any good, Vietnamese and us included.
We are murdering civilians by the thousands
And our boys are dying out in rotten jungles
And for what? A rotten government
That's totally amoral.
I plan to tell all this to Johnson,
Just exactly what I think, I simply
Hope and pray he'll take it like I give it.

I can report that pacification's moving forward,
We're taking action to eliminate corruption,
The morale of US troops is very high,
The ARVN troops are much improved
And the election has produced a good effect.
On my last trip I came back from there impressed.
After this one I can say that I'm encouraged.

What's our objective out there?

Well, before you build a country,
You must put down the insurgency.
Many Asian leaders tell me that the enemy
Is communism—militant—that's centered in Peking.

Is our enemy the North Vietnamese or is it China?

Well, the South Vietnamese know who's their enemy.
Those boys out there are being maimed and shot at,
They don't find it very difficult
To recognize their enemy at all.

224.

At all practical costs we should avoid involving
Any US forces in an Indochina war,
But if the makers of our policy determine
No alternative exists to such involvement,
We should not then be self-duped into believing in
The chance of our involvement being partial,
"air and naval units only," some scenario like that.
You can't go over Niagara Falls in a barrel only slightly.
If we determine that we ought to send in
Air and naval forces, it is difficult to see how sending
Ground troops in could ever be avoided.
Air strength to be sufficient would require big bases.
Protection of such bases and of ports would call
For ground troop personnel, and once that force
Had been committed we would have to have
Ground combat units in there for the case of any
Swift evacuation that was needed. We must
Clearly understand that there is no cheap, no restricted
Way to fight this kind of war once you're committed.

225.

It was 1936 and '37 and the early part of 1938,
I'd have been in junior high school, I had asthma
All that time though, other problems with my health
Those problems kept me out of school and I've been living
Off of what I learned at that time all my life
Because I stayed at home, I kept up with my
School work pretty well, and at the end
Of each semester I would take these tests

And pass them. At the same time I read everything
You could read on our government in Washington,
And I would listen to the radio, to every kind
Of commentator on there, you had Washington,
You also had the European situation roiled up,
War was coming. I was juiced up to the eyebrows
On that stuff when I was still in junior high school
And I stayed juiced, I knew everything
When Johnson started talking, reminiscing,
I picked up on every reference— mention
Zioncheck, I knew who that man was—
I knew the nuances of Garner's going home
Because he said he wasn't going back
To Washington again—he never did go back in fact—
But I knew all that stuff, I also knew the different slogans,
I knew all the minor actors of the dramas
Of the New Deal—those minute details
That I knew from being stuck beside the radio
At home, it was a freak, a kind of accident—
But all this was the stuff, you know,
Of Lyndon Johnson's life, he was a young man,
He was here, and he was deeper into all these things
Than I was, he was right here in the middle of it,
Fascinated always in a small town, maybe boyish
Sort of way, he knew significance, what things
Were aberrations, what were not. And from
The episodes in those days, some quotation
Always spun off, I could cite you those quotations,
I would recognize them. This was how we built up
Our rapport since I was versed in all those things
That were so meaningful to him, were still alive
To him, the days of his hot youth, here was
This fellow in the corner of his office he could
Sit with and relive all this, he was almost

Like a cow that needed milking, this encyclopedic
Side of him was crying for release
And you could say I was the puller of the teat.

Well, he fell into a pattern as the leader of our office,
He'd come in, he'd shout around, the whole damned atmosphere
When he was in the office was electric—
This was all through his career—then he
Would suddenly grow calm and he would either
Call me up or he'd call Mary, maybe Walter—
"Send Buzz in"—and so I'd go, he'd make
Some pretense of a reason why he'd called me,
He would say have you read such and such
Or I just promised so and so that you would call him.
But it always turned out somehow he'd go back
Upon his life, back to the Thirties, now he seemed
To see the Thirties as the good time, well before
He got elected to the Senate—Johnson rising—
And I got wrapped up for him with that good time,
I was the youngest of his boys, I guess the last one
Who had entered in the good time — as it was
I barely made it in before the gate got shut.
I was eight or nine years old when FDR
Became the President. I had picked up on him
In Chicago at the Democrats' convention.
FDR was up against a man from Texas,
My whole family was in favor of the man
From Texas, as you'd figure, there I was
In this environment and pullin' for the other fellow.
I was tuned in to the nominating speeches.
The excitement of the radio was something
Back in those days, just to hear them say
In signing off: "This broadcast has been heard
From coast to coast," it was a thrill, it gave me
Goose bumps, he was flying in from Albany,

They would interrupt the music, local programs,
To inform us that a farmer out in Daytonsville, Ohio
Heard the plane of FDR as it flew over.
It was a stormy day, the candidate should not have
Even flown in those conditions, all reports of him
Were crackling with suspense, and someone else would say
They'd heard the plane fly over, they'd report that,
It would touch down for refueling, it would take off,
Then you'd get some more reports.
Well, I was glued to this, and then I listened to his speech.

But to return to Lyndon Johnson, these spells
Of reminiscence fits that he'd fall into.
He would stage these little shows, a one man theater
Of sorts, it was his means of self-expression,
He was using it as late as in the White House.
He'd enlist me in these shows though,
I should not have called it one man,
I came in one day, I think this was a Saturday.
Now Saturdays for his staff were disastrous.
Every other office emptied out at noon,
The staff went home, but Johnson's boys—
He didn't see them as employees, he considered them
Co-equals, he assumed that they were dying
Just to stay there with him on into the evening,
Even Sunday. It was hell on any social life
You dreamed of. So he called me in this Saturday
And maybe Mary Rather, Walter Jenkins
Came with letters. He was building up to something
I could tell 'cause he was real tall at his desk
And seemed expansive, then when they came in,
He barked at them severely and announced
Some kind of damned fool rule that wasn't in effect,
You had to knock before you came in bearing letters
Like a shot across their bow: "Don't interrupt me!"

This was LBJ in prima donna mode, he was performing
Or preparing to. "You're close to history."
That phrase was like a leit-motif through all the years
I knew him since it summed up where he
Always meant to be, he even used that word
When he referred to Dallas once—which was sure god
Just about as close to history as anyone could think of.
He'd regale me with this repertoire of stories—
Close to history—young Lyndon—one was
FDR's inaugural address, how he was down there
At he Capitol to hear it, on the steps
Of the Supreme Court, he was hearing
That majestic voice again, he first had heard it
At the Democrats' convention back in 1928,
He was in Houston, he had bribed a kid
Who was a doorkeeper, he had bribed that kid
To let him have his job or some such thing,
So he was standing in the door, this great voice came,
It reached inside him, set him trembling.
I had first thought that this must have been a put-on,
This whole story seemed too good, but then
I talked once to a Roosevelt old-timer who assured me
That "the boss" had been the only speaker
Delegates could hear, this was the happy warrior speech,
In '28, we just don't realize what a difference
Public speaker systems made when they came in.
But getting back to Johnson's being close to history:
He liked to cast himself in humble little roles,
Some silent witness, no one knew that he was there,
But he was taking it all in, he said he'd once seen FDR
When he was on his way to veto some big thing,
It was the bonus for the veterans I think,
It was the Presidential kind of resolution
That had impressed this young man Lyndon,

Just the jawline and the way he set his face.
He had this presidential model set before him.

But to get back to this opera he was staging
For his office staff or rather just for me—
The closest brush with history he said he'd ever had
Up to a certain point at least—it was the afternoon
Of April 12 in 1945, he was a young man
But he'd wangled him the privilege
Of going to the little private office
Speaker Rayburn had, the Board of Education
Some folks called it though on Johnson's staff
We always just referred to it as number two-five-two
Which was the number that you dialed
To ring the phone there. He was with Rayburn
And I forget who else was there this day
To start with as he played this drama out for me,
He came around his desk, he fetched
A straight wood chair for me, he put that chair
Behind his desk, back in the corner, "You sit there,"
He said to me, I didn't know who I was playing yet
In Lyndon's little drama. Then he moved me,
It was not quite time for me to play my part yet,
Because he took that wooden chair and he sat down
In it himself as he was playing young man Lyndon,
He was sipping on a drink, he'd nod his head
And he'd be talking to the people in the room,
"Yes, Mr. Speaker, Mr. Chairman, Mr. Senator,"
But then he suddenly jumps up and goes back over
To his desk, he tells me now to go and sit down
On that wood chair in the corner, I assume
I'm playing him, young Lyndon Johnson.
Then the door opens, the imaginary door,
The Board of Education door. Who was this person

Walking in? Well, soon we knew 'cause LBJ
Was playing Rayburn now, he stood up and he said,
"Come on in, Harry. Hell, you're late."
So Johnson's coming through the door, he's playing
Harry Truman now, so in a whisper then he tells me
I should stand up, so I stood up. "Harry"
Went around and he was shaking hands
With every person in the room including me
And then he sat down in his chair right next to mine.
Now Johnson acting as the Speaker says
"Can I get you a drink?" Then he goes back
To being Truman: "Hell yes, why else do you think
I came to join you boys?" And then he laughed
And went on talking, looked at me and said,
"Well Lyndon, how has your day gone?"
It wasn't up to me to answer, Johnson answered
For himself, he re-assumed the role of Lyndon,
My big role was ripped right from me.
If this seems hard to follow now, just think
How hard it was for me to follow then,
Six weeks before I'd been in Austin,
Now I found myself caught up in this strange drama,
But you have to understand, this stuff
Was real for him, he'd lived it, it was not
Some thing he'd gotten from a textbook, he was
Steeped in it more deeply than an expert of the era,
Lyndon Johnson was the textbook.
He was playing Harry Truman and himself.
To myself I feel I'm only like a prop to him,
But suddenly he orders me to stand up
And to move that wooden chair toward him,
He edged it up and seemed to sort of calibrate
The distance with his arm bent at the elbow
Till he said "That's fine, right there." It was important
For the story that the distance be just right

As he remembered it. But then he jumped back up
And he's across the room as Rayburn
And the phone rings and he's saying
"It's the White House calling, Harry."
He jumps back across the room and then he's Truman
Once again. "I wonder what they want with me."
And he went over to the phone as Harry Truman.
"I'll be right there." Then he turns and says to Rayburn,
"Sam, the White House wants me now, I got to go there."
"All right, Harry. You come back in here tomorrow though,
You hear?" Then Johnson motioned me to stand up,
But then he spoke my line for me of course.
"Bye bye, see you tomorrow, Mr. Vice-President."
He was a stickler then for titles.
He would not have called him "Harry."
You cannot believe how caught up in this drama
He'd become as he enacted it for me,
I wouldn't say that he was crying,
But his eyes looked moist to me as he
Was summing up the moral of the story:
"Just think, son, such a tiny little distance,
That's how close I was to Truman when the wheel turned,
That's as close as any man can get to History."
He played this whole thing twice for me that year,
It seemed to mean so much to him, it was as if
He'd been entranced. But it seems strange
Or almost eerie that he later got a call like that
From History himself.

226.

God knows how very little we have moved things
On this issue all the fanfare notwithstanding.

To a C-, up from D+ if we're lucky, if we're honest.
That's about as far as anyone can say I've moved
The Negro while in office, he's still nowhere
And he knows it, that's the reason why
He's out there in the streets—hell,
I'd be out there in the streets if I was him.

227.

...Unbelievable and futile.

Rusk and Rostow think the enemy
Got beaten very badly during Tet.
No U.S. units got knocked out of operation.
Rostow says a certain document we captured
Shows the enemy as deeply disappointed.
Rusk reminds us that the enemy
Lost 40,000 men, and if we
Reinforce Westmoreland right away
He should be able to control things till
The advent of improvement in the weather
When we'll bomb them.

We delude ourselves to think North Viet Nam
Won't keep up pressure after better weather comes.
We're dropping ordnance now, the rate
Exceeds the rate at which we dropped it
During World War II in Europe near the end.
It hasn't stopped them.

We should cut back our commitment,
Just protect essential areas,
Not every district capital and province.

Let's consider an announcement:
We are putting in 500,000 men,
Perhaps as many as a million.
I'm not pushing this.

The virtue then of clarity at least
Would be achieved, that we were
Putting in the men to do the job.
Two hundred thousand five would have
No point, it's not enough, nor does it show
Our role must change.

I've heard reports that this request for
Two oh five is being argued over fiercely
In Saigon among our leaders.

I've repeatedly been honoring
Requests from all the Wheelers of the world—
Two hundred five—there's no assurance
That they'll make a bit of difference.
They may not even be enough to win.
There is no military plan to win the war.

Putting optimistic estimates aside
I think the people in our country
And the world think we have suffered
Major setbacks. There's a problem
How we're going to get support
For bigger programs, economic
And defense, if we've been telling
Our own people things are going
Very well there. How do we
Avoid suspicions that we're pounding
All our troops straight down some rathole?
What's our purpose? What's achievable?

We must re-think our position in the South
Before we make some new position or deployment.
But the President's sequestered at the ranch
With all the hawks—opposed to re-
Evaluation. Who will set forth all the doubts
We've been exploring? McNamara's
Not convinced that some large buildup
Of our forces in the South will do much good.
There are the moral consequences to consider,
Not to mention military, diplomatic.

Und so weiter.

We were both of us completely drained and shaken
As we drove back to the White House.

It really is all over don't you think?

You bet it is. The whole thing's crazy.

228.

It simply isn't working. It's disastrous.
We must find some way to get out of
This war. We must be watchful for some sign
The war is winding up again, not winding down.
In World War II "prevail we will" was working
Since we had the right conditions. Now we don't.

229.

Humphrey, who was then the Senate whip, remembered
Finding it impossible to move one of his colleagues,
This man wouldn't even talk about his vote for civil rights
And so the President asked Hubert
Did his colleague's mistress know of his position
Or his lack of one. "I didn't even know
He had a mistress," Hubert answered.
"She's the reason he won't talk about his vote,
Sonofabitch, since he's been screwin' with
A nigra woman lo these many years."
Whereat old Hubert sort of blanched.
"I didn't know." "Where is the Senator right now?"
"He's on the floor." "Make sure he stays there."
So the Senator got summoned to the cloakroom
For a phone call moments later.
Hubert stood where he could overhear him
Talking—at the President's suggestion.
Hubert never would have made so bold himself.
"I simply can't, dear, you must try to understand."
Was what the Senator was saying to begin with.
Then a couple minutes later: "Well,
I wasn't quite aware how much
This subject meant to you."
So Hubert knew he now had one more precious vote.

230.

"Unzip your fly," he said, "there's nothing there.
John McClellan cut your dick off with a razor.
It was so sharp that you didn't even notice."

231.

The Communists are plotting to destroy us overall.
It is a real and present danger, no less present
Than the plumbing or the furnace or the ice box
Going bad. It's a continuum,
You have the streets now being un-safe,
There are the strikes, there are the problems
With the colored, you have people taking dope,
You have the young folk leaving churches,
It's a breakdown of our standards pure and simple,
Of the way of life we've had and always should have.

232.

Marines were out there wounded in the trees
And screaming, fighting for their lives.
And our chief corpsman tried to leave the camp
And help them, but we had to hold him back,
We could not spare him. Damn near
Cried himself to death. When I would comment
That the battlefield behavior of our troops
Was by exception one thing admirable
To my mind in the conduct of the war,
She all but snorted: "That's mere loyalty
Of buddies, they're not fighting for a reason,
They're just out there and of course
They fight for friends. It's mere male bonding.
What's so admirable in that?"

233.

Now you take you some big sack,
You put your LBJ inside it,
Then you put your Hubert Humphrey in the sack with him,
And don't forget to put in RFK beside 'em both—
That's Little Bobby—then you adds you Richard Nixon
Who with Eisenhower ordered that the bayonets
Be brandished out in Little Rock,
Be stuck in people's backs, good decent people,
And you throw into the mix our fine
Chief Justice Mr. Warren, who don't have
The legal brains to try a chicken thief where I'm from,
Then you shake 'em up together,
Then for seasoning you toss in Nelson Rockefeller,
Socialist and governor of the country's
Most far-out and left-wing state
And then George Romney, also left-wing,
He was out there in the streets to show
He understood the demonstrators' wishes,
Wild Bill Scranton from the state of Pennsylvania,
Clifford Case another wild man from New Jersey,
Then a pinch of Jacob Javits, he's another
New York radical to watch for, mix them all up,
Turn the sack around and see who pops out first,
You pick him straight up by the neck scruff,
Drop him right back in that sack,
It doesn't matter who it is, they's not
One thin dime's worth of difference
In the lot of them, the national
Approved brand politicians.

234.

The zones the V.C. penetrate
Become like Harlem streets--you know,
The kind where when a cop walks
By himself, not in a group,
He gets gunned down along some alley.
When the reinforcements come,
They find a sea of staring faces,
Nobody knows of course what happened,
Nobody heard the sound of shooting.
Here in 'Nam what they deny
Is knowing any Viet Cong,
They've never seen one.

235.

—Sooner or later we will force them to the table,
We can't win an all-out war.
—But if we put 100,000 men in, won't they match that?
—Not if we step up our bombing.
—Do we want to take this chance?
—If you consider the alternatives, I'd say yes sir, we do.
It's get out now or pour more men in.
—Nothing else?—I think our allies
Might lose faith in us if we start pulling out.
—But I'd say few enough of those who are
Allied with us are helping out right now.

236.

There was a steady give-in to the pressure for
A military answer, only minimal sporadic efforts made
To find political or diplomatic answers to the problems
Since civilians were confused and couldn't tell you
Their objectives or suggest a cogent strategy,
These men were inarticulate. But then you also had
The self-enlarging nature of the military tactic.
Once you sent more ground troops in,
You needed air strikes to protect them,
Then you had to send more troops in after that
To keep the bombers' bases safe, it all just mushroomed.
And the military gains its own momentum
In the absence of directions from civilians.
Asked to save South Vietnam, not just advise it,
There was no way that the military wasn't going to press
For escalation. Once involved in Vietnam,
The different branches of the service ground their axes,
Proved their cases: not just fly power as important
Which the Air Force was prepared to warble
Descants on, extol ad infinitum, but supercarrier-
Based aircraft which the Navy hummed as its tune,
As its burden to the Air Force. But it wasn't
Just the jostling of the military branches—this was crazy—
Since Bob McNamara really seemed to rope
The rampant military in, you had the Pentagon
Controlled now by civilians, fancy that,
But in the face of this control a unanimity arose
Among the military factions, no more split JCS votes,
They would present united fronts on major issues,
In conjunction with their allies in the Congress
(Southern Senators, those moss backs) they presented
LBJ with one titanic bloc most difficult to move
Or get around, they had become a kind of

Flying wedge or phalanx, no mere President, one person
After all, could hope to muscle them aside.

237.

"We need those Polish votes to get Milwaukee.
The Senator's not campaigning in the core, that is the ghetto,
Or the Poles will think he's going soft on Negroes."
There were angry shouts of "Back to the Resistance!"

"Every single establishment in America's against me."
That a Kennedy should say this...

"The trouble with McCarthy is he thinks he's Jesus Christ.
And the union men felt threatened by the arrogant assertion
That the young and his well-educated people
Ought to rule the USA. That sort of shit
Works very well for conning money out of rich dames
Sporting saggy tits in sweaters,
But real politics it isn't."

"If he wants to win it, let him go ahead
And fight that war, let him keep
Sending all his son in laws and such like.
Just don't go start sendin' me, Jack,
I aint even got no job, what kind of stake
You think I got in fightin' Cong?"

238

With rising expectations we just cannot have these demagogues.
This country's quickly going off the tracks, we can't afford

This type of shouting, ranting prophet who assures us that
The promised land lies there across a rubble heap
Of looted, burnt out cities, we cannot afford
The type of politician who demands a tripled pay out rate
Of benefits to seniors, who advises that the duty which
We owe to Viet Nam be cast away to pay for
Make-work welfare programs in the slums of U.S. cities.
We can't let the draft be flouted. Negroes must obey the law.
We must discourage all this talk of free lunch handouts.

239.

The war in Viet Nam becomes
Increasingly unpopular the bigger it keeps
Getting, as our casualties increase—
There is a fear it's growing wider,
That the deprivations here at home
Will worsen, there's distress
At how much suffering we're visiting
On all the non-combatants
In the South and in the North
And most Americans can't figure
How we got to where we are
And with the benefit of hindsight,
Not sure why, they are convinced
We should have never gotten in
Or not this deeply. They all want
The war to end and they're expecting
That the President will end it.
End successfully. Or else.

240.

I laughed each time I thought
Of Senator Fulbright's phrase "the arrogance of power,"
Which may well apply to some in Viet Nam
Who still believe that we can throw the conflict our way
By our military force or by the weight of our
Assistance programs multiplied
By hundreds or by thousands.
But I think of some poor major
In his fly-specked little shack
In Binh Chanh province as he wonders how
To get his advisee to, for a change, do something useful.
Where's the arrogance of power in that picture?
Power's endless limitations are the lesson
One keeps learning all the time.

241.

There is one way we might start to get some change up there in Harlem,
If we made those Wall Street bankers ride in cars through Harlem
streets,
Both ways each day, to see the poverty first hand instead of
Sailing past above it in those air-conditioned train cars, just discussin'
How much money they've been makin' while they sip the next martini.

242.

The businessmen were quite right to suspect him
Since at heart he was a populist.
If he ever had the chance to put the knife into
A businessman, he took it, that was something

He could simply not pass up,
Was irresistible to him.
You must remember one key fact:
The sons of the wild jackass
Might at any time rear up in Lyndon Johnson.

243.

We cannot rebuild our cities
If we do not squarely face the isolation of the poor.
Bringing industry back to central cities is important,
We must generate new jobs, make sure
That Negroes can be hired.
But the central cities aren't enough alone.
There are too many people, there is
Insufficient land there, jobs and housing
Aren't enough to meet the need.
It's paternalism offering these programs
For the ghettoes by themselves
Because the crisis of the ghetto is connected
With the crisis of society *in toto.*
Private enterprise could help
To fix our cities, I do not mean to deny that,
Certain factories, a few more jobs result,
But then the ghetto's still a colony,
It will retain its economic and political
Dependence if its citizens are closed out
From society at large, cannot participate,
Break through. And private programs
Meant for rehab of the ghettoes
Leave in limbo our commitment to
Completing integration. Rehabilitation
Financed by a profit-making entity

From outside can become paternalistic.
We must attack the problem at its roots.
We must furnish modern transportation systems
Or how else can ghetto unemployed reach jobs
Beyond the outskirts of our cities?
It should not take three hours each day
There and back to get from Watts out to the airport
For a job that's there in theory for a black man
Who does not possess a car.
We have to implement reports that recommend
Six million units of new housing,
And the people who will occupy these units
Ought to have the chance to build them.

244.

The welfare system starting to erode the self-respect
Of mountain people. They're dispirited and whipped
As men lose jobs to automation in the mines.
West Virginia redivivus for the President in 1964.
He could not appear to make the right connections
With the voters on the issue of the poor.
He would have needed to compare the mountaineers
With urban Negroes since most poor folk
In the USA were white. He scheduled visits.
Photo ops with urban Negroes and with miners
In the mountains were proposed.
"I wouldn't do that, Mr. President," said Scammons.
"You won't get one extra vote by doing anything
For poor folks. Those who vote among them
Vote for you already." This caught Kennedy's
Attention. "I was thinking more of photographs
In cities with policemen." "You should go out

To the shopping malls on highways
Since the voters you'll be needing, I mean
Your folks, men with lunch pails,
They're all moving to the suburbs."
Information with a purpose
Was what Kennedy was after and esteemed.
The new mobility, the rural Southern Negroes
Coming North to live in cities, Catholic
Democrats removing to the suburbs now concerned
With how their property got taxed, how bonds
Got issued for their sewers. JFK
Closed in on one thing: if a Democrat
Began to make more money and was moving
To the suburbs, at what level might he
Start to vote Republican in 1964?
"It might be below 10,000," Scammons told him.
"I'll find out and let you know."
This was November 13, 1963.

245.

It began with conversation, senior officers describing
How heroically the pilots had performed.
But some lieutenant with an Irish name broke in
Or rather asked first for permission to
Contribute, which was granted.
What then followed was a furious assault
Against the bombing. All the men
Were being asked he said to fly through
Inconceivably effective antiaircraft zones
To strike at lists of targets which meant nothing.
"I've hit the same damned wooden bridge
Three times and they rebuild it.

I have flown through SAMs, through flak
And automatic weapons fire to hit
That measly bridge and in the meantime
I've seen goddamned Russian freighters
Sitting untouched and supplies stacked up
The length and breadth of wharves
Which I can't hit for fear of widening the war.
The war's too wide for me right now.
And idiotic." I of course knew
That the President was next door
In a stateroom and could hear this conversation.

246.

Silver and heavy glass wink out, the walnut-
Paneled bulkheads, the upholstered leather
Armchairs of a men's club with its humidors,
The officers and gentlemens' ideal
Within the limits which the Navy somehow
Manages to make this--it's like jousting--
Every day they touch the napkins to their mouths,
Unstated elegance almost and they go forth
Like knights of olden times, our nation's
Finest products, hang their hides out
Over Haiphong's SAMs, skeet-shooters,
Then return home to this club, its muffled
Finery, its Filipino waiters in their crisply starched
White jackets--unreal contrasts--
Could it ever get so bad, though,
That you'd literally start to lose complete control
And end up shitting in your pants?—
The standing joke was it's your laundryman
Who knows and only he, some little humper

Deeply buried in the bosom of the ship
Who knows for certain, has your number,
Undercutting knightly pretence--
Still they touch the unstained napkin
To their lips and sally forth, half blind
They ride the shrieking beast into the grey pearl--
Fire the catapult, you're off,
No turning back now, as a seaman on a catwalk
Hits the button, throws both hands up
In the air, that rather hopeless-looking gesture.
Just before he starts the big ride, though,
Full afterburn, explosion, in an exquisite
Refinement of correctness, just before
He grabs the stick to keep control,
The pilot throws him a salute, a raffish
Gentlemanly wrist roll debonairly
Which depending on conditions of the day
He might just top off with an upraised
Middle finger--he's entitled--
Lest absurdity go unacknowledged too.

The SAMs come up, the boys go down,
This is the next heave as they ride above
The river, SAMs were locked in on your plane
Or someone else's plane by radar,
They were coming up at Mach 3,
There was no way to avoid them
But by diving--diving brought you
Down so low though, into skeet range
Of the flak which seemed unerring,
Call it flying through a rain storm
While attempting not to hit a single drop.
And there were bomb-free zones,
Our government's attempt
To make the war in Vietnam seem more humane,

No hitting villages or churches or the harbor
If a foreign ship was docked there--
So of course they welded foreign ships
To docks in Haiphong harbor
And they stuffed the churches full-up
With munitions, made them arsenals.
To cut the harbor in Haiphong off
We were not allowed to mine it,
Just blow docks up, something simple--no--
We had to sever bridges like a surgeon,
Make our bomb runs through
Some fricking needle's eye--but this
Was futile, they'd just move the stuff
By barge across the water
Till the bridges got re-built.
What did it matter? No one ever gave us
Credit for discretion though the whole world
Snapped up stories of American atrocities
Regardless of the facts, the more
We stretched ourselves to keep civilians safe
The more they branded us as butchers
And the one time that they really
Turned us loose to do the job right,
When we tore that place apart,
The iron Triangle, a vital transport center
For the North--we ripped its gullet--
We got reamed next by *The New York*
Fucking Times for our atrocities,
The New York Times got taken by the North,
Became the mouthpiece of the North,
Were spouting VC propaganda--
War atrocities my ass!--it was a model
Operation for the North which we knocked out.
The North does not need any SAMs,
They've got *The New York Times* in their court.

The collapsing of United States morale
Was only happening at home,
You had the people getting brainwashed.
"Bill C. got it over Ha-Tinh, body
Bloody on the ground." Try taking that in.
In the face of which heroically we fight on,
Getting hobbled by restrictions
While the homeland we're defending's
Gotten flabby, turned defeatist.
We run great hops notwithstanding.
We came right down on the "Drive-In"
Christmas day and there were Charlies
Using Christmas day, the ceasefire
As a chance to move their baggage,
Quite amazing, traffic stacked up at
The ferry, people there could not have moved
If they'd been sure that I was going to
Open fire on them, they craned their necks
And stared in slow suspense, I could have
Chucked them by the chin hairs,
All those old guys wearing pantaloons
Looked up, they never let go of their wagons,
They seemed nailed to them, the wagons
Were so loaded up with shells
You didn't see how all those spindly old guys
Pulled them, they were jammed up with
The bicycles and trucks though, old cars,
Rigs of every sort, whatever rolled.
I should distinguish: Christmas day
I'd call a good hop, it revealed to me
A subset of the war, a little slice.
To say a hop's great calls for elements
Of jousting, sporting form to be precise,
One must avoid imperious death.
But once you had a hundred missions

On your resumé, you'd reached
The higher zone, the almost mystic
Sweet communion, some fraternity
Of those select few guys who really
Had it though we couldn't say what
"It" was, they had cut their ties
To ordinary mortals back on earth,
They'd gone through chambers
To the Castle of the absolute absurd...
The things they'd seen...that day we'd
Closed in on the target with the clouds
So thick they couldn't see the ships
In their own wing, the grey ghost
Loomed up, drifting straight across their path,
The smoke was pouring from the cockpit
And enveloping the fuselage that spinned,
The pilot cobbing it to try to reach the water
Where the rescue planes could save him,
But you knew he'd never make it, you had
Looked him in the eye for that one instant,
He'd implored you, then he'd vanished,
Sucked away, and though you knew the gunners
Down below now really had your number,
Dead aim fixed on your formation,
You continued to your target in a trance,
You had the brotherhood to face
When all was lost, you had the game
To still succeed at, never mind
Your sense of duty, love of country--
Love of sport was what impelled you,
You would hang your hide above the deep
Each day, then you would get up,
Hang it out again the next day, never
Question this succession, each new next day,
Every morning when you rolled out of the bed

In your nice stateroom, these components
Of the high-low game you'd play that day
Were lighting up your mind and you
Would calculate the fitness of your soul,
The stuff your bowels produced told all--
Haruspication--diarrhea was the worst sign
You could have, bespoke soul-sickness,
There was one sign worse than that, though:
If you vomited or someone else
Should vomit, you might hear him
Several stalls down in the head,
You'd wonder who, but it was better
Not to know, he might be riding
On your wing and this was all about
Maintaining your demeanor, saving face,
It was your laundryman who knew,
That little humper. Still the *sprezzatura*
Called for when you brought your aircraft
Back to deck shot up remained a grand thing
If you managed to maintain it,
"Check that stabilizer, will you,
I believe we caught a bit of flak, old chap."
Désinvolture. The gagged taboos.
The only place where you could let down
This reserve was in a bar, there you could
Roar (though still not violate taboos).
Gorilla fury. Now
The weather can't get better for protection's sake,
We're coming into Haiphong at about 200 feet
At close to Mach 1, bank for one quick turn
Around it, just another peaceful stroll
Through Haiphong Park, the weather's so bad
That the enemy assumes there won't be bombers.
But the overcast's too low, can't even
Contemplate a strike, third party ships

Are welded in there, so we'll take a look at
Cam Pha as we head home, just a little
Quickie run-by, maybe Hon Gay north of Haiphong,
Keep 'em honest. All at once I see a streak
Of orange shot up, Garth sees another--
Tracer bullets, they're to let the gunners know
Down there they're getting near the mark,
This stuff means business, there's a sound,
A sudden thwack, a good-sized rock
Has hit your car, no more than that,
Or so you'd say, they've hit the bottom
Of our nose, I have to cob it, all jets
Full blast, get it up above the clouds
Out towards the gulf where we can maybe
Get picked up, the plane's lights all
Are lit up red, I'm in control still,
Smoke is entering the cockpit,
So much heat that I can scarcely touch
Some sections of the panel, make attempts
To vent the cockpit. But they don't work.
Blow the canopy to try to clear the smoke,
This smoke's too thick, I still can't see,
The smoke pours in, I can't believe how hot
The metal is to touch, the stick's too hot.
Garth's in the back. Without the canopy
A hurricane has hit, a smoking hurricane,
His maps are flying off, he's going deaf,
Not even radio can come through
On his earphones, can we get back
To the ship without directions?
An explosion right in front of him,
Where Dowd was once a single pole
Sticks up, it's made of sections,
Like a telescope, it's strange,
He's never seen one. Dowd

Has punched out, that's what's left
Where he's ejected, Garth keeps staring
At the pole, then pulls his own ring.
Blasted forth with so much force
He now can't see. Jerked to a halt
Or to a slowdown by his chute,
Dowd just assumes that Garth is floating
Somewhere near him, he had told
Garth to eject--Garth could not hear
A word he said. Dowd was anticipating
Water underneath him as he came down
Through the clouds where they'd be
Picked up, not these islands,
But the wind blew in reprieve and he got wafted
Out from shore, he's been through
All of this in training, he prepares to shuck
His chute before he goes down in the drink,
You keep the life raft uninflated till you hit
So gooks can't spot you from the islands.
Then the water shocks him being too damned cold.
And the swells from up above it looked so calm.
It pitches up and down in front of him.
He can't quite understand it though,
He's being dragged down under it,
The parachute has wrapped around
His right leg in the swells' slosh
When he's thought he'd let it go.
He pulls his knife out, but the nylon cords
Are wet, the knife won't cut them.
It seems crazy that I'm now about to die,
To die from drowning in this pond
When I've survived this ten-cent
Weather recon shootdown. Such disgrace,
Such anticlimax can't be happening to me,
It's like an insult. Can the cosmos

Be so cruel? Abject self-pity floods my mind.
I don't DESERVE this. I'm affronted.
I refuse to take this sentence sitting down.
I give the chute one final tug
And find it's caught around my kneeboard,
Not my leg, the board attaches
To my flight-suit, I'd been using it
To jot down stats and figures--
Rip the kneeboard off my flight-suit
As I'm drowning...one last breath...
The chute is gone and I spring back up
To the surface grabbing air, my fate's
Been canceled, never mind, my raft's
Inflated, I'm not drowning any more.
I scan the water and the islands
Bobbing up and down in keeping with
The swells, I see no islanders with guns,
That head that's bobbing there is Garth's head.
He's survived too, we can fuck Fate up its ass.
They'll send Big Mother in to fetch us.

When they were back out on the Coral Sea,
They warmed themselves or tried to
Warm themselves by drinking coffee,
White cups, blue crests, blue bands
Wound about the rims, a certain dignified
Discretion. Then debriefing.
They were questioned, they gave answers,
Yet the two men who'd been rescued
Felt that something else was coming,
Some acknowledgement at least
Of what they'd seen, the loom's rough treadle.
There was nothing of the sort.
They asked for facts. No quarter given,
No slack cut, commander's jaws just

Mincing gum, the classic deadpan.
He detained them for a moment.
"Why did you two fly so low?"
Give us a break. And yet the code
Did not allow eschatological discussions.
At least the skipper finally said,
When he appeared,
"We're glad to have you two men back."
Made that concession. In its own way
It sufficed, implying many things unspoken,
Was a benison of sorts, a diapason.
Garth took one day off, was
Back out flying missions. Dowd
Had hurt his back ejecting,
He took two days off before he next
Got flung from off the skillet
By the slingshot.

247.

Far too much of our artillery fire in Nam
Was unobserved fire, H & I as it was called
And what we fired was ineffective.
Ammunition costs were simply through the roof,
We found that 85% of them derived
From unobserved fire, H & I stuff.
We could not say it was doing any good,
We poured it in, we poured it on,
And yet we said that we were people-oriented
In our mission—we of course did not discriminate
What people we were after from the people
Whom we said that we were saving.
We were devastating countrysides,

It made no sense, we overpowered them,
We did not resort to tactics,
We overpowered them extremely.
It was futile, it was madness,
Our techniques were wrong to fight
The kind of enemy we faced
Who would withdraw when we were coming,
This destruction was for naught,
It didn't hurt the Viet Cong,
It made us think that we were
Maybe getting somewhere.
In displacing native villagers,
We knew we'd get resentment and we did
Since they'd been living with the Viet Cong
And under them, supporting them for three years.
We were telling them to give up homes
They'd worked for, land they'd tilled.
They got to take along with them whatever
They could carry, pull, or herd,
What they could not take was retrieved
At some point later and delivered to
The relocation centers where we'd led them.
As the villagers moved out, the demolition teams
Moved in with every 'dozer you could think of.
They razed structures to the ground,
Collapsing tunnels and obliterating bunkers
Which the Viet Cong had used.
They'd scoop a big hole in the center,
Fill it up with high explosives,
Which they'd cover up and tamp down,
Then set off. This was to make sure
There weren't undiscovered tunnels underneath.

248.

But if I'm still a candidate,
They'll take my plea for peace
As some political maneuver
Aimed at Eau Claire and Sheboygan,
Some cheap shot to get me votes
In a parochial election, they'd
Diminish it, dismiss it. Abdication
Is the only course I've got.

249.

I don't pretend to any great political sagacity.
I hesitate to offer up my views then
Though I hold them with conviction.
I believe the course we're headed on right now
Will lead to Kennedy receiving nomination
By the party or to Nixon's being chosen
By the people in November—maybe both.
Because you're asking that the people vote
For this Administration to continue
Even though while this Administration's
Been in office, Vietnam
Has mushroomed monstrously, has grown
To take however many thousand lives per year
And 30 billions worth of wealth—and still
The enemy seems just as in control in '68
As he appeared in '64—no diminution.
If we've stabilized the government a little,
Made advances in Saigon, they've all been
Offset by destruction in the countryside.
The South Vietnamese perform quite poorly

As our allies, our associates, our lackeys.
Here at home you have the Negro
For whom some would say a period
Of fourteen years of satisfying progress,
Progress some would once have said could
Never happen, has unfolded, but not only
Does he seem to be ungrateful, he seems sullen,
Full of hate, potential violence is something
Which he broods on, always seething.
Our power in the sphere of economics
Has diminished, gold flow problems
Have restricted any freedom we once had
To act abroad. And Vietnam
Engenders sentiment against us
All through Europe, rabid anti-US feelings.
There's this sentiment that's hard to get
A hold of back at home, our youths are put off
By their elders, by the government, the system—
There's distrust. The drugs which youths take
Make it worse, offend their parents as
Un-patriotic notions youths pop off with also do.
There is the crime rate, people fearing
For their safety—public problem number one
As Nixon never tires of telling, the Administration
Seems to be quite helpless—to the minds
Of certain white folks the Administration
Can't knock any heads, it has to mollify
The Negroes whom it counts upon for votes.
Your culpability or lack of same relating to
These problems is beside the point,
It's still you who get blamed no matter what…
What Wallace offers is a violently different
Way of talking and performing and it seems
That 15 (give or take)% of the electorate
Might buy it. Bedrock Goldwater legionnaires

From '64. We cannot reach them.
Meanwhile Nixon will pretend that he's
More flexible regarding Vietnam—
No longer hawkish—and he'll put the blame
For problems on the war, our budget troubles
And an undefined unhappiness arising.
The Kennedy of Republicans is Rocky.
His change will be or will seem the most dramatic,
I predict that he'll go dove on Vietnam,
That he'll prescribe de-escalation,
Say get ready for political solutions.
Gene McCarthy's still the all-out dove proposer.
He'd provide a genteel, witty and
Distinguished front for pullout.
RFK of course is offering conversion to
A dove approach but he's campaigning also
As the tough guy who'd prevent
Our getting hurt by being softer.
He's more radical in changes he's suggesting
For the home front, he will say that he's
The one to bridge the gap between
The young folks and the old, he will be
Photographed with Negroes who have spent
Some time in prison but are trying now
To straighten out their lives, he's not afraid
Of being seen with them, the tough guy
With the heart of gold who puts a stop to riots.
He will try to be to you what brother Jack was
To the Eisenhower years: imagination,
Great vitality in contrast to a weariness,
A staleness, action stirring as opposed
To our entrenchment, hope of change
Opposed to baffled status quo, it is
That very status quo by which you seem
To be imprisoned, but you don't need to

Embrace that fettered status, you can
Show yourself as every bit as eager
As the next man for the kind of change
Bob Kennedy's been touting, just as restless,
And more deep by far in knowledge of
The problems, far more seasoned.
Viet Nam remains our paramount dilemma.
Change from status quo for it could mean
We escalate to 750,000 men or even more,
Up to a million, and with that force push
Still harder for a military triumph or:
De-escalate, change tactics, even bring
A few men home now. I'm still praying
That we choose the latter course
Because a military victory to my mind
Is beyond us in the ordinary meaning
Of that term and with the forces
That we have now plus the 25 or 30,000
More men we might add on.
Just saying as we have said that we'll win
Won't make it so and in the long run
Of the next three months we shouldn't
Even say it. And the opposition may confirm
That point which I've just made when they
Take back a few more towns. We cannot
Root the enemy out, changed tactics mean
We start to recognize that fact. Not that
He's going to throw us out of Vietnam,
We can continue to deny him any access
To the cities. We must force the GVN
To give responsible positions
To a greater range of outlooks and opinions
In their country, even NLF supporters…
No one who's connected to your effort
Should repeat the "Hanoi's watching" theme.

Hanoi for sure is watching this election
Just to see how well this government's supported.
Maybe two thirds of the voters are disturbed
About this war and to suggest that this
Concern of theirs is tantamount to treason
Is the right and ready path to make them hostile.
I would risk a lot of picketing and heckling.
Do not give up taking trips.
It should not be thought that Kennedy
And Rockefeller, Nixon, all the others
Can address the people freely and that you can't,
You don't want that kind of contrast.
There are cities you can go to
Where the peaceniks and the activists are fewer—
Cincinnati, Salt Lake City—
If you pick your targets shrewdly,
It will seem that there's no place you cannot go.
You might think that you will lose the Catholic voters,
But since Catholics have historically
Been with you on the war in Vietnam,
They may resist the dove pronouncements
Of the candidates who share their own religion.
There are Catholics whose support you ought to welcome
Like that I Corps chief of chaplains General Walt says
Truly understands the nature of this war. Don't court
The rabid anti-communist types of Catholics.
They're more trouble than they're worth.
Let Valenti, Califano make suggestions as to prospects....
What this memorandum's urging most of all
Is to present a moving target, on the issues,
Also physically. Don't stand still
And if you move among the people,
Show you're asking their support,
You won't be branded as a king who thinks
He has support accruing as his due.

Voters *will* support the Johnson of achievement,
Wit and openness who's done his level best
To end this war, who's working hard
For public order, social progress,
The enlightened Lyndon Johnson who's
Inventive, tough, not easily pinned down.
You have advantages your five opponents lack,
You have experience, achievement, and the office
Which you occupy. It would be possible
To waste them. You could take
The firm fidelity of voters to a war
That no one likes (this isn't World War II remember)
As a patriotic test, or even worse, make this
The key campaigning issue. That's one
Sure way you could squander your advantage.
Please don't take what Kerner's panel
Has reported and concluded as attack
Upon yourself, don't let self-pity get a grip.
And don't expect big celebrations
Of a parlous status quo about which
People feel uncertain. You could say
They've never had it all so good as at this moment,
Yet there persists this deep dis-ease, this strange
Uneasiness I've never known the likes of
In my lifetime....

250.

The idiot DC crime bill passed by Congress
Would have gratified the heart of Genghis Khan
It was so blatantly against the Constitution.
Still, it left the question open
Would the President now veto it, or sign?

McPherson wrote the rough draft of a veto,
But the President was contemplating saying
"I don't like it but I'll sign it" (sign the bill).
And there were people who were urging him
To sign it. "Let the courts
Do all the dirty work with this one,
You don't need to stick your neck out,
Everyone's opposed to crime,
You won't get criticized."
The days went creeping by,
And if he didn't sign in ten days, or oppose it,
Then the bill became a law without his signature.
We couldn't figure out what he would do,
We all were waiting.
Then at two o'clock the morning of the tenth day
My direct line to the White House
Started ringing. When it rang,
It made these three extremely loud bursts,
This bawump sound. So my daughter
Heard it ringing, she went in and picked it up
And heard this voice which said
"The President is calling for your father."
So she got me out of bed, I picked the phone up,
Said hello. The voice responded: "I just vetoed it."
"That's great news, Mr. President," I said.
"I just vetoed it and you have now destroyed me."
BANG. The phone came crashing down.
Still half asleep myself, I went back in
To where my wife was soundly sleeping.
"The President just said that I destroyed him."
The next day I found out that Califano
And McPherson got the same call after I did.
Same dire message of destruction,
Same abrupt bang. Roaring silence then succeeding.

251.

A tidal wave. He went right through the walls,
Came through the door and he would overwhelm
A room, just take it over…nothing delicate
About the man at all. He made you feel
That he'd been pawing you all over
St. Bernard-style. He would never
Simply shake your hand and leave it.
One hand shook your hand for certain,
But the other hand was always some place else
In an examination, exploration tactic,
He was working you all over, he'd assess you.
It was not the way he'd ask a person questions,
Give him lectures—not that only.
He'd reduce you to a wrung-out lump of flesh,
He had this way of leaning over you and looking.

252.

One evening it was quiet and the phone rang.
Secret Service on the line, or so the man said.
President Johnson wished to stop by my apartment.
He'd be there in fifteen minutes.
"Is that so?" I said, convinced this was a joke,
Some prank concocted by my buddies
In the press pool. But I went out in the hallway.
There was Secret Service out there
By the elevator door with that strange
Non-committal way they have
Of standing with their arms crossed,
Chewing gum. I was convinced now
That the leader of the free world

Was arriving in a moment.
I went back inside and tidied up
My place as best I could.
It wasn't many minutes later
That the President was standing in my door,
A sheepish grin on. Suit and tie on.
He came in of course, I offered him a drink.
His sudden advent was unnerving.
We made small talk, and the sound
Of ice cubes tinkling in that tumbler full
Of Scotch that he was holding in his huge hand
Seemed the loudest sound I think I ever heard.
The confession of his passion for me
Wasn't too surprising when it happened,
In this setting I had sensed that it was coming.
But the case he then went on to make was clumsy
Or bizarre: since I had always loved the Kennedys,
Why not transfer my affections now to him
As from one focal point of power to another.
This was how far his obsession with the Kennedys
Extended, this desire to have their favorite girl reporter.
It was not so much his wish to have me now
That struck my mind as his competing with his rival
Who was dead, he meant to one-up JFK in every aspect.
Besting Kennedy had now become his demon.
My reactions were a mix I'd have to say.
I can't deny that I was flattered.
I was startled, I was mortified.
Embarrassed for the President in some way.
And in need of thinking quickly on my feet
To ease the situation back down into neutral.
First one needs to take a deep breath.
"I admire you, Mr. President," I said.
"I always will. I stand in awe
Of what you're doing for the country,

But it stops there, has to stop there,
Goes no further." "I just wanted you to know,"
He said and polished off the remnants of his drink.
What could I say but "Well, I know now"?
Also "Thank you." Then he left.
The hall outside my door was empty.
No more Secret Service cohort.
That mirage had broken up.
Had I just dreamed of this encounter?
I think having been the lover of
The President that summer
Could have ended very badly,
Been the end of my career.
I had reasons people never could have guessed
For later writing that the President in 1964
Was looking not so much for votes
As to be loved.

253.

In talking to these business men
He put the greatest stress on civil rights.
He told these men the story of his cook
Who'd had to pee beside the road.
Bob McNamara later in the week
Expressed amazement: "Just imagine
JFK describing how his Negro cook
Had had to stop beside the road
Since there would not be public bathrooms
She could use. I mean it never
Would have happened." Bob knew

Many of the people LBJ had been addressing.
LBJ'S approach did far more
To convince them Bob was saying.
Elemental.

254.

I'm determined that this nation will be strong,
Secure the peace. We must be prudent,
Must stay solvent. But mere solvency
And strength don't make the heart beat
Any faster. That which makes a nation great
Is its compassion. We will have
That strength and solvency but also
That compassion—love thy neighbor—
Understanding for the plight of those
Less fortunate than we are.

255.

The odds I'd say are even that the DRV/VC
Will hang on doggedly, effectively,
Will match us man for man once we have
Factored in "guerrilla war, the ratio advantage."
In the meantime all our efforts won't suffice
To get the people of the South above the hill's crest,
Make the snowball roll our way, we might be
Facing further impasse as of early '67,
At a higher level more of same: stagnation.

256.

It seems they're only saying
What they've said to us before
And we should tell them we see nothing new
Arising from exchanges that we've had
And that the dialogue is over.
If they're thinking something different,
They can tell us so of course,
The channel's open still a crack.
But in the matter of the bombing I'm opposed
To our suspending it or ceasing it.
Hanoi would misinterpret
And would build up their supplies,
They'd take advantage.
We must not be thought
To weaken our resolve.
I wouldn't change the situation
In Hanoi and its environs,
Which might bear fruit in the future.

They may not have been forthcoming in exchanges
But I think that if the bombing were to cease,
They'd start to talk, and right away.
I would not cut off this crucial channel yet.
But the question's when we ought to have
A bombing pause. I think we need to probe
This possibility of talks, it might produce
Something. I do not believe the people of
This country will support us twelve more months.
I believe a pause would increase our support.
Cessation of the bombing won't affect the way
The war's fought in the South.

I don't underestimate the value of
Informal kinds of contact on occasions,
Unofficial kinds of contact have been helpful
In the past, I well remember how John Scali
In the Cuban missile crisis helped us
Misinterpret something Khrushchev sent.
I'm not sure about the wisdom, though,
Of Thompson tickling his man there in Moscow.
This whole effort doesn't smell like much to me yet
Since the offer we presented them
Was serious and generous. I would tell M
That my people back home don't think I
Have anything to show, I'd try to scare him.
I would say if he has anything,
It's time now to produce it.

I would recommend we keep this channel open
And await some sign from them,
So when they're serious they'd have a way to say it.

We cannot win militarily or so it seems to me.
I have asked the JCS for their suggestions on a way
To make it shorter, their suggestions
All pertained to something outside Viet Nam.
Which is no help. We've got to keep this thing in focus.
We can't win it by negotiations either, diplomatically.
Our proposals should be clear enough
To get clear answers back that we could take
And make a farmer understand.
I think we're right back where we started.
In the court of world opinion
In the last two months we've almost lost the war.
All the demonstrations show us we need
Someone else to lead us in this country.
People arguing for us to stop the bombing

Ought to know all we've been through
In this exchange. Some people sitting here
Are not aware of what has taken place.
We haven't seen a single change in their position
And they're filling all the airwaves
With their propaganda charges. I need answers
To their charges since the speech
At San Antonio which I gave did not get through.
I cannot mount any better explanation.
If we can't get them to sit down and negotiate,
Why not just hit all the military targets
Short of what would bring the Russians
And the Chinese in? I've really
Been astounded that our boys
Can keep morale up given all that's going on.

Pure vindictiveness. America gets angry
At an enemy that will not come to terms
And through the bombing cannot bring them
To the table, nonetheless we'll pour it on
And really punish them for making us look silly.
Bombing does not stop the flow of infiltration
Since the North can meet supply needs
In the South no matter how great
Interdiction efforts grow, so all the bombing does
Is pacify the hawks--our true believers--
For the moment since the North
Can re-build everything we smash,
But then the hue and cry from hawks
Becomes to smash them all again,
There is no end to this.
It makes so little sense.

257.

I first saw how committed Johnson was to civil rights—
I mean committed irrespective of political prestige
Or of the passage of a bill, deep down committed—
In the spring of '63. There was an impasse.
The public accommodations title
Of the civil rights bill Kennedy sent down
Had got the Southerners stirred up,
To them that title was obnoxious—it forbade
Discrimination being practiced in a place
That was accommodating people
Like a café or a restaurant, it was striking at
This sense of private property
The Southerners asserted, it imposed associations
Which they shouldn't have to undertake as "free men."
This was something that they wouldn't give an inch on.
I was sure the title had no chance of passing.
I was sitting up with Johnson in the V-P's Senate dais,
We were speaking of this bill and of its chances.
Senator Stennis passed by just then on his way out.
Johnson called him up to have some conversation.
"How do you like that civil rights bill title two, John?"
"Well now, Lyndon, you know just as well as I do
That our people couldn't take that.
Any man who owns a store
Or runs a restaurant has surely
Got the right to serve or sell to
Or refuse to sell to anyone he chooses."
"Then you don't think you'll support it."
"Oh no Lyndon, I could never give support
To such a clause." "I see. You know, John,
Something's bothered me that happened
Just a day or two ago when Helen Williams
And her husband who have worked for me for years

Drove my official car from Washington to Texas,
This car had the V-P's seal on it, Vice-President
Of USA, important. They were driving it
Through your state, they got hungry,
They pulled over on the edge of town, the colored part,
They bought stuff for their dinner at a grocery store,
Some beans, Vienna sausage, used a plastic spoon
To eat it. When they had to make a comfort stop,
They pulled off by the road and Helen Williams,
An employee of our second highest office,
Had to squat to take a pee behind her car door.
That aint right, John, there should be a law
To change that if your state don't want
To change that situation of their own free will
And wisdom." "Well now, Lyndon,
I'm quite sure that there are places…"
Johnson just said uh-huh twice
And turned his head away from Stennis
In a vacant sort of way. Discussion over.
"Thank you, John." And Stennis left.
And then the V-P turned his eyes toward me
And winked. It was the first time he'd conveyed to me
The depth at which he felt discrimination,
Just the basic human fact of it between persons,
For the monstrousness, indignity it was.

258.

Back when I knew Lyndon Johnson, he still seemed
To have the classic Southern attitude toward blacks.
I was a black sharecropper's son, I worked for
Johnson on occasion. It was painful. I was grateful
To the man of course, he'd helped me find

My postal service job and he would get me jobs
At parties which the big wigs threw in Washington
As waiter. I feared Johnson for the way…
You never knew when he would turn on you,
Start treating you like dirt in front of guests,
He'd often "nigger" at me most of all when Bilbo
Was around, old Bilbo liked to give these lectures
That the only proper way to treat a nigger
Was to kick him. I used to hate working
For Johnson whenever Bilbo was around
Because I knew that Johnson had to play the racist
For him then, he had to play a Southern part.
I simply hated Lyndon Johnson's racist side.
He was a different man in private just as long
As I did nothing that would anger him.
There was almost some affection in the way
He'd call me "boy," sometimes I felt that he
Was treating me…well, almost as his equal
Though in public he would never say a word
About a black without the nigger-word arising.
I never heard him speak of nigger women.
When he was speaking to his black cook
Zephyr Wright, a college graduate
Who could find no other work,
He would address her as "Miss Wright"
Or he would sometimes call her "Sweetheart."

259.

This whole damned thing is shiftin' and changin' so fast.
I got 38 percent of these young nigra boys
Out standin' on the streets, they got
No schools that they can go to,

Got no job that they can work at,
And by God I'm scared to death
What's gonna happen come July
And it gets hot, you get an old hard-peckered boy,
He gets inflamed—when you were 17 or 18—
I ran off to California, didn't think my daddy
Had one bit of sense, came out from Texas age 16.
You take an old hard-peckered boy
That sits around, he's got no school
And got no job and got no work,
No self-control, his daddy's no doubt
On relief, his mamma's prob'ly takin' morphine.
Why he ain't got one damned thing hurt
If he's shot, I mean he's better off shot dead
Than where he is and they're just fillin' up
The cities, you just wait till rats get goin'
In Chicago, up in Harlem.

260.

I'm just not really sure about Diem
Though he seemed tickled as could be
When I was pledging him a sum of forty million,
Or was mentioning new military aid,
But he was playing deaf and dumb
When I would talk about him speeding up
And beefing up some health and welfare projects.
I tried knee with him to knee, I bellied up,
I wanted no misunderstandings,
But I'm not sure I got through to him
Or maybe he was hiding his intentions.

261.

Roaring in across the treetops, choppers
Terrified the superstitious peasants--
Viet Cong--they simply turned tail, started running--
We would flush them out of hiding places, foxholes--
In the open they were almost sitting targets.

262.

We're sittin' on a powder keg,
About a dozen places, you cannot have
Any concept of the depth of what
They're feelin', I see some of them,
The boys that work for me,
2000 years of persecution,
Now they suffer from it,
Absolutely nothin' they can live for,
Unemployed are up to 38%,
They live with rats,
No place to sleep, they all start out
From broken homes, they're illegitimate,
They got narcotics circlin' round them.
We just have to find a way
To knock down ghettos,
Find some housing for them, work.

263.

A little after six I crossed the hallway
To an office where the President was standing
With his back turned toward me.

I could get my first impression unobserved.
He was a great deal more imposing than I thought he'd be,
Not only very tall but also burly, more than
Two hundred pounds upon a six foot four inch frame.
But he seemed somehow even bigger.
George Reedy said by size alone
He dominated landscapes, one could not avoid
The feeling of an elemental force at work
When one was in his presence—
A volcano or an earthquake or a hurricane,
One didn't know quite which,
Perhaps all three of them combined.
He might go off at any moment.
He appeared to be morose this night, ill-tempered.
The suit that he was wearing seemed funereal
As did his mood. A brooding monster.
He was awesomely intimidating, menacing.
A member of his staff had said
"He was the only other man beside my father
Who convinced me he might strip his belt
And strap me any minute." We proceeded
To another strangely stifling sort of room
Of bilious green in its décor for our discussion,
It was intimate but not exactly comforting.
"I'm going to have to run soon,
So you'd better ask me what you want to know"
Was how he started, inauspiciously to my mind.
Still I tried to do my best and asked a question.
"Mr. President, the Congress sitting now
Has been remarkable I think,
And one might argue it's the most important ever."
"There's no argument," the President replied.
"It simply is. If you can read.
You have three independent branches…"
Here began a nonstop monologue

Which I could only gape and marvel at
While scribbling down some notes as best I could.
I was reminded of the way he was described once
By a boardinghouse associate from college days:
"Well, he was very entertaining,
But if someone else would try to interject,
He wouldn't let them, he would quickly interrupt them,
God, his voice would just ride over you
Until you had to stop. He would monopolize
From when he first came in until he left, I still
Can see him as he reached up, kept on talking."
"Little got done here for years,"
Was how he started summing up
A quarter century or more of what he thought of
As inaction by the Congress. "All those liberals,
The ADA-ers, guys like Hayes and Doug,
They jerked, they talked, like local bullies
By the barber shop who said they'd make
A million but of course they never got there.
Not since 1937, '38 had Congress
Passed much legislation. The executive,
The Cabinet, they'd been through Bay of Pigs.
They'd had their washouts. We came in
And plugged the holes. Since the election
I have not talked of a mandate.
If you have great power, remember
Not to use it, think of FDR, his veto
Of the Bonus Bill exposed his overreaching,
He was suddenly perceived
To have some weakness.
We've cut down that fear that did in FDR.
People fear the President's terrible power.
Fear like that brought our Republic into being—
Fear of monarchs. When the people
Didn't like what FDR was doing,

He denounced them, called them
Economic royalists and money changers.
FDR had said they'd surely met their match
And that they now would meet their master.
We had people fighting and spitting at one another.
That's why we created bridges with the people.
We took titans both of industry and labor
And we bred them. I'm no confiscator.
Nor do business people think of me as such.
And labor doesn't fear what I might do,
They know I voted for the measures
Like the minimum wage that helped them."
He took a swig from his grape soda bottle and belched.
"Congress doesn't fear me, I revere them,
I am not out to denounce them.
Unlike Schlesinger I don't denounce
The members as archaic fools, buffoons
Whose shirts get stained with their tobacco drool.
This morning I was up at seven,
I was meeting with them over breakfast.
I show Congress no contempt. I gave
A dinner for the Court which I revere also.
I do not advocate impeaching our Chief Justice.
No man knew less about Congress than JFK did.
He never even knew enough to know how you
Get recognized by them. When he was young,
He always lit out for the weekend
Off to Florida or Boston.
I never saw him in the cloakroom once.
That's where the deals get made.
I never saw him eating with a fellow member once.
And Speaker Rayburn never knew him.
The only way that Rayburn knew to think of him at all
Was as a young man who might die of his malaria.
He was a Joe College type of fellow,

He had no rapport with Congress,
He had no affection for us.
And the Congress felt he didn't have an inkling
Where the ball was. When he got to be the President,
He only had these old leftover programs
From the days of FDR and Ike and Truman."
The evening news shows now came on,
The President would sometimes turn the sound up,
Focus in on them. At other times
He spoke against the sound, his startling
Talkathon continued, channel-hopping
Did not seem to stop the flow.
"We knew what we wanted to do
And we knew how to do it, I was like the pilot
Who has flown a thousand times across the ocean.
After all those times I knew how to close the door
And open the throttle. We called in
The greatest thinkers in the fields that were neglected.
We got the Mayos, we brought men in
From Hopkins, all the best.
Our stuff wasn't drafted by Corcoran and Cohen.
Highest quality went into it.
The press cut at us though,
Those superficial, shaller types of columnists.
We treat those types of columnists as whores.
Any editor who wants to screw 'em....
They'll be down there on the floor,
Their price is three dollars.
But they do not have too much influence.
I've started keeping records.
If a paper prints up five lies, then I write 'em.
One day last week the *Po*st had eleven.
When they say that they've been quoting
'Well-informed sources,'
That just means they've said the things

They want to say regardless, damn the sources.
We should pass a law preventing them
From using 'well-informed.'
They don't have the horsepower needed
To defeat me or they would though.
This year a hundred bills turn into law.
In any other year the highest number's twenty.
The Executive should lead, I do believe that,
I propose and they dispose.
But more than any other President
I've visited the Hill and more of them
Have been down here.
Every member's gotten two complete briefings,
All five hundred thirty five of them.
The least little member from the remotest district
Gets to ask his President for what he wants."
He watched an image on the news
Of some poor child in Vietnam with real concern.
There was a slight tic in his cheek
While he was staring.
"I like to see Marines do something else
Besides just kill—like helping palsy."

264.

—That'll really hurt me badly,
I'll have to get it back the hard way
If it comes right down to that
But all the time that it would take me
Scarin' funds up for that buildin'
Equals time I could be workin' on your programs.
Why not let us have a million,
That would get the project started.

—You don't want me to reward Shreveport, do ya.
I'd be run out of the whole United States
If I rewarded them before they start behavin'.
God A'mighty if we did that
We'd become the biggest laughingstock on earth.
—That's not how you got the whole bunch
Out in Texas on your side, you kept on
Wooin' 'em, pursuin' 'em, then finally got their votes.
—But Russell please my friend
I want to give you every damn thing that
You ask for in this world, but no Long's
Ever going to ask that I reward them
When these people cut my throat, they're just
The meanest, God A'mighty I've got literchoor from there
That is the worst, called me a crook, called me a rapist,
Called me everything and all that stuff is comin' out
Of Shreveport, I'd get ridiculed from that state
And from every other state and so would you.
—It's more than that. They'll run me out.
—They aint going to run you out of there
For this year. They aint holdin' no election.
—Mr. President I need it in the worst way.
It would build up Russell Long.
—I would do anything to build up Russell Long
But your old daddy would be turnin' in his grave,
That's not the way he gave rewards out.
You just tell 'em first apologize for callin' me a thief.
Then they have got to clean those Birchites
From that paper that was callin' me
A dirty low down thievin' worse than that son of a bitch.
—But Mr. President, we've got some good
Times-Picayune- type people that will try to buy
That paper. In the meantime it won't help us
If we're seen as hurting Shreveport,
You surrendered that whole section

When you signed that civil rights bill.
We can build support back up and by the time
You get some colored on the rolls
You'll carry everything down there.
—But it's a premium on DIS-loyalty by God.
You've lost the Long in you.
I won't sign anything for Shreveport
If they don't take back those charges
I'm a thief and I'm a thug. Because I'm not.
—You've got a lot of mean folks up in Shreveport,
I'll admit that, but you've also got
Some damned good folks up there
Who wanna help ya.
—Maybe 15 of a 100.
—And my mama's in the 15.
—I am surely for your mama,
Don't pretend your mama can't examine
Everything I said or did since 1933
That she will not give her approval to
As far as all the Long clan is concerned,
I am a populist like Huey was by God,
I'm for the poor folks, I'm going to pour
The education into all of them, I'll pour
The roads in too and pour in health care.
But I sure as hell aint for that Shreveport crowd.
You can't be either. You bin smokin' marijuana?
I just rolled that damned red carpet out for all of them,
You saw, I gave them souvenirs, lead pencils,
I did everything I could and then I picked
The paper up, I never read such stuff,
Notorious thief and so forth.
You tell Shreveport you yourself will try
To help them, they're in trouble.
—I won't fight with you. I see your mind's made up.
—Well, you saw what all I did when they came here.

Could I have possibly been nicer?
—I agree. But then you signed that civil rights bill.
—How could I have vetoed that?
—I won't dispute this any longer.
I've been takin' too much time.
—It really hurts me not to do
Whatever you might feel you need
But don't go pickin' out that bow-legged,
Stutterin' slattern cross-eyed gal
And bring here in here, try to tell me
She should be my beauty queen
And if I name her that'd help you…

265.

But Lyndon kept pounding and pounding
And pounding whatever the issue,
That was just the way he was
When he would start in on a project,
He poured every ounce of energy he had,
The project overrode his life,
He didn't hold back, he went after
Every person who could help him.

266.

Oh I could see the whole thing comin',
Recent history provided me with cases
How the bugle sounding ended
All the best hopes of reformers,
World War I was death to Woodrow Wilson's dreams
And World War II did in the New Deal.

Once the war began conservatives in Congress
Had their weapon, they took dead aim
At my programs. They had been against
My helping out the nigras or the poor folk
In the first place. But they couldn't figure
How to make their opposition to me noble
In a time of great prosperity for all.
They had the war though—
Oh they'd use it, they could talk against
My programs not because they had a thing
Against the poor, why they were generous
And advocated charity to poor folks—
But the war had prior claim as their concern,
We had to beat those godless commies,
We could worry later on about the homeless.
And the generals, what did they love most but war,
It was their chance to seem like heroes,
Bombs and bullets were the very thing they needed.
Mistrust military men, they are so narrow
In the way that they appraise things,
They see everything through blinders.
And the South Vietnamese scared me the worst,
They couldn't get themselves together.
Yet I knew if I got out of Vietnam,
If I let Ho Chi Minh run through the streets of Saigon,
I'd be seen to be like Chamberlain in 1938,
Conferring prizes for aggression, if I let
Communist aggression take control in Vietnam,
We'd have a firestorm of debate
That would destroy my term in office.
From the moment that the Communists
Assumed control in China,
Harry Truman and Dean Acheson were finished,
Their effectiveness was over.

I believed the loss of China
Paved the way for Joe McCarthy.
All those problems though were chickenshit
Compared with Vietnam were we to lose it.

267.

In 1958 he hired Lloyd Hand,
He was the Leader of the Senate,
But he felt he had to bring Lloyd Hand on board
At this late date, Lloyd was a student body
President in Texas, he was good at meeting people.
Lloyd has told me, though I guessed as much myself,
And he seemed baffled when he said it,
"In my interview he said 'Now you know how
To deal with people, how to meet them,
I can tell.'" But Lloyd was puzzled,
Asked the Leader what he meant.
"Well, like at parties and receptions.
See, I'll tell you what I want to have you do,
I want you always going with me
To these parties as my lead man,
Just a step or two in front of me,
It's better if I got a man to do that."
And that is really how he was,
There was a streak of some enormous shyness in him.
I know people will declare me off my tree
For even saying this but he was always
So afraid that in a gracious social setting
He would fall short in the area of manners.
He took over any party he attended for a reason:
If he didn't take it over, it might bite him
In the rear end in this area of manners.

That's why he was hiring Lloyd as his protector,
Someone running interference.

268.

Johnson was a man plagued by
A sense of inner emptiness.
To fill that kind of void he overate,
He oversmoked, he overworked,
He also womanized,
But nothing seemed
To bring him inner peace.
I never saw a man eat stuff like Lyndon.
He would snark up two large meals,
He'd gulp them down,
You would have thought
The man was starving.
There was nothing that could seem
To slow him down. He needed
Constant talk and motion.
He depended on a challenge
Which would keep him working
Day and night. Convulsive.
And his telephones were crucial,
He just had to be in contact
With the whole world every minute.
He had phones everywhere.
The walls of his houses
Were studded with telephone sockets.
One of the trees in his back yard
In Austin was wired, it had
A thirty foot extension corded phone.
One day in Dallas at the airport

Horace Busby found him pacing
Back and forth beside three phone booths.
Johnson shouted "Watch those phones!
In just a minute each will have a call
Come in to me long distance."

269.

...But LBJ had awfully strong class feelings,
They were not of someone from the lower class
Against the upper but...well, this was how
I sensed it, this applied when he was President,
It applied down to the end of his career.
He believed that there were people from
The upper classes elsewhere who just didn't
Understand that he was upper class back home
In Johnson City, upper class however strapped
For cash his family may have been at times,
It was aristocrat against aristocrat in his mind.
There were people who weren't giving him his due.

270.

That speech about the dental plan is no good,
It lacks somethin', I'd say empathy's the word
For what it lacks, so when I give it
I must know that li'l old lady in the front row,
Not one tooth inside her head,
Is going to feel my hand come creepin' up
Her skirt—you've got to touch 'em.

271.

Now I knew I couldn't make them
Want to integrate their schools
Or open up their homes to blacks
But I could make them feel right guilty
Cause they hadn't, and I felt compelled
As President to do precisely that,
To use the suasion of my office,
Make them feel that segregation
Was a curse they'd carry with them
To their graves.

272.

An unreconstructed 19th Century old school
Virginia gentleman, Judge Smith as he was called
Was what the Congress had to deal with,
What John Kennedy had to deal with.
"There stood Jackson like a stone wall."
So did Judge Smith. His whole legislative
Effort, his whole life had been
In warding off "encroachments,"
He distrusted any influence from outside
His own region—Yankees, carpetbaggers,
Foreigners, Republicans were threats
To his own people and the way of life they'd led.
He was a white supremacist and to the end
He fought off racial integration.
He opposed almost all federal reforms
Including health and welfare bills
And bills improving education.
He was a true believer in the Constitution

"as it was written," strict constructionist,
An advocate of states' rights. Adamantine.
Unassailable. Reactionary. Diligent.
Soft-spoken. Gracious. Courtly.
Rather brilliant. An enigma.

273.

—This damned Passman's pretty slick.
But I believe that he's a mental case, I do.
Why don't we Democrats have someone
In the House to do the job the way that he does?
It appears they all just go along with him.
They don't know how to use their heads.
—What should I tell them?
—Three point six for foreign aid.
And I have *not* agreed to anything below that.
They gave Kennedy three nine.
—You wouldn't get them up that high.
—I think that they're endangering
The future of their country.
It's a shame to have a cave man there like Passman.
I don't think he knows enough about our country,
How it works, and he's got problems in his head.
Unpatriotic? It might be about as bad as that
Although he does show fine facility with figures.
I just hate to see our country go his way,
I love it too much. I just wish we had the leadership…
—I'm afraid of getting caught up in a box.
—Well, we'll certainly get caught, we're in a bad one.
The ammunition out in Vietnam is not sufficient.
You got McNamara coming in tomorrow
After flying all night long. And we are

Not in real great shape, what can we brag about?
We should not let some mental case
Reduce us down from three point nine
To three in foreign aid.
Just talkin' to him got us in this mess.
I think we ought to just go out, appeal it,
Let the members vote it down.
I don't want the people thinking I'm a part of this.
I have to go to them, I have to tell them.
I know foreign aid's unpopular.
I didn't want to go to the Pacific
Back in 1941, I did it though.
And I didn't want to let those Japs
Shoot at me in a Zero but I did it,
And so now if I can't take a little Passman,
Let him beat me...that's all right,
I'll let him beat me. I get just as much in pension
At eleven months as at eleven years.
But we should fight him till he's shitty as a bear.
—I don't think that that's the point though.
He's got far too many troops with him—
—All right, just let him go with them.
And we just take our little squad and then...
I think that's all that we can do.
We can't agree to this. Would he
Agree to cut a hundred missiles out?
I think that when we had to sit
And look old Mr. Castro in the eye...
—We're trying to deal with impossible people.
—We'll have to let a hundred eighty million people
Hear the news that we have yielded to Mr. Passman.
—We're not yielding, all we've done
Is twisted arms all day to try to get more votes.
—Well, you can't do any good that way.
—We tried and tried to get more,

I've been up and down…the members say
They're out there on a limb on this one.
They've promised to cut out the communist sales.
You've seen times when you couldn't get
The votes on certain issues.
—I don't think that we can turn this country over.
I'm not letting Khrushchev have it.
But I think it's just about as bad
To let old Passman have it.
I will talk to Rusk about the wheat amendment.
But let me be the one to take the rap,
Then they can call me communist
Or maybe Nixon can,
And that will make them happy.

274.

One afternoon patrolling on the Mekong in a boat,
Our lookout saw a sampan as it moved along the shore.
A marksman fired three warning rounds across the sampan's bow,
The bullets skipping off the water's surface into tall grass.
Then the sampan turned around toward us.
The deep roar of the naval craft drowned out the sound
Its tiny outboard motor made as it putt-putted forward
And as we trained fifty caliber machine guns on
The boatman and his wife who pulled up sheepishly beside us.
According to our orders they produced the needed papers.
These were checked against a list of "known VC,"
Then handed back to them. A sailor said to open up
The hatch beneath the wife's feet, which the boatman did.
We saw there three small fish inside a bent cage.
"He could have had gelignite, rounds of mortar," said the sailor.
He bestowed upon the boatman and his wife a bar of candy

And some cigarettes before he waved them off.
Good God, I thought, this war might last forever.

275.

The war took on a weird warp from the standpoint
Of the people we were fighting for, was "affluent":
Hot food brought in on helicopters far out
To the soldiers in the field, the PX full,
Piled high with gadgets for our soldiers, flocks
Of trans-Pacific planes conveying troops
And massive quantities of weapons,
Spanning distances no object, bombs
And ammo used in excess, hours and hours
Of bombs and strafing by the planes,
Barrages triggered by the smallest pops
Of snipers; forests, lakes, and rivers poisoned.
Disproportionate responses. Watch the Rome plow
Pull a tree up with one spike-swipe.
Stench of diesel fuel, of burning human excrement,
Of scorched or rotting flesh mixed with
The odors of the decomposing jungle.
Some GIs said that the smells of local cooking
Were offensive--fancy that. Adhesive fear,
Pervasive hatred of an enemy called Charlie,
Who was faceless, who might be that
"Harmless" grandma you'd just passed
Along the road, whom you should think about
Destroying first lest she flip bombs at you
Offhandedly--or so the crazy thought presented.
There was no front, there were no lines,
And the only way to stay alive was ending tours
Of duty, getting out. How with this rage?

276.

--Westmoreland wants to take out all the SAM sites
At the same time. He's an old South Carolina boy,
He's been messin' in the jungle long enough,
He's gotten fed up, wants to end it, not lose
Boys of his shot down--a sort of firefighter outlook.
In addition you've got Wheeler and the Joint Chiefs,
Want to take out Six and Seven right away, they're actin' tough,
They'd like to take out every damned thing
They could find in Southeast Asia if we'd let 'em,
But they really want to take out Six and Seven
Of the SAM sites. McNamara also thinks
You've got to take them out right now,
That if you don't, you send a message to
The Russians--pretty soon we'll have no planes
Left in the air if we let Russia knock them down
Without reprisals. Still, despite his reputation,
McNamara holds the military down
Much of the time. Most people think
He's always raisin' hell to get us into battles.

--I think he's got most of the military cowed,
They can't express their true opinions.

--I've had the military over here for hours,
I just go round and round the table with 'em,
Some are downright irresponsible,
They scare you, they're prepared
To send a million in right quick.
Rusk thinks we ought to take those sites out too.
And Ball and Goldberg. I'd say Humphrey
Kind of wobbled on both sides,
But you know Hubert.

We think Russians man the sites,
We don't want that fact getting out though.

--I don't think so. I think Russians
Have their people there to show them
How to shoot them, it's the North Vietnamese
Who pull the trigger. I would never
Say I thought that though.

--We don't want them to feel
That they've been put against the wall
Where they might feel they have to fight.
I'd like to minimize this thing or play it down.
We told the Russians what our budget
For defense was, how we'd lowered ours
Two billion. They cut theirs then.
When we cut down on our nuclear production...
You remember when we talked about it last year,
You asked why we hadn't cut it down much sooner.
It was runnin' out our ears when we came in here.
They cut theirs down when they saw that we'd cut ours.
That's why I'm trying not to say I'm going to spend
A billion dollars, get me up some big announcement.
They'd be back in bed with China. Ho Chi Minh
Is trying all the time to get them back together.

--I'd take every SAM site out and I'd
At least take out one other if I knew
Where its location was for sure.

--But then you get into Hanoi if you do that,
Into civilians. World opinion turns against us.
I can't chase these other sites,
But they don't bother me a damned bit.
Six and Seven are in line with all my targets.

I can't keep on sending boys up
If I don't knock Six and Seven.
Hanoi aint your basic problem.

--I'd sure try to get one other if I knew
That I could knock it.

--You're goin' to hit the goddamned capital in that case,
You'd have Russia and the Chinese in the war
In fifteen minutes. I believe the North
Would like to trap us into that.

--Well, I'd say yes then, get the sites you can tonight,
But I would hate like hell to miss 'em
After notching this attack up.

--Chances are we're going to miss 'em,
They have strips of ground that look just like
Their SAM sites, they have mobile ones
They move in and can move out like a trailer.
Let me ask you somethin' else though.
I've been working out a deal
Where I give Westy what he wants
In three installments, thirty thousand at a time.
One whole division right away from your
Fort Benning, by the 2nd of December
Two more increments of soldiers.

--You have one damned first rate soldier
That I know of down there waiting: Walter Russell.

--He's in that crowd?

--He sure is

--And he's aware that he'll be going?

--Oh they all know they'll be going, they're just
Sitting down there waiting for the order.

--We don't think that we'll be asking
Too much money from the Congress
So as not to blow this up.

--I'm with you all the way on that one,
There's no need of pressing hard.

--I just don't think that we'll be writing legislation.
They can ready plans for calling up Reserves
In case we need them in the next year.
In the meantime I'll be doing all I can
Up at the U.N. with this Jew--
And every other place you'd think of in the world--
For us to get out though we wouldn't want to say so.
If we can't get out I'm stuck,
I'll have to think about Reserves
Along come January 1. But I don't think
I'll call 'em up now. Too dramatic.
It commits me where I can't get back on out.
It also puts me out there farther than
I want to get right now. Does that make sense?

--It does except it feeds into the argument
Old Ho Chi Minh might make
That we aint really going to stay,
That we'll just pull out when the time comes.
It may ease some of the pressure
We want Russia putting on them to get out.

--What do you think?

--Call up Reserves.
They'll understand that kind of language
Since they understood it spoken in Berlin.

--If I extend enlistments, put a hundred thousand
More men in the field, they'll understand that.
I'm afraid they'll understand it all too well.
I don't just have to call up those Reserves though.
I can double up my draft calls.

--You shouldn't send a lot more than
A hundred thousand over, Mr. President.

—That's right and I don't plan to.
I'm just going to send a little less, I think.

—And you've been livin' with this damned thing
Every minute. I just live with it at night.

--I never worked so hard on anything.

--It nearly drives me mad.
It's just the first thing in my life
To which I can't find some quick answer.

--Do you think I need to send
Some kind of message to the Congress
Once I've talked with all the leaders?
Or can I just get me some statement?
I don't need appropriations.
Could I just get me some statement which would say
I'm sending thirty thousand more men in at present,
I'll be sendin' in another thirty thousand
In the future for a total of a hundred thousand men

Who will be added. If I find that I need anything,
I'll call you. I don't want to rile up Russia.

--I'd just play the whole thing down
If that's the way you want to move.
I wouldn't cut down on the fighting though.
Those people over there...they play for keeps.

--I'm putting in a hundred thousand men. Hell,
I've just moved a hundred fifty thousand in
In ninety days.

--I'm still not sure
It wouldn't have a good effect
For you to call up some Reserves.

--But it would agitate the hell out of the North,
They'll go to pressin' for commitments
From the Russians if I force them.

--God knows we don't want that happenin'.
I would say the thing that's scarin' me the worst
Is that these damned Vietnamese,
I mean the South, are going to say this thing's
Your war, you go and take it. Then quit fightin'.
I have all along expected them to do that.
Like that little old man on TV with the moustache
He was on the other night, he seemed to say
That we should be the ones to fight
While his troops pacified the villages
Behind us. God, that scared me!
If they're going to try to fight that kind of war,
I'd be for getting out completely.
If the locals do not really plan to fight.
Even when their losses were tremendous,

Those Koreans kept on fightin', they were
Adding on to units. But in Viet Nam
They're letting theirs run down,
They're just not makin' any effort.

--You don't think I need to say this in Joint Session?

--If I wasn't going to call up those Reserves,
I wouldn't do that, I'd announce it on TV.

277.

"If it's no threat to the people of America
Or no threat to the economic future of our nation--
Or the moral--I would not propose
To sacrifice the life of one American
To lift the white man's burden so to speak."
"If it comes down to that I think we should
Assume it, Mr. President. To do so
Would be better both for us and for the world--
If we impose a peace upon it."
Making war for reason Wilson would approve of.
Waving big sticks. Best of both worlds.
Backing bluff up. TR honored.
High and low roads. Righteous remnants
And the cold steel of pragmatic thrusting in.
The peace restored by force of arms
And legal sanctions, law of nations
As our fig leaf. We're invited in
To re-establish order, never rushing.
We're not seeking to expand our own domains,
It isn't that, it's just hegemony we seek inside
An open global market

Which as well as us will benefit the next man,
Every nation, we're prepared to guarantee that.
What this adds up to is *gravitas*
Of judgment, measured force from
Our mature men, actions carried out
In sorrow, with restraint, extreme regret
And never anger. Legalistic/moralistic
As our flavor. Sober manliness our model
As our statesmen seek to serve the higher law.

278.

He was not good at distinctions
And this got him into trouble rather often.
As a salesman he was possibly the best we've ever had.
You know, a salesman doesn't care
About the tactics he's employed,
He wants to sell you on the spot,
But that can get him into trouble
Later on when he comes back
And hopes you'll place another order.
This is deadliest in politics whenever
You've sold something on a basis
Full of flaws, it tends to kick you
When the wrongness of that basis
Gets discovered down the line.
It's at that point that not only
Do you come out looking foolish—
You might have to scuttle programs
That in fact were very good.
I'm not sure that Johnson fully understood that,
The existence of this problem, I'd have trouble
When I tried to talk such matters over with him—

He disliked finespun distinctions—
It was not that he could not have understood them,
He could understand distinctions if he thought
They really mattered in a case we were discussing.
But he had so much resistance to this aspect
Of an instance that he'd often tend to skip it,
Run right past it from impatience I suppose.

279.

I had talked to many people who'd observed
Civilian matters there—they knew how dense
The whole thing had become, how many threads
Were running through it—unsusceptible
To ordinary treatment of a major power's
Commitment—I think having gained this insight
Made a dove of me—that label didn't mean much.
John Roche still was for commitment. He was bright.
So was Dean Rusk who was a far cry
From the simpleton that Schlesinger
And others tried to make him out to be.
And so an argument in favor of persisting
Still remained, could not be sneezed at.
Thus the President's reaction to the doubts
Clark Clifford had was really awful.
He did mind the fact that Clifford
Had reversed himself a lot, I would have
Minded it myself, been deeply bothered.
When you'd spent as much time struggling
With this war as LBJ had, had invested in it deeply,
Were convinced that nothing else, no other course
Could have been taken—then to open this abyss up!—
You'd already put five hundred fifty thousand

In the breach—and lost so many—
Twenty five thousand men were dead.
What if an error had been made?

280.

Evasive action meant fair game to shoot at.
It was not defined with any great precision.
It appeared to mean "if someone started running…"
So my unit had installed two MP sirens
On our chopper and we used these
To intimidate the people, get them moving.
We passed over once, some people in a paddy,
Maybe twelve, were just there working,
We flew low, but they did not take any action,
They were nervous you could tell,
But they stayed still, they did not run
Or try to hide, so then we hovered
Just a few feet off the ground
And cranked those sirens—that sound
Started them dispersing—we were free then,
Now we opened up and shot the whole bunch down
Who'd just been working there in peace.
Some guys thought of this as hijinks, fun and games.
Those gooks weren't human after all.

281.

I'd submitted all the staff work that the President requested
To reply to Ike's denial that in 1955 we'd made commitments
Of a military nature to Diem. I got a memorandum back
At 10 PM. "The President requested—no, commanded

Me to tell you that this staff work which you've done is not enough.
By the time he gets up in the morning he's expecting
That he'll have from you a copy of whatever may pertain
To all debates we had on SEATO, he wants everything Republicans,
Their Senators and Congressmen, were saying then—and likewise
All the Democrats—whatever shows that SEATO stipulations
Mean we have to offer arms to SEATO countries—
He will need the whole debate and every word that Ike said then
That builds a case up for us now, he wants the full text
Of the letters sent to Churchill and Diem, he wants the kind
Of brief Abe Fortas would be drawing up for Gideon,
Complete, full and convincing, he wants Mac
To get 'Goodpasture,' have him 'copter up to Gettysburg
Tomorrow so the General gets briefed about the battle
We just had in Vietnam, but he should take this letter too
And also copies of the stuff that Mac will dig up overnight.
Tell Mac to get Tom Hughes up out of bed
At State and make him do this job of research, all his people.
And that, poor friend, is almost all verbatim."

282.

November 24. He'd been the President for only two days.
It was a Sunday afternoon, he'd gotten briefed on Vietnam
By Cabot Lodge. He's in his office now alone, with only one aide.
He lies tilted in the chair behind his desk, it's his
Vice-Presidential office which he's still using.
Both feet propped up on the standard issue
Dubiously stained and streaked green waste can.
He's jingling ice cubes in his glass. It's now his aide
Who breaks the silence: What did Lodge say?
Hell in a handbasket out there very soon is what he promised.

Since the army will not fight and since the people
Can't decide what side to be on. If we don't act,
It may very well go under any day.
So what of that, the aide replied.
They'll think the US loses heart because of Kennedy,
They'll think that we've turned yellow, that we don't
Mean what we say. Who's they the aide asked.
It's the Chinese. And the Kremlin. They'll be sizing up
Their chances, seeing how far they can go.
What do you think we ought to do there then, the aide asks.
I'm going to give those fellas out there all the money
That they need. This crowd today with Lodge has said
They think a hundred million dollars ought to do it.
What did you say, asked the aide. That they could have it.
They could have more if they need it. I will not let Vietnam
End up like China, will not lose it. But I told them
Tell those generals out in Saigon Lyndon Johnson
Means for us to keep our word by God, but tell them
I need somethin' for my money and I need it in a hurry.
Tell them get up off their butts, head for the jungles,
Whip the hell out of some communists today
And after that leave me alone 'cause I got
Bigger things to do right here at home.
I hope they do the aide replied
And so do I he said while slowly swiveling in his chair
But right now I feel sort of like a catfish
Down in Lady Bird's and your home part of Texas
By the Taylor store. How so the aide now asked him.
I feel like I just grabbed me a juicy worm
That's got a right sharp hook inside it.

283.

Instead of fortifying any sense of self-esteem,
Of a consoling status (even if ascribed),
The place he came from just eroded
Any sense of who he was.
What after all could anyone expect
Of "just some poor kid" from
The Pedernales' banks? Not much of course.
This theme's familiar: what can anyone
Expect of just some cracker
Or a redneck or a Cajun or
A West Virginia mountain man?
There's no end to all the castigating labels,
All the titles, which are mainly tied
To place of birth and how you've been
Brought up and to your accent
Or your dialect and not to any personal
Achievement or to qualities of character.
The supposed traits that accompany
These labels, these pejoratives,
Are every bit as arbitrary, unfair
And contemptuous as the ethnic
And the racial. And such marks are
Unerasable, indelible, it doesn't matter
What you might achieve. The only thing
That's left to do is overcompensate,
Which Lyndon Johnson did of course
And did it with a vengeance
Since he worked himself and members
Of his staff almost to death, this was
His pattern of performance all his life.
He had accepted what the odds were,
Maybe bitterly, resentfully, but they
Were what he found he had to work with

Or against and so he did. He was
A poor boy from the hills, he'd gone to
Poor and shabby schools and then
A hick college. To attain the prize
A boy like this would have to run
Much faster than the golden-spooned,
The favored ones who had come from
Who knew where, perhaps from Austin first
Or Dallas. Later on it was an ill-defined
Northeast aligned against him,
Like "the Harvards," it was any place
Or no place, from wherever people came
Whom he though socially relaxed,
More intellectual and confident than he was,
Who were not compelled (it seemed)
To prove or justify themselves, they just
Belonged, they kindled jealousy in him
As well as envy, he was drawn toward
Their aplomb while at the same time
He felt forced to put it down, he was
Conflicted, loved to knock them
Off their perches, those who seemed to have
Refined taste or a smug sense of their status.
He'd reduce them with obscenity, of which
He was a master, or exaggerated crudity.
He drove his mother nearly to despair
With how he painted his own childhood,
He invoked log cabin myths and spoke
Of hardship, crushing poverty
And every disadvantage you could think of
Both in schooling and in culture
When the truth was he'd been pampered
And supported by a mother who
To her own mind was middle class,
Respectable, genteel, but his scenario

Of someone who'd been brought up
In the sticks, his dire distortion
Made the distance which he'd traveled
That much greater, his accomplishments
Improbable, pretending to have suffered
In his own life the effects of grinding
Poverty and all the worst discrimination.
Which wasn't true but still he did identify
With those who'd suffered from restrictions
To their chances. As a Hill Country boy
And as a Texan and a Southerner
He knew what it was like to have to
Start from way behind in life's
Ferocious competition. Unlike JFK he knew
What it was like to break a sweat.

284.

One big question plaguing Johnson was of course
How much his governmental stature helped the fortunes
Of their station down in Texas KTBC.
He could not exactly have escaped involvement
If he'd wanted to—not that he wanted to that much—
Because the members of his family were about
The only holders of its stock and Walter Jenkins
Kept the books. He tried to act like he was not
Too much involved, but he was watching
All the sponsors and was always on the lookout for
Fresh talent, most of all for Texas talent.
Walter Jenkins came to see me once
In February 1955 when he was taking care
Of business and we met somewhere for lunch
And Walter told me that the senator

Would like for me to go down there
To Washington to talk. This was a Friday.
So on Saturday I talked to Palmer Webber,
Asked him what I ought to make of this request
That I come down to see the senator,
And he said "Johnny, here's the simple score.
Lyndon Johnson's looking after his concerns
Quite well, old Lyndon walks around
Among the orchards with a basket in his hand,
He never shakes a tree himself, he lets the fruit
Fall heaped up high, though, in that basket.
His great failing is that he's not just suspicious
But he's also downright nervous
When he gets around those Easterners,
He calls them as we all do the Establishment,
And he stands somewhat in awe of them.
Now he's real impressed that you know
Edward Murrow, Walter Cronkite
And the writers for the papers. You've done well.
Now Lyndon thinks he's going to run in '56,
That he and Harriman are going to be the ticket,
They're the only ones that have sufficient money.
I can tell you they'll get beat but still
What Lyndon wants to do is get you lined up,
He wants access to your contacts, he's impressed
With how well known you are along
The Eastern seaboard. What you do is you call
Jenkins, let him know that you can take
Some Sunday off and make the trip down
For a meeting with the Senator whom you have
A great respect for. Now as far as Lyndon Johnson
Is concerned remember one thing: he does right
As long as it don't cost him money. He's for real
But he's the biggest opportunist, he's expedient,
And that would be the reason why the left wing

Scares him so, he's always scared to death
The left wing's not for sale, that they will
Go along with Lyndon when he's right,
Not when he's wrong, that they will not go
To the spring to draw some water
When it aint time." In summation Palmer said
"Yes, you get off, go down and see him
On a Sunday, and I can tell you just exactly
What will happen, Lyndon Johnson's
Going to court you, you have never gotten courted
In you life the way old Lyndon's going to court you.
He's going to have you by yourself, you'll be alone
With him, you only have to say one thing,
You tell him Senator I just turned 21 when FDR
Became the President and so I did not get
To play a part in that historical event
But I've supported you since 1938 and always
Given you my vote and if I thought that you
Were ever going to run to be the President,
I'd gladly give up much of my own life
Just to support you, sir." And Lyndon then
Will run his long legs out right there
In front of him and say" Well John,
I seek no other office than to serve
The Texas people. But I surely do appreciate
Your statement." But by that time
You will know you've got the hook in
Lyndon's jaw, that he will take you for a smart,
Perceptive man, you then can talk
About what you might want from Lyndon.
Not before then though, make sure you make
That statement first exactly like I told you."
It was the damnedest thing that followed.
I flew down there on a Sunday and the senator
Couldn't wait for us to talk, I had this feeling.

We sat down, he poured us drinks and ran
His legs out in the front like Palmer said he would
And I said Senator, the reason I've come down here is...
And I then went on word for word like Palmer
Told me, "I'm not interested really in a radio
Or a TV spot in Texas, if I thought though there was
Any slightest chance that you'd be running as
A candidate for President, the joy and the prestige
Of signing autographs for people up in New York
Wouldn't mean a thing to me, I'd come and join you."
Then the Senator as though he'd had old Palmer Webber
By his shoulder giving orders what to say next
Says to me, "Well John, I seek no other office
Than to serve the Texas people who have given me
Their trust, but I appreciate your statement
Since you come from just the kind of people
I'm from, we were born right up the creek
From one another, Johnson City isn't more
Than forty miles from where your place is."
Then he launched into a spiel about what Bird
Had been acquirin', how the two of them
Were building up a television empire—TV, radio.
And after that he asked me what I wanted
And I told him I was happy where I was,
I told him Texas couldn't pay me what New York did.
Palmer told me I should feel him out
On taking both a salary and interest in the station,
So I said I'd want some stock to make this move
That he suggested worth my while and he said
"Johnny, let me tell you I don't own a single penny
Of the stock, right after Bird and I got married
She was fortunate to have $10,000, KTBC
Was for sale, we took a gamble." Then he tells me
Only Bird owns any stock, "But Johnny,
This can be discussed, we want to see you,

If it works out rest assured that you'll be taken
Real good care of." Understand now up until this time
I had never talked to Bird about the station,
Just the senator who said he had no interest
In the station quote unquote, he was completely
Uninvolved. I said, "Well, Senator, I'll give this thing
Some thought," and I flew back to New York
All expenses paid . And then one Thursday Walter Jenkins
Called me up, was real excited, how the senator
Apologized for calling me so late but could I come
Tomorrow night to be in Washington the next day,
They were having this big party for the Speaker,
It was going to be Sam Rayburn Day in Washington D.C.
So I went down there, Walter met me and he drove me
To the Johnsons'. "Johnny, go to bed real early,
Get your rest because tomorrow is important."
I was given those instructions.
First the Senator was hosting some big breakfast
For the Speaker and the DNC at seven in the morning,
Then at nine there was another breakfast given by
The Texas Club. And then there was a break
And then at 6 o'clock that night a big reception
At the armory, the potentates attending,
Harry Truman and his wife and Mrs. Roosevelt,
Dean Acheson, and then there was a dinner
At which LBJ and Truman were to speak.
Well, we went to both the breakfasts and we had
A real big time and Lyndon courted me,
He introduced me all around to everyone.
By noon we'd gotten over to his office,
But it wasn't long before I said I'm going to the house
To take a nap, I was exhausted, so at least
I got some rest, by six I'm dressed in my tuxedo,
Lyndon's dressed in his tuxedo too,
So first we have this damned reception,

Mrs. Roosevelt, Dean Acheson, the Democratic Party
Since the New Deal reunited, it was wonderful,
And then we went to dinner, it was great too,
There were speeches, it was one o'clock or so
When we got home, my tailgate's draggin'
On the ground by now, I mean I scarcely had
The strength to pull myself out of the car
Despite the fact of having had that nap at midday.
Now the senator of course had had no nap,
He kept on steamin', and he wasn't set on stopping now
At all, he said to Bird that she should go on up to bed,
"I want to talk to John a minute"
Which was desolating news to me
Since I was on the brink of droppin' dead.
"Now I got somethin' here I want to show you, Johnny."
So he produced this air mail packet Special D from KTBC.
It contained the station's last two weeks' receipts.
You must remember now that here I had the leader
Of the Senate, it was one o'clock AM, he had
No interest whatsoever in that station out in Texas
Quote unquote and he now gave me a dissection
Of the workings and the status of the station
Which I doubt that any other station owner
In the country could have given, he was going down
The list of its transactions line by line. There was
A woman, an evangelist, her name was Mildred Wicks,
She did the laying on of hands, accomplished cures,
And she had bought herself commercial time
At night on KTBC costing fifty cents a minute,
Late at night, I think at midnight. Well, she'd canceled
Two commercials and the senator picked up on this
From all the stuff he's reading, "I'll be damned," he said
Since Mildred Wicks had up and canceled on him.
This represented one whole dollar in the company account.
I'd have to say I now felt scared to death, this woke me up

From my exhaustion which was total. I was sitting in
The presence of...what was he? He was not to be believed.
That he could pick this detail up when he'd been running
Fifteen hours in the company of Acheson and Truman
And had made a big splash speaking in his tux.
The man was not to be believed.

285.

Everything was chaos, we were all spinning
Around and around, we were trying to come to grips
With what had happened but the more we made
Attempts to understand it, then the more confused
We got, a bunch of cattle in a swamp with no direction
Simply circling round and round. I understood that,
So I knew exactly what we had to do or rather
What would have to happen. There is but one way
To get a herd of cattle in this state of being caught
Out of the swamp: the man with the hat on the horse
Has to ride from the swamp, he's simply got
To take the lead, assume command, provide direction.
In the period of chaos after Kennedy got shot
I was that man.

286.

I saw him running up the stairs to Air Force One in Dallas,
Secret Service had him running.
I saw Lady Bird then running up them after.

287.

The 31ˢᵗ of March, it's now 2:45 AM
And I've been croaking like a bullfrog.
A speaking tour with nine stops through Wisconsin
Just completed did my voice in and I'm bushed.
I think I'm more exhausted than I've been
In all my life and yet I look upon
The day with satisfaction. Clem Zablocki
Who has come out for the President just left,
Almost effusive in his thanks for what I've done.
He felt I'd made the greatest contribution
To the President's campaign of almost anyone
Who's been here. I did follow up quite hard
On what had happened back in Madison,
I put the whole thing squarely in the context
Of the right of all positions to be heard.
The McCarthy people treated me with kid gloves.
I believe I may have driven home in this state
The importance of the principles we stand for—
More important than what happens in
The primary campaign. But no one knows
What's going to happen and to tell the truth
I'm not too optimistic.
Crowds I drew were pretty good.
I started night before this at LaCrosse,
The Labor Temple with at most 100 people,
All the old folks, labor leaders,
Older farmers, they control the local patronage,
The normal, rather unexciting Democratic Party types,
The regulars, they're good folks, very solid,
And they represent a residue of power.
They were there at least—that's something—
All responsive, conscientious, not too active.
That was pretty much the picture. I had

Airport stops the next day in the morning,
Crowds were friendly, they were bordering 100,
Lots of work was done to turn these people out.
I had the college kids at Appleton.
I lack the strength to write at length about them.
It's a complicated problem, I'd say prospects
Wirth this group are not too good, they're not
Enamored of the President to put it very mildly.
Still they may well be a sleeper. Most importantly
I've heard that many older folks express
Real reservations toward the statements
Which they're hearing from McCarthy
And the Kennedy campaign, they say
"Exactly what do these men have to offer me deep down?
Give me some reason why we ought to change
This man, i.e. the President." I sense potential too
In many numbers of Republicans who might cross party lines,
I hedged my bet on that in speeches, I asked often
Who can say what the result is going to be,
You've got the wife of a Republican who's governor
Campaigning for McCarthy or supporting him at least,
She's been at rallies for McCarthy.
I bore down on him real hard today,
And I'll be curious to see what his response is.
I got the sharpest crowd reaction
With a statement that I'd thought about
Beforehand, I did not go off half-cocked with it
At Warsaw when I said that a McCarthy vote
Was voting for appeasement, while a vote for
Lyndon Johnson was for firmness. I have heard
That the Assembly member introducing me
Disowned me later on the radio tonight,
That is to say disowned my statement.
I've not verified this yet. But I not only
Called McCarthy an appeaser, I took issue

With his statement that the members of the Cabinet
Should stay away from campuses, confine themselves
To forums at the White House, state occasions
Well-protected. I have often called that kind of
Statement flippant—Gene is flippant—
Since the subject of the right that all sides have
To gain a hearing is important, it's the nub of things.
I've introduced most speeches with a statement
Of conviction: "I've come back here to complete
What I was saying several days ago
When storm trooper tactics wouldn't let me
At your own state's university.
What I have to say may not be too important,
But my right to say it is."
The response to this is uniformly good.
So perhaps my contribution is to nail
That concept down in such a volatile environment.
I should probably turn in.
It's been a while since we blew in here.
I should probably have gone to bed at that time.
I was wound up. Several people stayed up with me.
I had time to browse the papers.
It's too hard to reach a place and turn straight in,
You've been excited, gotten stirred up
By the speeches you've been making.
This is new ground for me, so many
Different kinds of people. It has been a real good day,
We'll have to see what happens,
Clem Zablocki thinks that Johnson will get 55%,
Without Republicans that is, among just Democrats
The President gets 60. That sounds over optimistic.
Clem is confident, a damned shrewd politician.
It would be a real leg up though if he's right.
In the meantime he's announced a special broadcast,
He's preempted time on TV for tomorrow.

The prediction for the Presidential speech tonight
Is more troops, more supplies to Vietnam.
As I have felt the situation on the stump,
I would prefer a 30 day pause in the bombing—
Strictly limited—I'm sure that that would be
Far more acceptable to folks, but he's the President,
The one who knows what's what, I have enough trust
In what he and Rusk come up with
To interpret it to groups as I've been doing.
When the pacifists get up and speak of leveling
Of villages and people being killed,
It does get to you in the stomach,
They're quite right to ask how long this thing will last.
What can we do? I wish I knew.
We can't appease or break our word.
We have commitments to protect those
Who have put their faith in us.
I have been saying that all day
And I believe it. But I do wish
We could find some way to end this.

It's the same day, it's 11 PM at home. Well now
The roof has fallen in on us, on all of us,
But who had seen this coming?
Jane and I just took a stroll discussing
What will happen next. The speech was in
Progress, with the President discussing Vietnam
But then the phone rang, not just any phone,
It was the White House phone and Jean ran off
To get it. Then the operator would not be denied,
She said I had to take this call at once
And in the middle of the speech, it did not matter
If I had the speech turned on (how could I not have?).
So I went angrily and took the phone from Jean
And it was Larry Temple calling me to tell me that

The President had wanted me to know
He was announcing in his speech
That he would not seek or accept the Democratic
Nomination, that he appreciated everything
I'd done for him. "My God," I said
And then went right back to the speech, which was impressive,
Deeply moving. Bill Wirtz called me right away,
Asked what I thought. I told him mostly
I felt frightened, I said something trite
Like power abhors a vacuum, I thought
All the special interest groups and pressure groups
Would surely start to rush in, make a mess.
Bill was not of that same mind or not completely,
He was hopeful that the country might respond
To this renunciation gesture that the President had made.
But Congress will not pass the tax bill.
That would be the acid test of their response.
This sure jams up the Presidential race though
And the one who's had his legs sawed off but good
Is poor old Hubert, that whole base he had with ADA
And labor, all the liberals, that's gone—
To Gene or Bobby. Johnson can't help Hubert out
Or he would violate his pledge to stay above
The field of battle. What is Hubert going to do?
He's down in Mexico tonight. He could come back,
Call in some friends and make decisions.
Wirtz is primed now for McCarthy.
I expressed concern that Kennedy might get it.
I said Kennedy impressed me in the Cabinet,
But far less as a Senator, and even less than that
In his campaign, he's been emotional, insensitive,
And negative and uncooperative.
At any rate the whole thing now is screwed up.
I got a call just now from Baker who is out in Indiana.
"What do you suggest we do now, Boss?"

He asked me rather plaintively. I didn't know of course.
My main thought was to batten down the hatches,
Move more strongly on our programs, plow ahead.
I'm afraid whatever chance we had to move them
In the Congress may be gone or very small
Without the power that a Presidential push would give.
I guess I'm kind of numb now.
I slept poorly through the night,
We had to get up very early for our flight,
We had the drive first to Chicago, I got in
At 3 P.M., I couldn't nap, I did some yard work,
Ate some dinner, then the President came on.
It's time for bed and yet my desk's piled high
With papers. I am overbooked tomorrow,
Off to Tokyo on Wednesday. Far too much.
And yet to go ahead with business
Is the only way to deal with such a shock.

288.

Bobby's going to have to shoot straight pool from this time forward
Since the game's no longer banking shots off Lyndon.

289.

—I think this is the best we could have done,
Pretend it's victory. They really rolled us good.
The time will come, though, when we've figured
How to beat them. I'm not sure
What I can do but I know this:
They make us report it and they make us all but advertise,
And every time we have to do that the Russians get angry,

And it's them I have to deal with.
—All it says is that you have to notify them
In the Congress that the wheat sale's in our interest.
—When you notify them, though,
They write a story you're pro-Russian
—You just put a little letter in the mail.
Don't that much notify 'em?
—They'd say you're yielding to the Russians.
H.L. Hunt puts out a news release.
I don't want to debate it with you, friend.
You have to trust me when I ask them
Not to make me give them notice
So it won't get in the papers
That I know just what I'm doin'.
And we really screwed it up.
This damned fool Humphrey put that paragraph upon us.
—He told me he would do his very damnedest
To remove that paragraph.
—I've got the language right in front of me
And it oughtn't to be there nohow.
Why should I want to tell the whole
Damned world I screwed a girl?
You screwed one last night
But you don't want to report it.
—Wish I had.
—That makes it come home to you, don't it though?
I'm the damnedest fool on earth now.
It just publicizes me as lovin' Russians.
Just when Nixon's makin' plans to run against me.
You can't tell me that that clause they've got's
A good one. You can't shit me.
When a Democratic President's
Required to give such notice
That our interest means it's good
To go for Russia, it can't help him

When he starts to run for office.
I'm humiliated, here I am the President,
I've got a friendly Speaker and a leader
Of the Senate, I've got Albert Thomas, Jack Brooks
As my friends, but Passman ends up being king.
I think it's awful, it's disgraceful
That a goddamned Cajun cave man
Got the best of us, surpasses us in power.
I will tell you fellas sometime
What we're facin' in the world
And it's a whole lot worse than last year.
If I woke up in the middle of the night
And saw a rattlesnake a-slitherin' toward Passman,
I aint gonna pull it off him let me tell you.
Now you go and tell those Texans
If they want to hit the Russians,
They should go and fight the Commies
For themselves a while, I'll dress those sons a' bitches up
As soldiers, let them fight. They talk a big game.
Hubert's got his damned amendment drafted wrong.
Tell him no more talkin' first and thinkin' after…

290.

The politician's talent as defined by Lyndon Johnson
Was to enter, to inhabit minds of many kinds of men
For which one needed to control all information.
The self he'd play to one man must be secret to
Some other, he could not let those who'd seen him
In the "right" role (vis-à-vis them) happen on him
In the "wrong" one at the wrong time somewhere else.
He had compartments. He'd be juggling
This whole massive apparatus of deception

If you will or of selective information,
Being many things to many kinds of people,
A political St. Paul, but when it worked,
Got good results, the very Senate he'd deceived
Heaped praise upon him as a leader
For the miracles he'd wrought,
So in his own mind he assumed that he'd be praised
For "pulling off" (as he described it)
Both the war in Vietnam and Great Society at home.
But he could not show how he did it at the time,
By indirections he would find directions out,
He'd contradict himself, finesse it,
Keep his dealing with a certain group,
The generals let's say, a well-kept secret
From some other, his domestic politicians.
It was the same thing with campaigning,
Tell the truth but tell it slant because democracy
Demanded good results, not big debates
That squandered energy and time,
Engendered conflicts.

He had worked so hard, had put so many years in,
He had reached the point not only of proposing
But of passing legislation, he possessed at last
Authority to use, he'd now help people
More than even FDR had, he'd achieve the dream
His father had embodied for him first—
Improving lives—the dream was there
For him to see and almost touch
And he was not about to let some puny war
Come and destroy it, he had no choice
But to keep his foreign policy a secret.
He refused to make a choice, he was determined,
He believed both in the war and in prosperity
And peace, he meant to have both.

He would not admit he could not have it all,
That he would have to make some choices,
Live with limits, set priorities, adjudicate
The conflicts that arose, he tried to compromise
The conflicts by his skilled manipulations,
Artful soothing, artful dodging, he'd be seeking
For a formula that satisfied all claims
As he had done when he was leader of the Senate.

FDR did not attempt to do the New Deal
And a World War at the same time.

291.

The poll tax fight went on for years and years
But Lyndon took no active part,
In fact he'd always vote against us
When it came up in the House
And I would bitterly reproach him.
He would put his arm around me,
He'd say "Honey, you're dead right
And I support you, I'm all for you
But we aint got votes right now."
He'd say "Let's wait till we get votes
And then we'll pass it."
This I would say was the essence
Of Lyndon Johnson. Maury Maverick
Always acted like a bull,
He just charged in there, he'd go
Crashing with his head against the wall.
But Lyndon wouldn't stick his neck out
Till he knew he had the votes,
He was a super politician, very cagey.

I believed that he and I were on the same side.
He would wait, though, over decades
If he had to, he had patience.
And of course he came from Texas
Where he had to forward oil's cause.
If he didn't he'd be sent home in a minute,
No more LBJ in Congress. He would
Have to fight the fight of oil depletion,
All those oil men had complete control
Of Texas. Lyndon never sat
And talked about philosophy
Of government or of the poll tax,
He just acted. There was nothing inarticulate
About him, he would talk a lot, he kidded.
We all knew how he adored Bird,
He was totally dependent on her help,
But you would never hear him say
How he loved Bird. Of course
He worked her near to death,
And all her women friends got mad
When he would brings those shoals of people
Home for dinner, not give Bird a bit of notice.
There are cousins she has back in Alabama
Who will still say "Bird was certainly
A sweet girl, we all love her, but that Lyndon!
It was terrible the way he went and worked her,"
And he did you know, he just took Bird for granted.
She was entertaining breakfast, lunch and dinner,
You would not believe the crowds that she would feed
And maybe put up over night. But I got sidetracked.
Lyndon never talked philosophy that I knew.
He was far too busy acting.

292.

Dorothy Nichols had to travel
In a separate car to keep track of his clothes.
He would shower every other stop or so
To get the grime off and at least change shirts
Each time, he wore these monogrammed
White shirts that had French cuffs
And always Countess Mara ties
And one time Dorothy even asked
About this regimen, she may have
Even chided him a bit about the need
For such resplendence. He replied:
"My people down here aren't just sendin' me
To Washington D.C. to have my nostrils
Sprouting hayseeds or my ear-lobes
Sprouting onion shoots.
They want someone representing them
That they can take some pride in,
Not some yokel from the country
In a dirty shirt with snuff juice
Dripping down it from his chin."
But he would alternate between
Refined and crude, he'd be obsessively
Immaculate by day but in the evening
In an overnight hotel room on the road
He almost seemed to take delight,
He liked to shock the more protected of
Our cadre, he'd present himself, a hunk
Of lumpen flesh with all its needs,
He'd be there belching, breaking wind
While he was talking, he would stalk
Into the bathroom there to urinate
Or defecate, he never shut the door
Nor did he ever lose the thread

Of his remarks or he'd launch into
Long descriptions of utopias
He meant to bring to pass, in which
He'd have the central place,
Romantic visions of the man
That LBJ was meant to be:
That cruddy piece of clay whose every
Urge we'd had to witness would be turned
Into a living work of art.
He was what Shakespeare
Would have called the thing itself though,
He'd be shaving in the morning,
He'd tell Phipps to call "the girls"
And both the Dorothys, Dorothy Nichols,
Dorothy Plyler would appear,
They'd bring their notebooks, he'd be
Standing there before the mirror to shave,
He'd have a towel around his middle
Loosely draped, they'd take turns standing
In the doorway making notes of his
Instructions, he'd be barking out the orders,
Both girls scribbling, but the towel
Would tend to slip off, he'd just keep on
Shavin', talkin', it seemed nudity,
Especially his own was no concern,
It was a simple state of nature.
The man was something of a cyclone.
He had secretaries working in a relay,
There were three of them and they'd go
Alternating off for weeks of rest,
They'd set a schedule to survive.
When you were working, there'd be
Meetings in the evening, re-cap meetings,
Then the next day's schedule had to be

Assessed, you'd get to bed at 3 AM,
But he was up again at 5.
The people working for him had
To get some kind of break from this.
The congressman himself of course continued.

293.

The poor in our cities…
They have merely been the wards
Of our political machines.
The machines had need of poor folks
To exist, the poor folks needed
Those machines to just survive
And the benevolence of all the politicians
Toward the poor kept this arrangement
On the tracks. Then we discovered
That these poor folks wanted more
Than some illusion of their really being in,
They wanted power, wanted some sense of
Control, they were revolting,
They weren't satisfied
With condescending head-pats any longer.

294.

Of all the opportunities to disengage we missed
I think of one we missed in 1964, a crucial
Turning point. The President had asked
His chief advisors to prepare for him
As wide a range of options to consider
Post-election as they could, he wanted

Every course of action they could think of
On the table, no omissions, all scenarios.
What followed in effect was Lyndon Johnson's
Bay of Pigs, a long drawn out one.
His advisors all effectively converged
On only military options juxtaposed
Against two other very phony kinds of options
(blow the world up in effect or run-and-scuttle).
Thus the President was faced with unanimity
For bombing in the North among the counselors
He relied on. He may not have been
Too confident in dealing with affairs
Beyond our borders, he was not
That well-informed concerning matters
That pertained to Southeast Asia
(although you might have asked who was
Among the men who served around him)
And the kind of unanimity
The President was faced with had submerged
The searching questions he or someone
Should have asked when you considered
What a mandate he'd been handed by the voters.
What's the worse that could have happened?
That a neutralist regime had taken over
In Saigon and asked that US forces leave?
When you consider all the lives
And all the dollars wasted since,
That kind of outcome seems a dream
Of some lost paradise we spat on
Or disparaged.

295.

I returned in June of 1966
And I reported to the President,
The options out in Vietnam I thought
Were either Fourth or Fifth Republic,
That with luck we'd get the Fifth,
If we had bad luck we would end up
With the Fourth: I thought some semblance
Of democracy was possible out there,
That is procedures could be put in place
And maybe made to operate.
But stability could not be guaranteed.
I also offered up a lot of caustic
Comments on the presence of Americans
Which I found unbelievable.
I may have been the first to push
For Vietnamization though it didn't
Have that name yet, what we needed most
Was getting Viet people into action,
What had happened in July of '65 was
McNamara got the war as his to run.
He and the I.S.A., his sort of
Mickey Mouse-type state department,
Spun this nice scenario: the war could be
Quite limited, would only take two years
And at the end of two years things
Would be just fine. Now they envisioned
Getting children off the streets,
That is the fundamental premise
Was to get the Viet people off the streets,
They thought they'd run them in
And sit them in a balcony with box seats
Where they'd watch us while we won
Their war for them, "They're just a nuisance,

If you've got them there, you're then obliged
To train them, they're corrupt."
What was happening when I was out in 'Nam
In '66 was this huge input of Americans
And our impedimenta piling into
This small country, ripping up its social fabric.
We should have cut down two thirds
On the size of our commitment
With an increase in efficiency of fifty,
Maybe more than that per cent.
I have a sort of warm nostalgic glow
Abut PX's from my time in World War II,
But I don't think you need eleven
Of our GI's in the tail for one up front.
That's overdoing it. The Holy Roman Empire
Making war, you had feudalities, the A.I.D.
Had its turf, and the others,
It had made Saigon a shambles,
Just the whole damned thing a shambles.

296.

He was capable of childish temper tantrums,
That's the only way I think you could describe
The fits he had. He was titanically ambitious,
He was so aware how easily the train
Could go off course, a little penny on the track
Might well derail it. He did not want
Anybody putting pennies on his track,
He was afraid of that. If anybody
Really came a cropper, made a huge mistake,
He could exemplify compassion.
It was the small mistakes he could not tolerate.

I think he realized if you really made a cropper,
There was little he could do to make you feel worse.
He was a man who never quite learned
To control tremendous force within himself,
This heaving temper, this emotion,
Bubbling fountain of desire and of emotion,
Aspiration, it just flowed from him,
A great explosive force. When it was thwarted,
He would throw a temper tantrum like a kid,
He'd turn on anyone, without restraint
He'd really lash out. But I've seen him,
On important things, behaving more restrainedly
Than Job himself had been, he'd be
A monument to patience on a pillar.
On the lesser things, though, he could grow
Volcanic, it didn't always seem to make
A lot of sense or halfway jibe
With what the situation was.

297.

He'd read something in the paper or a briefing memo,
Things would catch his interest, he would
Call the guy involved and ask him
"What does this phrase mean?"
Or "What the hell are these folk
Doing to us here?" And he did not just
Pick the phone up, he would grab it
Out of secretaries' hands while they were talking,
Cut off conversations he had just instructed them
To have on his behalf and dial some other number—
That meant *his* number—he'd reduce these girls
To tears. I think it almost did him in

When he would try to watch three TV channels
All at once and at the same time
Talk on two phones since he only had two ears.
He would have called up Jesus Christ
At any time except he didn't have his number.
There wasn't any hour at which
He wouldn't call you up at home,
There'd be that voice of his pursuing you.
He'd have some subject on his mind,
He'd have the stuff about it right there
On his desk, you wouldn't have it
At your house, he'd be expecting you
To have it in your head though, be conversant.

298.

Sometimes he'd enter my office
And he'd offer observations. Like
"I see we've gained a pound or two."
You knew then that you'd better
Start a diet. He'd be planting
These suggestions. If you
Hadn't had your hair done,
He'd stroll in and say
"It must be getting windy."
He was adamant about the state
Of stockings, he could see
A mile away if they had runs.
I'd be so nervous every time
I'd walk away from him, I knew
That he'd be looking up and down,
I mean the treatment was complete,
We're talking scrutiny and then some.

And if you had a tiny little run,
You'd better change those stockings.
It was always best to have
An extra pair inside your desk.

299.

He had a phone/microphone, a sort of horn
Atop his desk so that the utterance,
When it would get to my phone, seemed a riot
On Fourteenth Street being picked up through
The subway grates at Times Square,
More than garbled, you could not make out
The half of what he said, I'd hold the phone
Out there at arm's length, let him rave.
From time to time it helped if you said
"Yes, sir," let it go at that. So many people
Didn't understand this, they would take
These rants as personal attacks when they
Were not that, he was screaming at the universe,
Not them, your only function was to stand there
Bearing witness, keep him company at that point.

300.

The entourage had staggered through the door of our hotel
When this incredible long day, this surreal marathon
Of motorcading ended, northwest Indiana, countryside
And cities flashing by us, nine whole hours of this.
Germond and I had headed for the bar to have a nightcap.
We were balanced on our stools when in came Kennedy himself
Who didn't often do the bar scene late at night with us reporters.

He declined the seat we offered, he just stood at our
High table call it musing. "I've done all I could," he said,
"It simply may not be my time. I'm sure of one thing:
That old Democratic coalition, labor and the South,
Cannot be looked to any longer as the answer,
We must rather bring together whites and blacks
Here in the North, the social barriers between them
Must be broken." He was also deeply bothered by a sign
Which read YOU PUNK, the man who brandished it
Ran out and got ahead of where the car was,
Then turned back and grabbed his hand as it came by.
"He squeezed so hard, I was convinced that he was
Breaking every bone of it on purpose."

301.

The man who taught me most of all was Alvin Wirtz,
A Senator from Texas. Now at one time he
Was trying to persuade the local power groups
To put in lines to reach way out to rural areas
To help the little farmers, it required a lot of effort,
But he organized a meeting and the power guys
Were there as were consumers' representatives.
The power guys were playing hard to get,
Were being difficult. At one point this young
Ardent jackass of a populist who thought
He knew it all got up and blew his stack
And gave the power people hell,
And his performance caused some stir
And won him praise—except the meeting,
When it broke up, had arrived at no decision
And I noticed that my friend and mentor Wirtz
Did not look toward me with much praise

And admiration. "You had better come
To my office "was as far as he would go
Until we got behind closed doors.
Then came the real stuff. "Lookee here, Lyndon,
I worked more than one whole year
To get that meeting pulled together,
You have simply got to realize who in this world
Owns the power, we won't get a single kilowatt
Of it unless those men that we were sitting with
Agree, you might feel good about the ruckus
You just raised, that real fine speech that you
Just made, but let me offer this advice:
Never tell a man to go to hell unless you're sure
That you can send him there yourself."
I learned that democratic politics was summed up
In that speech that Wirtz had made to me,
The opposing forces have to reach consensus
And it isn't only flattening your adversary this day,
He's the one you have to live with every
Next day after that, I mean that son of a bitch
You just knocked off his perch.
You ought to think that thought before you go to bed,
Ask how to keep that fella friendly.

302.

It's not enough for me to stand before you and condemn
The riots. I would also at the same time, to be morally
Responsible, have to talk about conditions that convince
The people rioting that the only way for them to gain attention
Is to take part in these violent rebellions.
A riot is the language of the unheard,
And let's ask ourselves the question

What America has failed or is refusing now to hear.
To put it one way very bluntly whites are making
No attempt to overcome their racial ignorance,
They are convinced they have so little left to learn,
And real investment, bringing Negroes up to standards
Of the present, gauging sights to having Negro neighbors
Next door and to real school integration is a nightmare
For the most well-meaning white which he suppresses.
This is what it means for blacks to be unheard,
The white suppresses their desires. There's a loose
And easy language of equality that's bantered,
There are resonant, high-minded resolutions
Touting brotherhood of races, these sound pleasant,
They may gratify the white ear, but the Negro knows
That every time he makes some even smallest type
Of progress then the white says "That's enough,
You should be satisfied with that, why ask for more."
Each forward step accents a tendency to backlash.
It would almost seem, I'm driven to regrettable conclusions
That the Negro's greatest stumbling block as he attempts
To stride toward greater freedom isn't Ku Klux Klan
Resistance but the white well-meaning moderate
Devoted to tranquility and order, not to justice.
"I agree with you in all the goals you're seeking,"
Is his message to the black man,
"It's your methods that are making me uneasy,
Your direct action." It's paternalistic presence
As he sets some kind of schedule he approves of
For the freedom of another, of the black man,
At a "more convenient season." Whose convenience
Is at stake here? Men of good will showing
Shallow understanding are in some ways worse,
More baffling to the Negro than the men of ill will
Shutting off benighted minds completely.
Lukewarm acceptance versus outright rejection,

Which is worse? I'm not sure which
Includes the greater form of insult.

303.

"It doesn't seem that we can win by military means
Or diplomatically. We've tried all your suggestions.
The demonstrators want to show
We need somebody else to lead this country.
People who call for a halt in the bombing
Ought to know what we've gone through
In this exchange, the Paris channel, by negotiating.
The hawks are throwing the towel in,
I'm getting hit from every side.
The San Antonio formula had no impact,
But I cannot mount a better explanation.
We must show the people
We have tried and failed but that we've walked
The extra mile in their defense."

304.

—...That I thought would do me good
And I would ask the U.S.I.A folk
If they knew anyone who wanted you to broadcast
And I'd go up on all the TV if they wanted you
You know and I would go to any of the young folk
Even those that march against ya
But you've got so much good sense
And sense of humor, you can laugh 'em
Out of it, I'm not concerned about
The kind of thing they'll do to you but anyway

It seems to me you need a damned good staff
And have a personal occasion, get yourself
Some real good press, you'll look real substantive
For workin' on these things, for goin' over
At the President's request and don't apologize
For any goddamned thing, take the offensive

—Yessir, that's exactly what I have in mind to do.

—I'd just say that our position is
We'd like to stay exactly where we are
And not change NATO but we think
That every nation ought to do what it's agreed to,
You can tell 'em we will do it but it's hard
When all the rest of them have not come up to us
We have to rotate one division, they can
Count on us to keep up with the one,
Tell them our President does not believe
In changin' it at all, we don't believe we ought
To have an invitation for those sons of bitches marchin',
He does not forget what Khrushchev, though,
Told Kennedy when they met in Vienna..

—No sir.

—We don't wanna be encouragin'
But they encourage 'em for sure
When they jump over us out there in Vietnam,
That kinda stuff, the weaker they are
Then the weaker NATO is, they ought to
Have the sense to know that if they think
We're just a bunch of country bumpkins
They're a bunch of goddamned fools,
They ought to end all these attacks on us,
Now I'd get in there, I'd tell Wilson,

Pull in every damned back bencher,
I just talked to him last night about the bombin',
They got in last night and bombed a bunch
Of our folk, bombed and killed 'em,
No one says a word when they bomb,
If they'd stop this goddamned bombin' for a while,
Then we'd lay off our bombin' too…

—Well, I think that I can do a bit of work on them

—I'd just take this old back bencher, just say
You're not going to yield to any liberal ideas
From a goddamned one of 'em
That you were facin' this same fight
When you were killin' German fascists

—Yessir

—Europe, when you had to go across,
The battle of Britain, you had shoesteads
In your state and every city in the US
Raisin' hell then and you got the same type now
But that the time has come to stand up
To the people who are tryin' to provoke
This kind of tyranny, enslave folks
And would do it by aggression,
That you did it when you had to there
In Greece, in Turkey, that you did it
Where it rears its ugly head and just because
It isn't there in their back yard's no reason now
To think by God it's all right goin' off inside of
Someone else's yard, now we will try to get it
Cleared up for the weekend, my position
In the broad sense is I won't give up an inch,
Won't give a soldier, I don't wanna give

A damn thing, I want every one of them
To do what they agreed to do
And they have done it since they want to,
My own Congress wants to bring 'em all
Back home, I'm gonna play around
And rotate one division but I'll have 'em,
It won't mean a goddamn thing,
I'll have 'em in an' out, my airplanes,
They won't need but one day's notice,
I'll have all divisions there, I hope
That I can keep my own damned Congress
From withdrawin' them, I know I can
If Germany stands up and does its part

—Well, I'll be able to discuss these matters openly
With Leddy won't I Monday of this next week,
That way get a lot of solid information.

—You can do it, talk to anyone you want to,
Trouble is though that your staff
Gets this stuff out and I been readin' in the papers
How the Democratic party, take what have you,
Every columnist throughout the whole
Damned country, they just got the greatest stuff,
Not only Allen, Maryann Means too

—Oh I know, I know, I read all about that stuff
They had with Allen, not a person you can find
On God's green earth has ever talked to him

—No but they talk to other people
And they pick it up from others and they do talk
Cause I never talked to anyone about it
But to you but then goddamn it I start readin'
In the papers, you just tell your little boys,

It's true, and every VP we have had has had this problem
They all think that their man's gettin' overlooked
And when they get a goddamned inch
They take a mile, they haven't got enough
Good sense and if they leave that up to you
Why then you'll make their mile and do it
In a hell of a way if they don't bomb ya
And torpedo ya and Rauh now what I'd do
Is stay away from goddamned columnists
And papers, tryin' to blow yourself up big
To Evans, Novak, all that bunch,
They've got you anyway,
Then I would get me a damned good outfit
And I would get me some damned good speeches
And I'd make a hit with TV and the radio
And stuff out there, and I would take
A good group with me if you want to
In your own plane, you could take one of
The big planes, I'd remain reserved
And dignified, the best way you perform
Is not too friendly, too forthcoming
And a little bit reserved, a bit judicious,
Now I never saw you better than today
And it's because you were the last
And 'cause you didn't wanna keep 'em
And because you didn't get your hockey hot,
You didn't get yourself worked up,
You just were perfectly judicious,
That's the way I'd go and treat this goddamned press,
I'd make it look like you're a big man,
A judicious man, a statesman
And you won't go and get perturbed
By little nit pickers goin' round
With all the peace speakers,
I'd never refer to them by name,

Whenever they referred to me
I'd simply smile and go on otherwise,
But I would show I was the man, my only interest
Was in keepin' this alliance pulled together
And preservin' what could easily have been
A big disaster and our own Congress
You had Mansfield and the whole committee,
Russell, you had all of them unanimous to bring
The boys back home, now we've averted that,
You've got to let the British know
They can't just simply up and run out
We understand that they've got problems,
All they've done since I've been President
Is send us Douglas Hume
And he comes over here and tells me
What they've got to do for Cuba,
They send Wilson over here,
He has to tell me how he won the Nobel Prize,
The people called up in the middle of the night
And then by God he says there's nothin' he can do
Unless we give him all the funds he needs to do it
Then the next day he lends Cuba 40 million,
We're behind him in those money matters
He's got all messed up in, then he lectures us
On keeping him informed, we haven't done it,
Then he issues what's a truly damned fool statement,
He's an inch away from peace, just with
The slightest little turn he would have had it,
That's a mile high load of bullshit,
Any fool who's read the letter of the Pope
Is well aware, now Wilson oughtn't to
Be giving us those lectures, I just
Wrote a wire and told him, I could not give this guy
Power of attorney so that he could show his ass,
So that's the picture, we still like him,

But we're foreign, always will be with the British,
But he's got to understand
I've got a hell of a lot worse problems
Than the British, ask how many men in Vietnam
Does he have, how many mothers has he got
That call him up and so if he can't hold his own out there
He isn't very strong and by God Churchill
Took the battle of Britain on, he took it
Waiting on us too by God and so if this guy
When he doesn't hear a sound can't take the heat,
I mean he couldn't take a seismograph
And find one goddamned rumble of an earthquake there
In London, he hasn't got a single man there
And we're payin' all the bills
And we are losin' all the lives
And so by God he's simply got to learn to shimmy,
He can't squat there wettin' ground
Like our friend Adlai and pull his bloomers up
And come back over, tie his belt

—Well I think that I can work on him,
Be helpful, Mr. President.

—And you tell Kiesinger we love him and the Germans,
We put Germans number one,
I am the most pro-German President
The Germans ever had, but their man
Can't remain as President too long
And have the Chancellor say
He's in complicity with Russia, not conferrin',
By God I've given the Germans more time,
Willy Brandt did not have one foot out my door
When that damned fellow started saying George McGee's
Been camped out here and on behalf of German interests,
Old Erhard showed up here before the ink

Had started dryin' on my oath,
I took him home with me for Christmas,
Had him talkin', then for them to say
We haven't been conferrin',
And I had than damned disarmament man
Bill what's his name

—Bill Foster—

—Yeah Bill Foster, he was over there to see 'em,
He stuck their nose up their ass every day for months
By God he's out there namin' me as in complicity
With Russians, I have made no damned agreement
With the Russians, I check everything with him
He'd better lay off usin' names like that
To call us in the papers I know how to call a man
A goddamned four-square headed son of a bitch
In ten more languages than those guys ever heard of.
I just got more manners, I mean
That's what you've got to tell him
If you want to cuss each other out in papers
By God this guy he's a goddamned mountaineer
And he knows how to do it,
He can call you a shitass seven different ways,
And he wouldn't ever use that word complicity,
He doesn't wanna do it cause he likes ya but
This is no way to try our cases, in the papers.

—Well, I hope that I'll be doing you some good.

305.

It was only seconds after LBJ had thrown the towel in,

Young folk boiling down the Hotel Schroeder's corridors
In search of celebration, rapt with glee, this was
Their moment, one poor kid who may not yet
Have turned 18 all by himself, no one to dance with,
With his brilliant yellow sweater, tousled hair,
He loped and swiveled, shook his balled fists disbelieving.
"I have helped to unseat LBJ the President," he whooped.
OK I wondered (wished him joy) but what comes next?

306.

Roosevelt redivivus—I'm sure that's what
He was dreaming he could be, the whole
Nine yards, the great progressive
On the home front and the sorely burdened
Father of his country fighting wars
Around the world. Beloved as both.
It wouldn't wash, the times had changed,
The people didn't want this act
A second time, his fondest image of himself,
It shocked and hurt him, it's the hardest
Thing to do, unset your mind
From some scenario the ducks of which
You know are going to line up as they ought to
Then they don't.

307.

Of course Clark Clifford's doubts upset him greatly.
Who would not have been upset if he had spent
As much time agonizing over Vietnam as LBJ had,
Who'd invested his whole soul in this.

He knew his place in history depended on
The outcome of this war no matter what else
He had done, on whether he'd been right
To escalate the war, so having me,
An English major type of lawyer who was sniping
At his choices from the comfort of the sidelines
No doubt galled him. Things got worse though
When the Wise Men came the second time
To open up the chasm of this issue once again.
Christ, you had put five hundred fifty thousand
U.S. soldiers out there, of those
Twenty five thousand soldiers now were dead.
What if it's wrong? What if you've made
This massive error? All the wisdom of the time
Was that the choice of building troops up
Was the right one. Looking back on it,
The situation's weird in '65, you might have thrown in
Every factor you could think of to the mix
And turned the blender on, and it would still
Have come out belching with the answer saying "Go."
It really shocked him when The Wise Men
Turned against him, he had never heard
These people say such things, I mean
Dean Acheson and Dillon, men of that stripe,
Men of stature who'd been stalwart up till then.

308.

There was the factor of ego investment
Since these guys have taken part in a decision
Which they thereby gain a stake in
And that stake of theirs increases as they go on
Taking steps, make more decisions.

Now you might dissuade a man
Of strong self-confidence if you still
Have him confined upon a low rung of
The ladder of decision—maybe, maybe—
But the higher up he goes it gets much harder
Since a change of mind up there
Means walking back a string of previous
Decisions, asks for self-repudiation, magnanimity,
Or as a wise man (maybe LBJ) once said,
By simply starting up the ladder or the pole
You have exposed your ass already.
At the heart of our calamity in short
You have a group of able, dedicated men
Who have repeatedly been wrong.
Their standing at the present time
And more importantly in history
Depends as they perceive it on their
Being proven right. Do they dig in
Or do they back down? These are not the men
You'd call on when the time arrives
To extricate the USA from error.
They can't lose face.

309.

"If you support Lyndon, you will get the housing project
And your paper too will prosper.
If the paper don't endorse him,
You will never see those housing funds down here."
Now my response to this appeared June 25th.
I wrote a column. "If we want to get
Those federal funds out here, it's good to have him
On our side. In my opinion though a part

Of any federal funds is mine, it's just as much mine
As it's Roosevelt's or Johnson's. And I'm hanged
If I am going to be bamboozled into voting
As they want me to to get my hands on money
Which is mine, at least a part of it is mine.
So rugged, ornery and gall-durned independent—
Those are Texas traits for sure though we've been
Loyal to the Roosevelt administration almost
To a fault I'd say but we reserve the right
To think and vote as we see fit."
So we endorsed Johnson's opponent
Although I told my readers vote for whom
You please for your own reasons.
Of course our housing project never got
The federal funds which we requested.
I ran into Johnson later at a barbecue he hosted
For the whole town. His face hardened
When he saw me. "What the hell right
Do you think you have to be here?"
Was the burden of the message he conveyed
By that expression of annoyance—maybe worse.
He demanded that you cave in to his will.
I may very well have forfeited my right
To even live at least in his mind.

310.

I was told when I arrived
You won't believe this man, this Johnson,
He's not real, I mean he's absolutely not.
But I for years had heard the Lyndon stories
(stuff of legend) at a hundred backyard gatherings
On summer nights in Austin

When the conversation slacked
And someone raised his voice and asked
"Well have you heard the latest thing
That Lyndon did [or Lyndon said]?"
And we would draw our chairs in closer, that way
Adding great enjoyment to that evening's
Watermelon we were having for dessert.
Many conferences among the staid old
Austin banker-types and Austin businessmen
Would end when LBJ, a representative
At that point, junior Congressman, would feel
He'd had enough of going nowhere,
He'd just stand up, tell those patriarchs
They all could go to hell—or it was sometimes
More explicit, he'd be spinning out his scheme
For postwar growth when some old fossil,
Who was not exactly bullish on the new world
Or on anything since maybe 1910,
Informed the Congressman that he for one,
His family and his friends were very fond
Of Austin just the way it was, could not conceive
Of any need for it to grow. A long nose leaned in,
Almost touched the old man's face,
And then a voice: "Your brain's been clogged
For thirty years," the brash young Congressman
Began, "and it would be a signal service
To the city if you poured a can of Drano in
To get the blockage moving."
I once heard a lawyer well-disposed
Toward Lyndon say, "No tellin'
Where that boy would go if only
He could somehow rein it in"—he meant
Could someone help young Lyndon get a grip?
But even old-line-family Austinites
Repeated all the stories though they often

Added others they'd invented to confirm
Their oldest bias: Lyndon Johnson
Lacked all breeding, he exemplified
The riff-raff which the better sort of people
Had been plagued with by the New Deal's
Revolution, Franklin Roosevelt's betrayal
Of his class. But LBJ provoked
A kind of fascination, politicians could
And did not act the way this fellow acted.
Everyone in Austin wondered just how far
This guy could really go, how long he'd last
When he rebelled against the protocols
So freely, so persistently. By any kind
Of calculus a fall was in the offing.
At the same time he provoked a kind of envy,
Secret envy in his fellow politicians,
They'd have liked to say what they thought
When they thought it just like Lyndon
And to not put up with fools
And not to toady to the patriarchs
Whose rings all politicians had to kiss,
But no one else had the audacity,
The carelessness of Lyndon, the political
Realities meant nothing to this man,
He just defied them. Lyndon Johnson
Was apostate on the issues,
So the Statehouse whispers went,
Did not defend true Texas dogma,
He spoke well of federal aid to education,
He lacked fervor in defending Texas tidelands,
He was soft on civil rights, he didn't shriek
When socialized medicine was mentioned,
Didn't seem to mind the tempest
He unleashed in his home district
On the two or three occasions he suggested

Co-existence of a mild sort with the Russians.
He was cavalier in dealing with the state's
Main sacred cows: big oil, utilities, employers.
It was thought no politician could defy
These powers and live, yet Lyndon did.
Out on the stump, when he campaigned,
Few men in Texas were his equal,
He would orchestrate applause
To his words' rhythms, he would cue up
The emotions of the crowds, he got them
Hissing when he mentioned his opponents,
He'd be mobilizing marchers to the polls
To smite down enemies. Before I ever met him
I'd go stand beside the downtown Austin park,
Out at its edges, just to hear him
And to watch this man in action from a distance,
He'd be shouting, pounding, whispering
And thundering his message, he'd be
All around the stage disdaining microphones
And speakers, you could not resist this man,
On summer nights he'd take sedate crowds,
He'd transform them into...well,
I guess you'd have to call them mobs,
They'd be perspirin', stompin' feet.
He wasn't careful with his voice
As politicians ought to be,
He let the words come raw and grating,
This just added something guttural,
A convincing kind of meanness
When he took out after PUP, a term
He'd fashioned for Petroleum,
Utilities and Privilege. When he'd finished,
People did not want to leave, they crowded
Toward him, he came lunging out
Among them, coatless, drenched with

Perspiration, touching people, being touched.
Sometimes he'd fall clear out of sight
Beneath the crush, the young and old folks
Who were struggling to be near him.
But in 1946 his greatest test came
When election time rolled round
And there would be no FDR
Back at the White House to support him
Or to save him. All the past
Closed in upon him, his defiance
Of the rules of Texas politics of course
And his revolt against the protocols.
Big oil, the power trust, the business lobbies
Brought up all their gathered forces
To annihilate this man, they had
The well-born, well-placed, well-fixed
Folk of Austin on their side who thought
They'd now be shut of Lyndon.
For a year at least or longer,
In advance of this great battle,
The consensus was that Lyndon Johnson
Did not stand a chance. But he bet
Everything on getting to the people
Though at first he just went AWOL
From his district, he remained aloof
In Washington, serene above the battle
Out in Texas, solely focused on the business
Of the nation in support of our new President,
He had no time for politics at all,
You could not lure him toward campaigning,
Two months, one month, it went right down
To the wire, no sign of Lyndon,
Down to two weeks, Lyndon Johnson
Was not seen, then came announcements:
The agenda of the nation would permit him

To return the last ten days before election,
He would have the time to come and "visit" now
With friends in county seats and thus
The virtuoso whirlwind of performances began.
The spectacle of Lyndon so demurely (almost)
Waiting out his doom had brought the voters
To the edges of their seats, they wondered
What would happen next.
The news that Lyndon was returning
Brought them leaping to their feet,
The little people, they were turning out
In even greater numbers than before
For their boy Lyndon who would give them
What they wanted. PUP laid claim
To his opponent Hardy Hollers,
But the people, they had Lyndon,
Ever faithful public servant toiling selflessly
With no thought of himself or his advantage.
Now the little people got to shake
Their fists and stomp their feet
When their barnstorming boy arrived,
The tears were running down their cheeks.
It was another time and place.
On closing night of this campaign
The opposition spoke before an empty park,
So we were told, with an array
Of old-line family guests lined up
Like wooden dummies on the platform,
More of these up on the platform
Than were out there in the non-existent crowd.
On almost every city block, though,
At the same time, you had water melon parties
Being thrown with Lyndon Johnson
Dropping in on them. He brought along
Gene Autry as his partner to these fêtes.

What mere opponent could compete?
The next day 73% of voters in his district
Went for Lyndon.

311.

Well, the President…his attitude toward LBJ was funny.
Strangely mixed. He really liked his roguish outlook
And as an operator who could not respect him?
As a politician Lyndon was the man who got things done.
And he thought Lady Bird was neat.
But there were other times I'd say, and you could feel it,
When the presence just of Johnson in the room
Would somehow bug him. It was not noble.
It was there though. And a single word at certain times
Might hint at this revulsion. He had never known
Another man like Lyndon he would say, but then he'd add
That he found Lyndon somewhat monstrous—
With a comic side—outlandish. That word "monstrous"
Seemed significant to me, it gave a darker
Psychological game away almost, suggested
Greater depths of feeling, depths roiled up
By this relationship in Kennedy who mostly
Liked to keep a cool façade.

312.

From the train that carried Bobby back to D.C.,
Of the many sights, the honor guard of people
Keeping vigil by the tracks, I best remember,
Since they tore my heart in two and took my breath,
There was a wedding party standing in a meadow

Down in Delaware--of all the days in all the years
That some poor girl had picked for getting married!--
All the bridesmaids in their right hands
Held the hems up of their dresses--green
And red flashed--in their others hands
They held up their bouquets, their arms
Extended in a gesture, who knows what,
Some strange abandonment or drunkenness,
Despairing, love's last reel, and when
The last car of the train, the one that carried
Bobby's body in it, passed, they all together,
Stepping forward, dashed those sprays
Against its side as if to christen it or something.

313.

The President was in favor of a pause
Around Thanksgiving, he was "60-40 for it"
After that we'd knock the hell out of the North.
But first we'd pause for preparation.

314.

Long-whiskered beatniks, dirty clothes
Worn down by willingness to look
Just like a beatnik in the vanguard of
The marchers, not entitled to respect,
They're the antithesis of any definition
Of a patriot you'd offer.

315.

At three o'clock and every hour thereafter
I kept going to the door and saw this big hulk--
A Marine--and I kept saying I was freezing.
He said "Yes, sir," but the big hulk never moved.
It was the President, remember,
Who had entered this complaint.

316.

I've been told that there is no time to reform South Vietnam--
Just win the war first--that reform is something
We can get to later, it's a luxury almost.
But the Viet Cong have understood
You cannot simply separate the two.
That's why they're winning.

317.

The captain to his prisoner said: "Americans are kind,
They do not kill, they always tell us not to kill you.
You will see, I'm not so kind, and I will kill you."
Then the interpreter to me: "You know the VC
Takes these boys, and it convinces them
Americans will eat their hearts for breakfast.
But the captain's right. You have no taste for war."

318.

One of our complaints was that we couldn't
Understand the air controller. He suggested--
That is McNamara's man did—
That we learn Vietnamese and then
We'd understand the air-controller fine.
We said we didn't have the time.
Stay two whole years, he said,
Though he had scarcely been there two whole weeks
And soon would fly back to the States,
A brilliant man. He's lucky still to be alive.
I mean we had to hold back guys
Who would have killed him.

319.

That upstart Bobby's come too far too fast.
He skipped the grades in school
Where you learn all the rules of life.
He never liked me though that's nothin'
Next to what I think of him.
But I don't need that little runt to win elections.

320.

Light at the end of the tunnel--hell!
There isn't even any tunnel there yet,
We aint dug one. I can't finish off the war
With what I have. I can't get out.
What can I do?

321.

It seems you have a choice,
To lose the war now or to lose it after putting in
100,000 men. The latter seems the better way
I'd say, for U.S. politics at least.

322.

I am a little bit surprised
That formal treaties over periods of years
Should catch our people by surprise
When things get tough. I'd hope
The Senate would not ratify
Alliances they don't intend to honor.

323.

Unlike many politicians Clifford knows just when
To grab opponents' balls, to hold on tight to them,
To squeeze and twist them hard, to not let go.

324.

A confusion of the self
With all the interests of the nation--
Quite magnificke but a harm-inflictor too.

325.

The question isn't whether I lose face if we pull out
Of Viet Nam but rather do I lose my ass if we stay in.

326.

"Halleck has got it going,"
LBJ complained to Shriver,
"He's outsmarted you.
He tried the Nigrah thing first,
That did not get off the ground,
But now he's got you on religion."

327.

Soon after he was President Dick Russell
Was reported to have given him advice on Vietnam:
Spend anything it takes to put a government in place
That's going to ask us just to pull up stakes, go home.

328.

...a test case of United States ability
To help a nation stand against
A "war of liberation" which
The communists were leading.

329.

The decision to employ force if we need to
Backed by resolute deployment and conveyed
By every means we have at hand against our foes
Gives us the best chance of avoiding
Any real use of that force.

330.

In making this decision we face two risks,
First the risk of escalation toward a major Asian land war
With the use of so-called nukes and two,
The risk of some reply South Vietnam itself might make
To force that country to be lost to neutralism,
To a neutral situation and eventually
To communist control.

331.

...to force North Vietnam from sheer self-interest
To desist from its support of the insurgency down south...

332.

This looks about like just where we came in.
Remember it was Pleiku where they hit us
In the barracks and we first began
To strike them in the north.

333.

There's not a boy in this whole crowd
That wouldn't gallantly march down
And don his country's khaki uniform,
He'd march down to the station
If he thought his country's flag
Was in some danger since
The blood of many Carolina sons
Has gotten strewn throughout the nations,
They've been carrying that flag
Around the world and they have brought it back
Without a stain upon it.
When you lead that boy of yours
Down to the station and you send him
Off to boot camp and they put
That khaki uniform upon him
And they send him to a country
Which he just might not come back home from,
They don't ask about what party you belong to.
It's that flag that you're defending and you go.

334.

It's rather hard to fathom, in a week
The years of Johnson will be over.
I cannot help thinking looking back upon them now
That all the forces he was being asked
To deal with were the worst, the most tumultuous
Conjunction that this country's had to suffer
Since the 1850's just before the Civil War.
How can you judge his performance
When you can't begin to judge or understand

The force of currents that engulfed him?
He tried to act as the crises demanded
At a time when no one really knew
Exactly what the crises were.
Perhaps it will be said a lesser, simpler man
Than he was would have also gotten crushed
Or swept away but he especially was liable
Since he stood up so titanically to face them
And got broken though perhaps
The era didn't really matter in the end
And if the times had been more halcyon,
The Johnson era might have ended up
Perplexing him, perplexing us about as much
Since it's as Creon said to Oedipus
At some point in the play: "Such natures
Chiefly are a torment to themselves."

CPSIA information can be obtained
at www.ICGtesting.com
Printed in the USA
BVHW030359090520
578872BV00001B/1